In and Out of the West

Page-Barbour Lectures for 2002

In and Out of the West

RECONSTRUCTING ANTHROPOLOGY

Maurice Godelier

Translated by Nora Scott

University of Virginia Press
CHARLOTTESVILLE

University of Virginia Press
© 2009 by the Rector and Visitors of the University of Virginia
All rights reserved

Printed in the United States of America on acid-free paper

First published 2009

9 8 7 6 5 4 3 2 1

LIBRARY OF CONGRESS CATALOGING-IN-PUBLICATION DATA
Godelier, Maurice.
  In and out of the west : reconstructing anthropology / Maurice
Godelier ; translated by Nora Scott.
      p.   cm. — (Page-Barbour lectures for 2002)
  Includes bibliographical references and index.
  ISBN 978-0-8139-2707-7 (cloth : alk. paper)
  1. Anthropology. I. Scott, Nora. II. Title.
  GN25.G628 2009
  301—dc22
                                                      2008034463

Contents

IN AND OUT OF THE WEST

Introduction: Anthropology Today— What Have We Done and What Should We Do?

The present volume is based on the Page-Barbour Lectures, a cycle of four lectures organized each year by the University of Virginia, which I was invited to give in 2002 and which appear here as chapters 2, 3, 7, and 8. To these, I have added chapters 1, 4, 5, and 6, which continue some aspect of the lectures or open onto other problems. It was, of course, an honor and a pleasure for me to give these lectures, for each was followed by a rich and lively debate, a friendly discussion between colleagues and students speaking on behalf of anthropology and the other social sciences.

Two distinct positions appeared. One side affirmed that it no longer, or had never, believed that any scientific credit or particular authority should be attributed to the analyses of anthropologists, or to those of historians, Orientalists, or other social scientists that populate the universities of the West. The other invoked the various accomplishments of anthropology—such as the discovery and inventory of the range of kinship systems known to date—maintaining that anthropology could not be reduced to a simple intellectual undertaking in the service of Western expansion and domination of the rest of the world, and that its methods and results contained elements which made it a scientific discipline, even if the degree of scientificity was modest in comparison with that of biology, or chemistry, or physics.

This debate was not really new. Beginning in the late 1980s, when George Marcus, James Clifford,[1] Michael Fischer, Paul Rabinow,[2] and Stephen Tyler (and others with or after them) exhorted their colleagues to adopt a reflexive or critical awareness of the discipline, it has become a habit to "deconstruct" anthropology down to the last nook and cranny, and to invent a new way of practicing it and communicating its findings—that is, "New Ethnography" and "Writing Culture"—which would allow many voices to be heard beyond that of the ethnologist, who henceforth could make no claim to any particular authority to interpret the facts gathered.

For some, field material could and should no longer be "represented" but only "evoked," poetically if possible. Along this dividing line, many claimed that anthropology and literature would meld and produce various sorts of narrative-fictions. To these calls for a new ethnography and the overall deconstruction of the old brand, other emblematic figures were summoned, but their voices came from the other side of the Atlantic—Jean-François Lyotard, Jacques Derrida, Michel Foucault, Gilles Deleuze, Jean Baudrillard, and Paul Ricoeur among them. Their collective work became what is known in the United States as "French Theory"—a purely American invention, since France recognizes no such unified body of thought.[3] In France there are thinkers—such as Lyotard, Foucault, and Derrida—who, beginning in the 1970s, wrote different books; who changed their theoretical paradigms several times in the course of their careers; who were sometimes deeply opposed to each other (as was the case with Foucault and Derrida), and at other times were united; and whose influence, once the fad wore off, did not make them gurus or visionaries who illuminated the whole field of ideas, but rather thinkers whose views were sometimes adopted by other researchers, insofar as they were useful for addressing an aspect of reality or a particular set of problems. In short, France produces and exports many brilliant thinkers, but at home their ideas are usually consumed with moderation and pragmatism, and on the whole no one individual among them is allowed to stand in for all the others. We will return to these points in due course.

Crisis, an Obligatory Passage

The question before us is clear then. Are these debates, contentions, and deconstructions agitating the field of anthropology and other social sciences the signs of its "twilight," as Marshall Sahlins[4] asserts, and thus heralds of its death? Or, on the contrary, are they the indirect proof that anthropology (and with it the social sciences in general) is—in a contradictory, and turbulent, but perfectly normal manner—going through a transition period from which the discipline will presently emerge with a greater critical awareness of its methods, its concepts, and its limits, and with greater analytical power and rigor? In short, are we witnessing the birth of an anthropology that is more than ever necessary, one that is capable of analyzing the complexity and contradictions of the globalized world in which its practitioners, and those with whom they live and work, must lead their lives? Our answer to these questions is equally straightforward. The crisis of anthropology and the social sciences, far from leading, by dint of deconstruction, to their disappearance or dissolution in the soft forms of "Cultural Studies,"[5] is the obligatory passage to their reconstruction at a level of rigor and vigilance that did not previously exist. Let us turn to why this is so.

Until the mid-nineteenth century, ethnology was merely an accumulation of narratives and descriptions produced by the soldiers, civil servants, missionaries, traders, and explorers of all stripes that had, since the sixteenth century, been enlisted in the interests of the colonial and commercial expansion of a few European countries, even before the birth of large-scale industrialization in the nineteenth century ensured these countries their ascendancy over the rest of the world and pitted them against each other in what was often bloody competition. All of their accounts obviously served more or less directly to establish this domination, and most of them implicitly or explicitly allowed that the West was both the measure and the mirror of human progress. Nevertheless, there were a few philosophers and poets who saw reflected in the customs of "savages" the paradise lost by the West through the advances of "Civilization."[6] In short, during these centuries, ethnology was primarily an ethnography steeped in Western ideology.

✕ ✕ ✕

Anthropology did not begin to emerge as a "scientific" discipline until the latter half of the nineteenth century, when its founders, Lewis Henry Morgan and Edward Tylor,[7] undertook a comparative analysis of the customs of other peoples and, in so doing, consented to temporarily suspend their own cultural judgments and assumptions, deliberately decentering their thinking with respect to the categories and value judgments of their own society and time. This enabled Morgan, following a systematic survey conducted first in the United States and Canada and then throughout the world with the help of hundreds of correspondents, to discover and catalogue the various forms of kinship found both in Western and non-Western cultures.[8] He analyzed these forms in such a way that he was able to grasp their "logic" and to recognize that they constituted "systems," different from but just as coherent as the cognatic principle found in the West, which derived from that used by the ancient Romans. Morgan was obliged to invent new terms to describe and define his discoveries. He began to speak of a "matrilineal" descent rule, and of "classificatory" kinship to designate kinship terminologies that used a single term for the father and father's brothers, and another for the mother and mother's sisters, and so forth. Some of the other general terms he used to characterize types of terminology, such as "Malayan" or "Ganovanian," were not adopted by subsequent scholars, and were replaced by such ethnic designations as Hawaiian, Iroquois, Eskimo, and Sudanese.

But Morgan's work—the decentering of his perspective and the systematic analysis of his correspondents' questionnaires—was interrupted and even negated when, later in his life, he used his conclusions to construct a fictional metanarrative of human evolution. This account posited that humankind advanced from its original primitive, animal state to an initial "savage" state and then to a "barbarian" state which resulted here and there in the culminating "civilized" state. This final stage was embodied first and foremost by the European nations, and most explicitly by the United States of America, which was free of the feudal (and other) relations that hampered the development of the Old World from whence the future conquerors of America set out.[9]

The lesson to be drawn from the existence and the succession of these two Morgans is clear. From the outset, the development of anthropology was rooted in contradictions that mixed rational practices and ideology, and the discipline was therefore doomed to struggle within and against itself. This is where we remain, but in a radically new context. And since anthropologists are made, not born, it is indispensable to consider the world in which individuals become anthropologists and then pursue, now and for some time to come, our profession.

Today's World

Today's world came into being following three transformations, each of which left its mark. The first occurred in the wake of the Second World War in the 1950s, when after centuries of domination (but also numerous acts of resistance[10] on the part of the subjugated populations), the colonial empires of England, France, Holland, and Portugal disintegrated and disappeared in a more or less rapid, and more or less bloody fashion. Spain had already lost its colonies in the nineteenth century, and Germany's followed in 1918, after the First World War. But once they proclaimed their "independence," these local populations and societies did not return to the same circumstances and relations that existed before colonization, but rather were "integrated" into the borders and structures of the states created by the colonial powers. And as these states came into being, they disrupted or destroyed chains of relations—such as empires or trade routes[11]—that had previously drawn such groups together, subsequently displacing or reorganizing whole populations, and creating an entirely new living environment.[12]

These newly independent, artificial states had to become "nations," to construct or lay claim to a shared identity that had never existed between the earlier local societies which practiced different customs and religions, and were now caught between new borders. These emerging nation-states became "secular" in character, like those founded on the separation of religion (or religions) and politics in Europe and America following the French, English, and American revolutions, when the views of the Enlightenment philosophers—that neither the sciences nor society should be forcibly subjected to the domination of religion and theology, or to the power of kings and dominant classes or the ideologies that legitimized their rights and their authority[13]—became part of their social fabric. It was to these former colonial frameworks that the newly independent countries would be obliged to turn, reviving or reinventing their traditions to fashion a future in an increasingly globalized world where new forms of dependence would soon replace the relations of direct domination once imposed by the colonial powers. And though the Vietnamese War marked the final disintegration of the old colonial empires in the 1960s, this did not pit a former colonial power, France, against one of its Far Eastern colonies, but rather the capitalist Western world and its allies against the communist world.

This happened because, after World War II, a second fundamental transformation divided the globe into three blocs: the capitalist world, the communist world, and a third world made up of large countries seeking independence, whose desires were given voice by such great, charismatic leaders as Jawaharlal Nehru, Gamal Abdel Nasser, Sukarno, and Patrice Lumumba. The "socialist" countries claimed to be building a way of life for their peoples that was opposed and superior to that of capitalism. Doing away with private ownership of the land and the means of production, and promising equal access to education and jobs, they aimed to invent a "new man" who embodied utopian dreams, or the hopes of those who criticized "bourgeois" values and the promotion of the individual at the expense of society. And they denounced the myth of the optimum distribution of resources and wealth among all members of society that would automatically result from allowing the market its head, unfettered and totally free of state control.

In reality, the "superior" democracies of the communist countries rapidly turned into bloody, one-party dictatorships, and apart from building industrial infrastructures, the planned, centralized economies proved to be incapable of significantly raising the standards of living to match and surpass those of Western Europe, the United States, and Canada. The socialist countries were thus ultimately unable to compete with the capitalist countries, save in the production of the scientific knowledge and technologies needed to put them on an equal military footing with their adversaries. Forced to bear the weight of the arms race with the capitalist West, and the accelerated development of countries such as Russia or the Central Asian "republics" (which had very little industry in 1917 at the time of the Bolshevik revolution), or Rumania, Bulgaria, and Poland (but not Hungary), and China and Vietnam in the postwar era, the socialist system started to crack and crumble and was quickly dismantled after the fall of the Berlin Wall in 1989.[14] And though China, Vietnam, North Korea, and Cuba still consider themselves socialist, their economies are increasingly involved in the capitalist world economy.

It was during the final years of these regimes, when their creaking signaled they must either undertake a thoroughgoing reform or disappear, that the intellectual world of Western Europe, which embraced structuralism, Marxism, and existentialism, also began to break apart, due largely to the assaults and critiques of Lyotard, Foucault, Baudrillard, and—in a somewhat different fashion—Derrida and Ricoeur. Foucault, who along with Althusser had proclaimed the death of the Subject (a cause to which Lévi-Strauss also rallied), turned to the writings of Heidegger and then Nietzsche to help him formulate the new setting for philosophy and the social sciences, a situation Lyotard was to call the "postmodern condition."

Lyotard saw this new state of existence and thought as an inevitable consequence of the death of all "metanarratives," those theories claiming to offer a general explanation, in terms of the action of "last" causes, of the various historical realities experienced by the individuals and groups that make up a society. The first metatheories targeted by Lyotard were, naturally, Marxism and Lévi-Straussian structuralism. Within a few years, the fall of the Berlin Wall cost Marxism its privileged status, and the resurgence of the subject and the "subjectification" of the individual relegated structural analysis to the realm of abstract games, which offered little insight in understanding the complexity either of historical realities or of individual identities.

The demise of the colonial empires, and most of the socialist regimes twenty years later, gave some the impression and fostered the illusion that we had reached the "end of History"[15]—that no form of society and economy other than one that combined capitalism and parliamentary democracy was henceforth likely to arise. According to this view, humanity had entered the final phase of the global expansion of the capitalist market economy and the generalized establishment of liberal democracy in the exclusive service of "human rights," values that had taken the place of those that in preceding centuries had been assigned to Christianity, the one "true" religion.

This was more or less what some had come to believe prior to September 11th, 2001. But the al Quaeda attacks on the Twin Towers and the Pentagon once again turned a spotlight on the existence of violent forms of resistance to Western domination, and more generally the rejection of the Western lifestyles that had permeated numerous non-Western societies. In fact, it was not altogether an accident that certain al Quaeda Web sites[16] quoted criticisms from the works of Western Orientalists[17] and, more broadly, the assertions of certain postmodernists that any knowledge of the Otherness of the Other is radically impossible and inaccessible to the social sciences, to support their claim that the West has never understood the first thing about the

East or about Islam, and has never done anything but dominate, disparage, and mischaracterize the Orient.[18]

Since 1989, the capitalist economic system has extended itself to all local societies and all states. The world is becoming economically globalized, such that no state or local society can reproduce itself and develop materially without becoming increasingly implicated in the market economy. At the political level, by contrast, the trend is in the other direction, as new nation-states have multiplied due to the disappearance of colonial empires and the disintegration of the Soviet Bloc, and the accompanying reassertion of local, ethnic, religious, and other identities.[19] This is the case of the Czech Republic and Slovakia, of Croatia and Bosnia, of Ukraine, and of other places where the two opposing forces reconfiguring the globalized world in which we live and exercise our profession as anthropologists play out—a trend toward the integration and globalization of economic activities and relations within each society and between societies, and a trend toward political and cultural fragmentation that divides and subdivides preexisting political-economic structures, often violently, and engenders new states that must then go on to become nations.[20] This second tendency usually gives rise to a new cultural and political life in numerous local societies, reflected in the rediscovery or reinvention of local traditions which many ethnologists have regarded as pure fictions, and thus shown little interest in at the outset.

But the multiplication of independent states joining the United Nations one after the other has not eliminated their inequalities of political influence and autonomy—quite the contrary. A new hierarchy of old and new nation-states has emerged, dominated from the outset by the hegemony of the United States, self-proclaimed Big Brother and Big Stick of the world order, which was virtually unchallenged following the breakup of the Soviet Union in 1989.

The 9/11 attacks put a brutal stop to this state of affairs. Using violence, weapons of terror, and attacks targeted at one and all, al Quaeda declared jihad (or holy war) on the West, on Christians and Jews, on the "materialism" of the Western way of life, on the humiliations and the exploitation that Westerners had inflicted for decades on hundreds of millions of Muslims, and on all Muslims, the world over, who aided or cooperated with the West.[21] Yet one of the reasons for Muslim "resistance" stems directly from a core principle of Western societies— namely, the separation of religion and politics, the secularization of the state, and the freedom of all to practice a religion or not to have one.[22] This separation of religion and politics has also been the principle of the socialist regimes, but in the guise of their brand of Marxism, dubbed "scientific" materialism, that became a quasi-state religion, imposed on everyone at school, in the factory, in the stadium, and in scores of other places.

But it is not only Islam that aims to make religion the basis of the state and of society, though this has long been the case in Saudi Arabia, where through the influence of the fundamentalist Wahhabist branch of Islam, Shari'a is the basis of the legal code, as well as in Afghanistan, even since the defeat of the Taliban. The Hindu fundamentalists of the Bharatiya Janata Party (BJR), which managed to win the Indian national elections a few years ago and governed the country for a time, have for decades been denouncing the secularism of the Indian state and the religious tolerance instituted by Nehru, holding him responsible for all of the country's problems. They appeal to the "soul" of the Indian nation, to its eternal "essence"—its Hinduness (*hindutva*)—which they maintain is rooted in and draws its force from Mother India (Bharat-Mata).[23] Although they argue that Hinduness is more than the Hindu religion, asserting that it is also a way of being and thinking that is shared by Muslims, Sikhs, Christians, and the like, its glorification has resulted in no less than 18,000 Hindu-Muslim riots over the last twenty years.[24] These clashes have caused thousands of deaths and culminated in the destruction of the holy mosque in Ayodhya in December 1992, when Sangh Parivar Hindu militants, in association with the BJR, claimed that the edifice had been built on the birthplace of Rama, an avatar of Vishnu. Here, as elsewhere, each camp demonizes the other.[25]

In Sri Lanka, Theravada Buddhism and the Singhalese language—rather than Shivaite Hinduism and the Tamil language—are regarded as the essence of the people and the nation. Archeological excavations and linguistic and historical studies are undertaken to lend "scientific" proof to this nationalist policy, which sparked the armed Tamil uprising and their "separatist" demands.[26] In Burma (or Myanmar), the army, which seized power following a coup d'état designed to prevent the duly elected opposition party from governing, also invokes Buddhism to rule, continually broadcasting legends of the ancient Kingdom of Burma, restoring the ancient Buddhist monuments, and even ensuring the loyalty of the populace by procuring a "sacred tooth" of the Buddha from Beijing (which was kindly lent by the communist authorities) and organizing a huge procession throughout the land from one sacred site to another, which drew considerable crowds and was the occasion for all, from senior government officials to the humblest peasant, to make gifts in honor of the Buddha. The junta thus offered everyone the chance to store up merits for the afterlife, and to have their names appear in the local papers (or, for the most generous donors, to be announced on radio and television).[27]

The massacres and destruction committed in the name of the "eternal essence" of a human group, placating its desire to "cleanse" the society of everything that contravenes, insults, humiliates, or provokes its "soul," are numerous and endless. To be sure, when members of a group are denied access to schooling, or land ownership, or a military career, or high public office because they are Jewish or Christian, or Black, that part of their identity takes predecence—in the eyes of others, not necessarily in their own—over those aspects that repress, reorder, and subordinate all other identities possessed by each human group and each individual.

To those who accuse anthropologists of having reified the identity of the groups they study by describing them as frozen and inward-looking, passing through time with little or no alteration, most ethnologists (and most historians for that matter) have stressed to any and all who would listen that there is no such thing as an "eternal" essence of a people or a human group, and thus that its identity is always the product of a particular history, a multifaceted "construction" that is amenable to borrowing from others. When such borrowings are not imposed from the outside, they are usually chosen and integrated into a cultural configuration which they then modify, and which in turn modifies and gives them a new meaning and character. This vision of cultures, which extends from Franz Boas to Raymond Firth to Frederik Barth to Marshall Sahlins,[28] does not preclude the possibility that, in certain historical contexts, groups that have previously been on relatively good terms will suddenly shut themselves off and advance an aspect of their culture as their *fundamental* identity, one that is presumed to give them, now and in the future, exclusive rights to certain resources. Generally speaking, the elements people put forward to define their identity are those that testify to some longstanding part of themselves, like being the first occupants of a particular place, or having always been Shi'ite rather than Sunni.

Issues of identity are thus not merely theoretical concerns in people's lives, problems hinging on an abstract definition that historians or anthropologists, tracing their origins and comparing the facts, regard as suitable or fictional. The identity to which people lay claim is "true" or "real" to them because it is the reason they live the way they do and often act the way they act to change their way of life. How, therefore, could their identity be false? We must also bear in mind that groups or individuals always define themselves by reference to others of the same or opposite sex, or of the same or another religion, and so forth. It is in this more fundamental sense that no identity, whatever one thinks or wishes, is closed in on itself, and closed to the outside.

The world in which anthropologists work today is not only characterized by the integration of all economies into the world capitalist system, and the massive diffusion of liberal ideology that holds private property to be the foundation of society and the individual to be its most basic unit. It has also witnessed the multiplication of old or new nation-states that have unequal influence on the evolution of the contemporary world, and that are more or less subjugated by such powerful forces as the United States, which—since the disintegration of the USSR and the disappearance of its European or Central Asian satellite regimes—exercises a political hegemony over the rest of the world that it justifies by declaring itself the leading defender of democracy and human rights (the rights ascribed to individuals as private persons rather than as members of a particular ethnic, religious, or other community).[29]

Hence we come, in simplified terms, to the third transformation that produced the world we live in today, where most of the 192 member states of the United Nations do not (or no longer) enjoy the sovereignty typical of the nineteenth or the early twentieth century.[30] Today, scores of forces—international organizations like the World Bank, the International Monetary Fund, and the World Trade Organization, as well as transnational companies, the international expansion of religious sects and movements, worldwide migrations and diasporas,[31] and the 20,000 or so nongovernmental organizations (or NGOs)—all intervene directly, in various ways, in the internal workings of many states and local societies. NGOs, by way of example, are usually active in poor countries where the state is unable to provide the population with access to education or health care, building schools and hospitals and bringing along their ideologies and rules for living.[32] Though not all of these international organizations stem from the West, the vast proportion do, and thus constitute new forms of Western intervention in the lives of the peoples of Africa, Asia, Latin America, and Oceania, as well as Central and Eastern Europe. And all of these organizations, even those that are Islamic or Buddhist, intervene, in the name of various ideals, beyond the borders of the countries in which they originated.

Deconstructing the Social Sciences, Not in Order to
Abolish Them But to Reconstruct Them

Given this snapshot of today's world, it is thus understandable that societies can neither be thought of or analyzed as closed
totalities nor as finite sets of localized, unchanging social relations, walled off from the outside by their particular identity and
peopled with individuals who share the same representations
and values and are incapable of acting on themselves or on their
relations with others or with nature. Such societies have never
existed, and such theoretical views have no empirical basis or
scientific foundation. Clearly these views must be critiqued and
rejected, something that the champions of "New Ethnography"
do with pertinence and eloquence. But repeating these critiques
ad nauseam is unproductive, and accusing or suspecting all our
anthropological forebears of having analyzed the societies they
studied with such presuppositions is quite simply erroneous and
highly demagogical. Let us briefly consider Raymond Firth's
publications on Tikopia, by way of illustration. For more than
thirty years, using field observations made during the course of
three successive stays between 1928 and 1962, Firth described
the changes in a small-scale society that, according to oral tradition, came into being only in the past few centuries. In 1928, the
inhabitants of Tikopia were still performing their rites under
the authority of their chiefs and of the Te Ariki Kafika (the head
of the high-ranking Kafika clan). Thirty years later, most of the
young people had emigrated to New Zealand or to other islands
in the South Pacific, and even to the United States. Nine books
and dozens of articles trace the history of these transformations,
which accelerated after 1962.[33]

Today such groups as the Tikopia, the Nuer, and the Kachin
still exist, but their societies are no longer those observed by
Firth, Edward Evans-Pritchard, and Edmund Leach, respectively.[34] They are increasingly tied into the globalized world,
where the influence of the West predominates. But why should
we find these changes so surprising, or see them as unprece-

dented? And why should these facts oblige anthropologists to turn their attentions elsewhere? Might the answer be that these societies are no longer "primitive," and that the course of history, which provided anthropologists with such objects of study during the West's colonial expansion, then suppressed them with decolonization and independence? If we accept this line of reasoning, perhaps it is now up to sociologists, economists, and development experts to step in. Obviously no anthropologist can claim to analyze and understand all aspects of the life of a local society. However, if its economy rests on the production and sale of a cash crop, such as coffee, the anthropologist needs at least to learn how the price of this product fluctuates on the world market. This sort of interdisciplinary cooperation does not invalidate the anthropologist's approach to research, immersing him- or herself for years at a time in a particular culture to discover and understand the way its members think and act, as well as the nature of their social relations and the way they represent these relations and their places within them. Though a sociologist, or an economist, can study all of this as well, anthropological fieldwork gives rise to a very different, if complementary, approach.

Yet other voices question the capacity of sociology, anthropology, economics, and the rest of the social sciences—because they emerged and developed in the West—to understand how non-Western societies think and act. These concerns are raised by members of newly independent societies, who demand the right to study their own rediscovered or reinvented traditions, and to propose their own interpretation of their history, their culture, and their society. This perfectly legitimate demand, which should lead to a better understanding of these societies, echoes what A. R. Radcliffe-Brown said to M. N. Srinivas when the latter announced his intention to return to India and study his own society. Though Srinivas felt obliged to stop calling himself an "anthropologist" and declared himself a "sociologist," Radcliffe-Brown felt that his decision to go back and work in his own country afforded anthropology the possibility of adding new understandings of Indian society to those that might be produced by an ethnologist from outside.[35]

But things are never this simple and "idyllic." The Oxford-trained Srinivas was accused of sharing the representations of Indian society held by the Anglo-Indian elite, who had supported the struggle for independence and the vision of India's past and future developed by Nehru and the Congress Party.[36] These representations excluded struggles with and forms of resistance to British colonial power, which were not patterned on such views but instead had their own cultural logic and their own rationale. The critiques of British historians of India and the nationalist sociologists of the Nehru period, who glossed over such concerns and denied them their rightful place in India's history, have led to a new and fertile field of research, of which the twelve volumes of Subaltern Studies published to date—inspired by the work of Karl Marx and Antonio Gramsci, and making use of analytical grids inspired by the postmodernist theses—are particularly notable.[37] These deconstructions hold the promise of more rigorous reconstructions, and with it a more complex and complete understanding of the diversity and complexity of the Indian subcontinent.[38]

Voices have also been raised here and there—in the United States and the Fiji Islands, in Mexico and Great Britain—that claim the exclusive right to speak and to say what their society "really" is because they know its "essence." This is a familiar argument found in all human groups struggling to find an identity, one that, delivered more or less violently, sows doubt and arouses guilty feelings in those who, counting themselves as outsiders, are quick to question their own experience. The logic is simple: Only women can understand women and talk about them. Only black women can understand black women and talk about them. Only black Brazilian women can talk about black Brazilian women . . . and so forth. This series of qualifications (and disqualifications) can go on infinitely, and can be applied to any area of social life where relations of domination and exclusion exist between social groups and individuals based on such differences as caste, ethnic group, religion, gender, or skin color.

The withdrawal of each individual into his or her own identity, and the resulting incantatory, solipsistic, and often arrogant discourses, runs counter to our sought-after goal. If no one can understand anyone else or be understood by anyone else, by what means can we hope to change the relations imposed on us by others?[39] By violence alone, which won't stop at mere words? If no dialogue is possible, then no common struggle with other social groups confronting other sorts of discrimination and humiliation is possible. The belief that nobody but a particular individual is qualified to speak about him- or herself leads not only (as Stuart Hall has shown in the case of the Black struggles in Great Britain[40]) to a dead end in practice, but also to an unfounded, arbitrary denial of the viability of social "sciences," even if no one denies that their "scientific" character remains limited but can grow.

Yes, we need to deconstruct the social-science discourses and findings. No, we cannot deny them every vestige of scientific character. Yes, we can affirm the existence of cores of rational knowledge produced by researchers conscious of their methods and their limits. Yes, we need to deconstruct anthropology and the other social sciences so as to reconstruct them with greater rigor and analytical effectiveness than before. This is the attitude researchers need to adopt when grappling with the conflicting issues, the contradictions, and the complexity of the globalized world in which we practice our trade. But to deconstruct the social sciences and dissolve them in narcissistic discourses, reveling in the refusal to theorize, and in deliberate irony, inconsistency, and incompleteness,[41] on the pretext that to theorize is to claim an authority that does not exist and to impose it on others by means of a few rhetorical devices, is to refuse to accept one's responsibilities when one has chosen to give life meaning by taking up knowledge-based professions—unless the goal, in such games, is perhaps to amass prestige and seize power in one's own academic or literary area.[42]

We can therefore gauge the responsibility accepted by George Marcus when he wrote that, during the entire colonial period, the relationship between a Western ethnologist and the men and women who were his or her informants boiled down to one of complicity in the production of "fictions that each side accepts." Stephen Tyler went one step farther when he wrote that "ethnographic discourse is itself neither object to be represented nor the representation of an object" because "no object of any kind precedes and constrains ethnography. Ethnography creates its own objects in its unfolding and the reader supplies the rest."[43] According to Tyler's deliberately opaque formula, an ethnographic narrative "is a reality fantasy of a fantasy reality."[44] Here, too, we discern the theoretical position adopted by Jacques Derrida and Paul de Man, for whom it is imperative to "deconstruct the illusion of the reference, the possibility that a text refers to a non-textual reality."[45]

Placing himself at the far end of the deconstruction of anthropology and the social sciences, Tyler, unlike Marcus, regretted that there was *as yet no instance of a postmodern ethnography.*[46] The future proved him right on this point. But then the real world, outside of anthropology, intruded harshly on the United States on September 11th, 2001, such that it could not be reduced to a television show (*reality fantasy*) or to a hallucination to be treated by psychiatrists (*fantasy reality*). For some, on that day the world was clearly divided into two camps, Good and Evil, and decisions with real (and not imaginary or symbolic) consequences were taken in the name of this fantasy that once again made the West the mirror and the measure of human progress, and legitimized what it saw as its rightful claim—to govern the rest of the world.

In writing this, I am not placing "Americans" on trial. France is similarly capable of proclaiming itself the country of "Human Rights," even as the *banlieues* of its major cities burn in rioting by populations who feel excluded, sentenced to a lifetime of unemployment and poverty. Nor am I conflating all those who have rallied to or are accused of having cheered on "Postmodernism." Marcus is not Rabinow, Clifford is not Tyler, and Clifford Geertz differs from them all. Moreover, their views are not static, and over the years there have been several Marcuses, and several Tylers. There is thus no such thing, for any society, or individual, as an immutable "essence," an eternal identity.

Death of a Few Celebrated Anthropological "Truths"

The stakes are therefore clear. We must continue to deconstruct anthropology and the social sciences in detail, down to their last self-evident "Truths." But for each "self-evident" truth that is deconstructed and has thus lost its force and status as such, we must derive the means to reconstruct another representation of the facts, another paradigm to account for the complexities and contradictions previously disregarded or neglected. I have been engaged on this path of deconstruction-reconstruction for years, and will briefly consider some of the results that I hope to have achieved in the pages that follow. These results challenge a number of established anthropological "truths" that have been celebrated for decades as scientifically "self-evident," the following theses foremost among them:

1. Kinship relations and the family are the basis of all societies, particularly those without classes and without a state, which were formerly deemed "primitive."

2. Economic relations constitute the material and social basis of societies (a point which is less generally accepted).

3. A man and a woman make children by having sexual intercourse.

4. Societies are founded on exchanges of persons and of goods, which take two forms: those involving commodities and those which make use of gifts and countergifts.

5. The symbolic takes precedence over the imaginary and the real (an assertion that is truly wide-ranging).

Taking these points in turn, and in light of my research, I have come to the following conclusions:

- There are no societies based on kinship, nor have there ever been. Kin relations, even in the guise of the family, cannot constitute the bond that unites different groups to form a society (a point we will consider at length in chapter 2).

- No society has ever held that a man and a woman alone can make a child. Rather, they produce a fetus, which is endowed with a breath, one or several souls, or other such animating forces by agents more powerful than humans, such as ancestors and gods (the focus of chapter 3).

- Alongside those things one sells and those one gives, there are things that must neither be sold nor given but kept for transmission, which are the material support for identities and endure the passage of time longer than things given or sold (a conclusion we will explore in chapter 1).

- Those social bonds that make a set of human groups and individuals into a "society" are based neither on kinship nor economics, but on what we in the West refer to as "political-religious" relations (our principal concern in chapter 6).

- All social relations, including the most material ones, contain "imaginary cores," which are internal, constitutive components and not ideological reflections. These "imaginary cores" are implemented and enacted by "symbolic practices" (which we will discuss in detail here and in chapter 6).

- Human sexuality is fundamentally "a-social." In every society, the gendered bodies of men and women work like a sort of ventriloquist's dummy, expressing and legitimizing its power relations and particular interests. Moreover, these relations operate not only between the genders but also between such social groups as clans, castes, or classes (the crux of chapter 4).

From these points follows an essential question: If neither kinship nor the "economic" relations contracted between human groups and/or individuals have the capacity to make them into a society—to gather them into a whole that adds to each an overarching, shared identity, distinct from their particular identities, which becomes an obligatory condition of their particular existence—then what are the social relations, institutions, and practices that can accomplish this? What, in the end, distinguishes a society from the different communities that compose it, each of which is constituted by and around one or several distinct identities? What is the difference between a society and a community?

As luck would have it, the Baruya, among whom I lived and worked for a total of seven years between 1966 and 1981, did not exist as a separate group known by that name a few centuries ago. The story of how they became a society, with borders that are known if not always recognized by their neighbors, led me to raise this kind of question and provided me with a few theoretical elements to find an answer. In fact, Firth asked himself the same question when he learned from the Tikopians that their society had not existed a few centuries earlier, and that it had been formed from several waves of immigrants that arrived separately and at different times from the islands of Ontong, Java, Pukapuka, Anuta, Rotuma, and Tonga.[47] Over time all these groups became integrated, with different roles and statuses, in the overall framework of the rites designed to ensure the good will of the gods and the fertility of the land and waters, which Firth describes as the "work of the Gods in Tikopia."[48]

The analysis of these examples (and others, such as the state of Israel) demonstrated that we should look to political-religious relations (so called, since political power was rarely separated from religious power in most of the societies that were known at the time) for the answer to our question. But this answer is too vague as it stands. Taking a closer look at the facts led me to see that it is *only* when political-religious social relations are used to define and legitimize the *sovereignty* of a certain number of human groups over a territory and its resources, which they can then exploit either separately or collectively, that these relations have the capacity to make these groups into a society.

The Imaginary and the Symbolic

But as I explored these problems (and others, such as the analysis of a few kinship systems), another major fact became clear: At the heart of all human relations, whatever their nature—

political, religious, or economic (to use Western categories once more for simplicity's sake)—there are cores of "imaginary realities" that serve as their essential components, give them meaning, and are embodied in institutions and symbolic practices that endow them with a visible social existence as well as the status of self-evident "truths."

It appeared to me that there was considerable theoretical confusion concerning these two domains, and that while the imaginary and the symbolic are closely connected and complementary, they are by no means the same. Though Geertz and Lévi-Srauss have each explored these areas in their work, as have Victor Turner, Roy Wagner, and other colleagues,[49] none has clearly defined the distinction between the two. Here, then, are some of my thoughts by way of clarification.

The *imaginary* domain is made up of thought. It comprises all those representations that humans have produced and continue to create—of nature and the origin of the world around them, of the beings that inhabit it, and of humans themselves—conceived with regard to their differences and/or their representations. This is first and foremost a *mental* world (*un monde idéel*), a world of ideas, images, and representations of all kinds that spring from the mind. Since all representations are at the same time the result of an interpretation of what they represent, the imaginary is the totality of the interpretations (religious, scientific, literary, and the like) that humankind has invented both to explain the order or the disorder prevailing in the universe or in society and to draw conclusions as to how people should behave with respect to each other and the world around them. The imaginary is thus a *real* world, but one that is made up of *mental* realities (such as images, ideas, opinions, reasonings, and intentions), which I have subsumed in the French term *réalités idéelles*.[50] Insofar as they stay inside people's minds, these realities remain unknown to others, and thus cannot be shared by them or *act* on their lives.[51]

The *symbolic* domain comprises all of the means and processes whereby mental realities are embodied both in physical objects and in practices that endow them with a concrete, visible, social mode of existence. It is by becoming embodied in and symbolized by such practices and objects that that the imaginary can act not only on social relations which exist between individuals and groups, but also on the new relations that modify or replace earlier ones. The imaginary *is not* the same thing as the symbolic, but it cannot have any visible existence or be socially effective without being embodied in symbols and practices of all kinds, which give rise to institutions by which they are organized and to spaces, buildings, and other settings where they are enacted.

Let us consider the example of ancient Egypt, one of the earliest (if not the first) state-based societies to appear in recorded history, organized around the person of the pharaoh, who was perceived and experienced as a god living among men. The pharaoh was the product of the union of two gods, Isis and Osiris, who were brother and sister. For this reason, he too was expected to marry one of his sisters, and thus reproduce the union between his divine father and mother. His breath, *khâ*, was believed to impart life to all living beings, not only humans but also all animals great and small. Every year, when the waters of the Nile were at their lowest, the pharaoh would sail his sacred boat upriver toward the headwaters to perform the rite that prompted the god of the river to once again send his waters, depositing their silt on the tilled lands.[52]

In underscoring what for us is the imaginary character of these representations and symbolic practices, we should not forget that their social consequences were neither imaginary nor purely symbolic. The peasants who worked the land, and were thus responsible for producing enough to feed not only their own families but also the temple and palace employees and the gods (who received daily offerings), were indebted from birth to the pharaoh, who had given them the breath of life. But they were also beholden to him for the annual return of the waters of the Nile, which carried the silt that fertilized the land they tilled. It was this debt that legitimized and lent meaning to the obligation to supply labor to build roads, temples, and palaces, and deliver a portion of each year's harvest to those who governed Egypt on the pharaoh's behalf. Such obligations to a god generally inspire a certain degree of consent on the part of those who find themselves so obligated, and reduces the need to resort to force to obtain their compliance.

Here the question of the relationship between violence and consent, in the genesis and continuation of the relations of domination characteristic of hierarchical societies, is posed and illuminated by the interplay between the imaginary and the symbolic. In ancient Egypt, where political-religious underpinnings played principal roles in the formulation of society, the interplay between the political-religious and the economic domains is particularly clear and striking, as the Nile's waters were not wholly controlled until the levee system was completed under the pharaohs. It was hardly surprising that the pharaoh wore a double crown, which represented the two regions of Upper and Lower Nile and their capitals and proclaimed the unity of a country once divided into chiefdoms that quarreled over the control of a stretch of river.

Analysis of the need to distinguish between the imaginary and the symbolic in order to understand the actual role played by each domain in the production of social relations (and the various institutions that implement them) demonstrates the extent to which the opposition between *cultural* and *social* anthropology (and between cultural and social history), as proclaimed or simply accepted by many anthropologists and historians, produces partial (in both senses of the word) approaches to the social and historical realities that the social sciences endeavor to analyze and understand. To set up an opposition between an anthropology devoted to the study of relations between individuals and between groups, without seriously taking into account the ways these individuals represent their relationships and their (and others') place in them, and an anthropology devoted exclusively to the study of these representations and the symbols that express them, without analyzing their role in the production of one or another kind of concrete relationship between individuals and between specific groups, is a dead end, and accumulates false problems that spawn endless, sterile debates between specialists.[53]

This is quite simply because a social relation, whatever it may be, cannot arise and be reproduced unless it has one or several meanings, for both those who produce and those who reproduce it. Thus, in societies where marriage exists and is a precondition for two individuals to have legitimate sexual intercourse, a man and woman cannot marry without knowing what "to get married" actually means. Whenever individuals and/or groups enter into any kind of social relation, it exists not only *between* but also *within* them. Parts of this relation, then, are the forms and contents of the consciousness of those who produce/or are subjected to these relations. And these forms of consciousness constitute the conceptual or mental (*idéel*) portion of this social relation.[54] Of course, certain (but not all) symbols have the capacity to endure beyond the historical context from which they emerged and the society that used them for generations and centuries, retaining their original meaning or taking on new significance over time. An example of this is the Christian rite of baptism. For Christians, baptism is a sacrament, an essential moment in life when a child or adult becomes a member of the community of those who believe in the divinity of Jesus of Nazareth. Clearly, the world of the twenty-first century, populated by two billion Christians, has nothing in common with that of ancient Palestine, which was a Roman province in Jesus's time. But these representations of a god who died and rose again to save humankind still have meaning for believers, even if this meaning is surely not the same as it was for the first disciples of Christ.

It is therefore important to stress that symbols survive and continue to be socially effective only if they retain meaning for some or all of the members of one or several societies. In spite of the assertions of Lévi-Strauss, who affirmed the primacy of the symbolic over the imaginary and the real,[55] it is shared imaginary elements that, in both the short and the long run, keep symbols alive. But taken together, the imaginary and symbolic *do not exhaust* the content of the social realities that humans produce and reproduce in the course of their existence. Social relations, whatever their imaginary, conceptual content and their symbolic dimensions, are constructed in response to concerns that are themselves neither simply imaginary nor purely symbolic. These are evident in a series of questions to which each society offers its own answers, which may or may not converge depending on the place and the time. Here are a few of the issues at stake: In a society, who can communicate with the ancestors, the spirits, and the gods? Why and how do they do this? Who has access to land or other material resources that the members of a society need to produce their material conditions of existence? Why and how is this determined? Who can wield authority over the others? Why and how is this accomplished? And so on.

On What Conditions Are the Social Sciences Possible?

The answers to such questions can be perceived in the social institutions and symbolic practices of different societies and implemented by some or all of the groups and individuals that compose them; and it is just such institutions and practices that anthropologists, historians, and other social scientists strive to analyze and understand. But for their analyses to be "scientific" in nature, the following conditions must be substantiated by experience—not merely of anthropologists or historians, but of any person who lives in society and is obliged to learn to interact with others in ways that are meaningful to others and to him- or herself:

- That the social and historical otherness of others is *never* absolute, but rather is always relative and therefore decipherable and intelligible, under certain conditions.[56]
- That whatever humans have created for the purpose of interpreting, and acting upon, the world around them and themselves within it, can be understood by other humans— whether this is Mahayana Buddhism, or the Aboriginal Dreamtime, or European Marxism—without necessarily

espousing them and being prompted to put such principles and precepts into practice.

Our experiences, as social scientists or as members of society, confirm that these two conditions exist and invalidate the assertions of those who argue for a fundamental incommunicability between cultures. This obviously does not imply that knowledge of the otherness of others is the purview of social scientists alone. Everyday life would not be feasible without the possibility of knowing something of others, and the notion of otherness is similarly explored by artists, novelists, poets, musicians, painters, and the like. Hamlet, Oedipus, and a host of other imaginary characters brought to life by Shakespeare, Sophocles, and scores of less illustrious authors "tell" us things about others and teach us something about ourselves. The difference between the perspectives of artists and those of social scientists is that no one can really revisit and add anything to the character of Hamlet (save by interpreting the dramatist's text), or criticize Shakespeare for the way he made him make no sense, whereas elements of Bronislaw Malinowski's analysis of the *kula* (the legendary exchange cycle he documented in the Trobriand Islands) have been criticized, rectified, and expanded in light of research conducted half a century later, not only in the Trobriand Islands (Annette Weiner) but also in Gawa (Nancy Munn), Muyuw (Fred Damon), and other parts of the Massim.[57]

In short, in the world reconfigured by the demise of the Soviet and various colonial empires—one that is economically globalized but politically divided, where nearly two hundred old and new nation-states have unequal amounts of power and harbor thousands of local societies rarely willing to let go of their identities, and often their internal conflicts—we must rely, now more than ever, on knowledge produced by the social sciences. Among these, anthropology occupies a special place because, owing to its origins, it has sought to discover, to understand, and to help others to comprehend the different ways that the societies and communities which coexist on the face of the earth think and act, and organize their shared life. The same questions that arose at the birth of the discipline echo today: How can we understand something we haven't ourselves invented, something that has never been part of our culture, of our way of thinking and living? What methods, what concepts make this possible? The answers to these questions are important, for what we know of others applies to ourselves, as well. Theravada Buddhism may not be part of our culture or experience if we are Muslim or Christian, nor the ways that the black communities of the Paris *banlieues* think if we are middle-class Parisians, but understanding these differences is of no small consequence in a world beset by globalization.

Breaking the Mirror of the "Self" and Constructing a New and Other Ego, a Cognitive Ego

The question of how we can understand what has never been part of our culture and society is not addressed to Western anthropologists alone,[58] but to all ethnologists, wherever they were born or trained, regardless of whether they come from the East or the West, from Central Africa or Central Asia. The objective is the same for all anthropologists: to produce knowledge that is not the projection of one's own cultural and political assumptions, hidden within official-sounding scientific jargon. Bearing this burden of ethical and political responsibilities, we must ask ourselves what we should do to produce fragments of "rational," nonideological knowledge about what makes others "other," the sort that concerns and challenges the identity of the individual who simultaneously produces it and acts as an other for the others he or she has come to know.

We have known the answer to this question for a long time, though it is hard to put into practice. Like the historian who sets out to explore past societies, the anthropologist must strive to break "the mirror of the Self," or at the very least stifle the inevitable temptation to use this mirror to decipher the acts and words of the members of the society in which he or she is immersed. What is the "Self"? It is the unity of the various

"Egos" that make up an individual, which change over his or her lifetime. An anthropologist must forge a new, Cognitive Ego to join the Social and the Intimate Egos. The Social Ego may be inherited at birth (as is the case when a person is the son or daughter of a Brahman in the Indian caste system), or formed over a lifetime. The Intimate Ego is fashioned, from birth, by pleasant or painful encounters with others, a lifetime's singular and indelible interactions. This ego embodies the desires, suffering, and pleasures that have shaped an individual's sensibility, and the way he or she interacts with others. The Social Ego and the Intimate Ego are inextricably intertwined, and in this way the anthropologist is no different from any other person.

It is the Cognitive Ego that sets anthropologists apart from others, enabling them to perform the "work of knowledge" they have fixed as their goal. This is first and foremost an intellectual ego, one acquired in such settings as the university, which places an anthropologist at a historically precise point in the development of the discipline, in a social field where institutions, publications, and remunerations often confer power, social status, and material profit. The Cognitive Ego is formed, prior to fieldwork, from mental components—prevailing concepts, theories, readings, discussions, and controversies—all of which bear the stamp of their time. Thus one may be a structuralist, a Marxist, a poststructuralist, or a postmodernist, depending on when one was educated. But regardless of the epoch, and whatever the intellectual training, all anthropologists learn first to "decenter" this intellectual ego with respect to the other egos that make them who and what they are.

In addition, they must also "decenter" themselves with regard to the ways their own society views the other and others, and maintain the state of critical vigilance against the intrusion of these views that is necessary to observe and understand other ways of thinking and acting. This is what Morgan accomplished during the first part of his life, when he discovered that Seneca kinship relations—which reckoned descent through women, dictated uxorilocal residence after marriage, and employed one term for both the father and the father's brothers—followed a logic that differed from the cognatic rules of his own society.

"Participant" Observation: Fantasy and Reality

It is, however, not enough for an anthropologist to learn about concepts and methods, and to be ready to abandon or modify them if they cannot account for what is observed on the ground. They must be tested in the field, through what is known as "participant observation." *But what is one supposed to observe and participate in, and how far should one go?*

Let us briefly touch on some of the myths and confusion that surround these strategic aspects of the ethnologist's trade, and which are even more cumbersome than the problems that arise when an ethnographer writes a book or produces a film to communicate what he or she observed in the field. Before "writing"[59] about a society and a culture, one must first uncover its complexity by observing the interactions that occur in concrete situations, and learn from the individuals and groups involved how they represent the nature of their relationships, as well as the place, the stakes, and meaning they ascribe to these connections.

To discover all of this, ethnologists have to do more than win over a small number of individuals to act as "informants" and spend a few months chatting with them around the fire. They also have to make systematic, months-long studies and surveys of various aspects of the social life of the group with whom they are living: their material and ritual activities, their forms of power, their sources of conflict, and so on. These studies will reveal whether people say what they do and do what they say, and systematic surveys conducted or repeated several times over several years provide the ethnographer with insights that he or she would never get from a single short stay or a few "samplings."[60] Far from excluding or marginalizing the value of getting to know individuals, ethnological inquiry always begins by observing the interactions between individuals and groups on an ongoing basis, returning each time with more accurate knowledge of the logic behind their actions and therefore the nature of their relations.

But in what way is observing actually "participating" in the life of others? Participation does not mean going hunting a few times with a group of Inuit, and on such occasions helping to feed oneself and others. Nor is it sufficient to understand the language to comprehend the ritual chants. Does this mean that ethnologists have to fully "behave like the others"—for example, marry into the societies with whom they live, have children and raise them, and be involved in all of the particulars of life, the better to understand the rules people follow, the goals they pursue, the strategies they invent when they marry? The answer to this question is no.

After some time and much careful reflection, ethnologists manage to understand up to a certain point, to share "mentally" the ways those with whom they are living think and act. But there is a fundamental difference between ethnologists and those they live with when it comes to using this information. For informants, as well as for the other members of the society under observation, myths, rites, descent and marriage rules, hunting practices, and other sorts of knowledge are essential in day-to-day life, to produce and reproduce *their* society. But for ethnologists, the knowledge they work so hard to acquire, which is always incomplete and only probably but not certifiably true, does not contribute to, or help to perpetuate, the society in which they have immersed themselves. Such information helps the anthropologist to understand others, but not to act and interact as they do. This kind of participation does, however, enable ethnologists to reproduce themselves as ethnologists in their own society.

The ethnologist's consciousness of the "others" with whom he or she lived for a time can thus never coincide with their consciousness and knowledge of themselves. This does not mean that anthropological knowledge is purely and simply "false," or a series of "fictions" constructed with the complicity of informants;[61] rather, it tells us something about the place occupied by ethnologists when they are in the "field," one that is hard both to construct and to maintain, and puts them *at once* outside and inside their own society and the one in which they have chosen to work. This place is both concrete and abstract: *concrete* because fieldwork is conducted within a specific area (such as the Highlands of New Guinea) and at a fixed time (beginning, for instance, before the country's independence and continuing after it has become a nation); and *abstract* because the ethnologist's life differs from those who lived there before and will continue to live there after he or she leaves or returns, and from the life the ethnologist leads in his or her own society between trips into the field. The place occupied by anthropologists reflects a twofold distance and a delicate balance between two societies and cultures, and makes fieldwork an original and singular experience of the relations a man or a woman can have with others and with themselves.

On the Need to Understand in Order to Compare, and to Compare in Order to Understand

There is something else ethnologists must do, which creates even more distance between them, the members of the society they have lived with in the field, and the people back home. A moment arrives when an ethnographer must sit down and compare the organization or the workings of the group being studied, such as its kinship system, with neighboring peoples, or with those with whom they have no geographical nor historical connection but who employ the same type of system. This intellectual process is essential, since comparison of societies occupying different spaces (anthropology, sociology) and different times (archeology, history) is at the very root of the social sciences. But does such comparison have any concrete use, and does it even have any meaning for the members of the society the ethnologist has studied? Of what practical use, we must ask ourselves, would it be to the Baruya of Papua New Guinea to know that their kinship terminology has the same structure as

that of the indigenous Iroquois, and to further explain to them
that the Iroquois traced a child's descent through the women
whereas the Baruya trace it through the men? The answer is
clear: it might interest them, but it would be strictly of "no use."
This kind of knowledge would afford them no reason to change
their ways of thinking or producing their concrete conditions
of existence. But the fact that the comparison of societies and
the resulting discoveries may be of no immediate use to the
Baruya does not mean that this comparison is either useless or
meaningless.

Though such information has little value in the daily life of
groups like the Baruya, it is of no small consequence to social
scientists, whose research can be used, directly or not, and immediately or not, to analyze and eventually help solve concrete
problems confronting the members of a society. It is this sort of
fundamental research, the kind that develops without the obligation to be immediately useful, that makes the social sciences
most like other sciences.

Without such comparative research, there can be neither
critical deconstruction nor a more rigorous reconstruction of
anthropology and the other social sciences. This was my goal
when I compared some twenty societies from Oceania, Africa,
Asia, and the Americas and, to my great surprise, concluded that
kinship relations did not provide a common basis for making a
society in any of them. This discovery exploded a "self-evident
truth," the anthropological axiom that there were such things as
"kin-based societies,"[62] and cleared the way for research focusing on what we in the West call "political-religious" relations.

Comparative research in anthropology is therefore not only
necessary but possible, because the social otherness of others
is always relative, never absolute; because what one culture has
invented to give its social existence meaning is comprehensible to others, even if they are not about to adopt such ways of
thinking and acting; and because all of humanity's cultural constructions, ours and others', are different and often diverging

responses to the basic, interrelated, existential questions every society asks itself, such as what it means to be human, to be born, to live and to die, or what forms of power are legitimate.

Nonetheless, recognizing the universal character of these existential questions by no means implies that all societies ask—or answer—them in the same ways. In fact, the multiplicity and diversity of mythologies, religions, and philosophies, as well as the forms of thought and codes of behavior and action they lead to, suggests the contrary.

What these questions and answers have in common is not what they say—even though a good many say very similar things—but what they aim to do. They give meaning to the realities that all human beings confront, regardless of where or when they are—the fact that they are born, die, cope with natural forces, are subject or subject others to various sorts of power and violence, and so forth—and thus provide the framework for relations between people, and with the environment. It is these inevitable, eternal realities that constitute the focus of all of existential inquiry, despite the differences of time and place, because they transcend differences.

If "relativism" in the social sciences means recognizing that the specific meaning of the questions asked and the answers given by different societies at different times thus derives from distinct cultural worlds, then it is hard to see how anthropologists and other social scientists could help practicing "relativism." But if we take such relativism further and affirm that these social and mental worlds are radically different and alien to each other, literally incomparable and inaccessible to all but those who produce and experience them, then we deny or destroy the very premise of the social sciences.

By social sciences, I mean the various forms of reflexive thought that enable us to analyze and understand the nature and functioning of the range of human societies, and the ways of thinking, acting, and feeling to which these forms of social life lead or have led. This is a difficult process, in that its practitioners must place themselves between parentheses, deliberately decentering themselves with respect to the social and cultural assumptions that have guided them from birth. This suspension of judgment is necessary, to be sure, but it is not sufficient to make comprehensible the rationale and logic that typify other human groups. We must also conduct systematic studies to gauge how individuals act—according to such factors as sex, age, or status—in the various settings they encounter in their lives, and so discover whether they do what they say and say what they do, particularly when confronted by similar circumstances. Adopting a critical distance from one's own cultural assumptions ensures that the outcome of such studies are not purely subjective projections of the observer's prejudices, or dogmatic affirmations of his or her preconceptions, but conclusions exposed to outside criticism, validation, and invalidation.

Let me offer a final remark about these existential concerns. The questions and answers they express are posed by specific individuals, not by society (since a society—Durkheim notwithstanding—is not a subject, a superindividual endowed with the capacity to think). This has been the case across time and space, as particular people address such concerns by drawing on their shared culture, reproducing or altering it according to their specific genius. And though the creators of the wonderful bodies of myth found in Africa, Asia, Oceania, and the Americas will forever remain anonymous, we clearly know how the Buddha, Christ, and Muhammad, drawing on established religious beliefs, broke respectively with Hinduism, Jewish tradition, and the pre-Islamic ideology of the Bedouin tribes.

But in order for the questions and answers elaborated by such individuals to seem obvious and to endure, ever extending their influence and rallying increasing numbers of believers and followers, more than the force of genius or truth is required. Unlike a mathematical theorem or a physics demonstration, the success and diffusion of mythology, religion, or philosophy stems from their capacity to confer meaning in individual lives, a meaning in which they have faith and which is daily tested, and affirmed. To analyze the power and the collective and individual consequences of belief is an arduous task, which we will explore in chapters 2, 3, 4, and 6.

The Anthropologist's Scientific, Political, and Ethical Responsibilities

After study, and fieldwork, at last comes the moment when an anthropologist must elaborate and publish the material that he or she has accumulated either through participant observation or from other sources such as public or private archives, travelers' accounts, and colleagues' work. The ethnographer must describe facts, events, and institutions, and report testimonies and opinions, and analyze all this in terms that establish his or her right to interpret these facts, citing sources, identifying those to whom he or she has talked or turned, documenting the context of the events reported and the identity of the protagonists, and so on.

The problem at this stage is not limited to writing, and questioning the choice of the rhetorical devices used to arouse readers' interest and convince them of the "truthfulness" of the interpretations proposed. It is also both epistemological and ethical—*epistemological* because ethnologists have to offer empirical and theoretical proof of their interpretations, and *ethical* because they have the duty to discuss their conclusions with the people with whom they lived and collaborated, and to be aware of the potential consequences of publishing a book or producing a film based on their research. These ethical concerns apply both to the host society and to the one to which he or she returns thereafter, where such publication disseminates not only the image the anthropologist has created for him- or herself, but also knowledge of the visible, less conspicuous, and hidden workings of the group described (as, for example, the secrets of rites gradually revealed to Baruya initiates as they pass from one stage to the next).[63]

The ethnologist's Cognitive Ego is therefore not just an intellectual ego, but also an *ethical* and a *political* one—ethical because ethnologists must follow a code of professional con-

duct, and political because they must be aware of the historical context in which they are working, conscious not only of
the interests, stakes, power relations, contradictions, and other
sources of conflict within both the society under study and their
own society as well, but also of the relationship between these
two societies (particularly if they come from a Western colonial power and study a group that was formerly colonized). An
anthropologist who knows nothing about history, or shows no
interest in learning about it, cannot fully discharge his or her
professional, ethical, and political responsibilities.

With these points in mind, let us return to the problem of
writing. When writing about others, it is altogether desirable
that ethnologists possess skills that enhance the clarity and the
rigor of their analyses and foster their readers' empathy for the
men and women whose ways of thinking and acting they discuss. But these literary qualities, these rhetorical devices, do not
make an ethnographic text something akin to literature, amenable to as many interpretations as it has readers (or spectators, as in the case of tragedies by Sophocles and Shakespeare).
Firth's *We the Tikopia* and Malinowski's *Argonauts of the Western
Pacific* are ethnographies, not novels, and cannot be treated as
works of literature for two reasons. The first is that unlike the
characters of Macbeth and Oedipus, which sprang from a dramatist's mind, the kula existed well before Malinowski arrived
in Kiriwina, continued after he died, and is still evolving today.
The second is that the worlds found in the works of Sophocles and Shakespeare, though compelling, are products of each
author's imagination. As we have noted, the very idea of revising
or "completing" Shakespeare's work, other than as pastiche, is
absurd, a point that does not hold for the kula, which was documented and analyzed by such ethnographers as Fred Damon,
Nancy Munn, Annette Weiner, and Jerry Leach in the decades
following Malinowski.[64] Remarkably enough, their research
did not invalidate his descriptions, but rather confirmed and
enriched them by pointing out the importance of two Trobriand
concepts—*kitoum*, or "valuables," and *keda*, or a kula "road"—

that Malinowski mentioned only in passing. They also explored a number of subjects that Malinowski glossed over (such as the role played by women in the funeral rites and the continuity of the *dala*, or matrilineal clans) or completely missed (such as the fact that in the other islands of the Massim, all lineages can take part in the kula, not just the chiefly lineages as in Kiriwina; or that women may even enter the kula via their brothers in Muyuw, according to Fred Damon; or that archeologists have unearthed proof that kula-type inter-island exchanges existed a thousand years before the first Europeans arrived in the South Seas). And these ethnographic accounts show that the kula is still a strong, going concern where today, paradoxically, the most successful man in the competitive exchange of armbands for necklaces is Billy, a "white man."[65]

The kula example demonstrates to skeptics and detractors that anthropology is indeed a scientific discipline, by virtue of two features. First, the realities observed by ethnologists are not fictions invented with the complicity of informants, but phenomena that existed before and endure after fieldworkers have come and gone (as in the case of Siberian shamanism, which is currently undergoing a full-blown revival in new forms). And second, like that of any discipline which voluntarily subjects its concepts, methods, and interpretations to a process of critical deconstruction, anthropological knowledge is accumulated and enriched by the two classic paths of science: the discovery of new facts and the invention of new paradigms.

It is therefore both erroneous and demagogical to reduce the history of ethnology to a mere succession of fantasized, contemptuous representations of others invented by Western intellectuals to legitimize dominion over the rest of the world. It is also insulting to those non-Western informants who have cooperated with anthropologists so that they might come to understand their ways of thinking and acting, to cast them as naïve, or worse as cynical, manipulating ethnologists by telling them what they want to hear and getting paid for their lies (something that very rarely happens in the field). If we had to pass judgment on past anthropological field research, we would thus echo what Firth concluded in 2001: "Be all that as it may, for me ethnography and social anthropology in general as they have developed, have been the creation of both alien Western and indigenous contributors."[66]

Firth made this observation when he was one hundred years old, just a few months before his death. He had just received the Nayacalou Medal, awarded in Fiji to those who have made the greatest contribution to "knowledge of the life of the Pacific Islanders." We all know that Firth was never particularly drawn to "grand theories" such as structuralism or Marxism, and that he had been keenly aware of the colonial context that was the framework of his research both in Tikopia and in Malaysia. Hence, neither blindness nor demagogy were his legacy.[67]

Anthropology is No Longer Indissolubly Tied to the West, Its Birthplace

Anthropology, as we have seen, is neither in its death throes nor about to disappear. Rather, it is in crisis, a positive sign[68] that the discipline is reconstituting itself in response to the new global context where it will be practiced. It is to these changes that I turn once more before concluding. As we have seen, the events that produced the world in which we live began with the end of the Second World War, and the dissolution of the colonial empires of England, France, Holland and Portugal between 1950 and 1970 (as well as the end of apartheid in South Africa in 1992). These changes accelerated with the rapid disintegration and then disappearance of the communist regimes in the USSR and its European satellites at the end of the 1980s (a process that is still taking place in Central Asia and the Far East, where the economies of China and Vietnam are daily being drawn into the world capitalist system). That decade also witnessed the critique of structuralism and Marxism, and the rise of a postmodern "New Ethnography."

These major changes deeply altered relations between the West and the rest of the world, as well as those between the thousands of local societies where anthropologists had worked and continue to work. The end of the colonial system led to the rise of newly independent states, whose structure and boundaries had been posed and imposed by the colonial powers. To be viable, however, these artificially constructed states had to become nation-states rooted in often reinvented cultural traditions, incorporating the diverging and even opposing interests of local groups that had hitherto served the interests of a foreign power. (This process recalls the independence struggles that occurred in certain countries as early as the eighteenth and nineteenth centuries, which led to numerous forms of opposition to the West and produced leaders who denounced the claims of those who colonized in order to "civilize.")

The disappearance of "real" socialism reinforced Western domination,[69] since "socialism" was a Western idea at the outset, and represented a powerful critique of the West by Western thinkers. In the nineteenth century, Marx and Engels denounced the forms of exploitation of the working class and other social groups that arose in Europe with the overwhelming ascendence of industrial commodity production. They also denounced the living conditions of the laboring masses, who were housed in the new cities that sprang up in mining and industrial areas, and emphasized the hold that the new bourgeoisie exercised on the state following the disappearance (or obliteration) of the aristocracy that had governed Europe for centuries. They proclaimed the right of peoples to rule themselves while their own countries were setting out to conquer the world and carve out colonial empires. But the "socialism" that took hold after the Bolshevik revolution addressed none of these problems. It replaced the market economy with a bureaucratic one that was largely ineffective outside the military sphere, and imposed dictatorships governed by one party and a ruling clique.

In short, when the Berlin Wall came down in 1989, some in the West, like Francis Fukuyama, proclaimed that "the end of History" had come,[70] and with it the irresistible tide of globalization, the overwhelming domination of the capitalist system, and the universal imposition of Western parliamentary democracy. The preeminent task became the global enforcement of "Human Rights," which were declared "natural and universal," and either replaced or (depending on the country) were added to Christianity, hitherto portrayed as the one "true" religion that accompanied the imposition of "true civilization" in the countries colonized by the West.

But things did not turn out altogether as some were hoping. To be sure, capitalism has become the first and only system to dominate the world economy, such that no country and no local society, great or small, can produce its material conditions of existence without every day becoming more and more integrated in the market economy. And with this comes the modern values developed in the West—individualism, consumerism, and monetization of relations and social exchanges—in short, a set of actions and principles that clash, often profoundly, with more traditional modes of living and thinking, and with values and forms of social organization that still prevail and are actively maintained in many non-Western societies.

It was against this backdrop that 9/11 occurred, and with it the familiar and immediate consequences of the wars in Afghanistan and Iraq, and of the U.S. occupation. The attacks on the World Trade Center and the Pentagon, and those that followed in such countries as Spain, Great Britain, and Saudi Arabia, were deemed legitimate acts of resistance by their authors, a violent response to the violence, humiliation, and exploitation inflicted on the Islamic world by the Western powers and the regimes that governed many Muslim countries and were perceived as corrupt, traitorous, and allies of the West.

In sum, the "end of History" was short lived (from Berlin in October 1989 to New York in September 2001). Since then, the world once again finds itself divided into countries that claim to embody Good and those seen as the "axis of Evil." And these accusations are reciprocal, since Islamic fundamentalists struggling to impose the true religion, that of the Prophet, on the rest of the world believe that the West embodies moral decadence, cynically exploits the wealth of others, and arrogantly imposes its own values—which result in feminism and lack of respect for men, recognition of homosexuality as a normal alternative, refusal to recognize God in daily acts of life and the cynical invocation of "Human Rights" to justify intervention in the life of others (especially those others who possess the strategic resources upon which the expanded reproduction of capital and the consolidation of the economic and military power of the West and its allies depend). And these pressures are evident beyond the open conflict between radical Islam and the Judeo-Christian world. In China, in the aftermath of the Maoist period where the state sought to obliterate "traditional," "feudal," or "bourgeois" forms of thought and power, involvement in the capitalist world market has led to the development of a strain of neo-Confucianism that similarly criticizes and seeks to surpass the philosophies and values imported from the West.[71]

Since 2001, the twin processes of integration in the capitalist economic system and segmentation and multiplication of political and cultural identities have gained ground and started to spread. These forces, which social scientists will henceforth encounter as they attempt to decipher so complex and contradictory a world, call for a reflexive anthropology, one that is aware of its analytical powers but also of its limits, that is pragmatic without being eclectic, that adopts tools which are useful rather than fashionable, and that is conscious of its political and ethical responsibilities.

This is the anthropology that is being reconstructed, even as it continues the process of deconstruction to emerge with more vigor, more analytical effectiveness, and more modesty, and with renewed awareness of its dependence on the other social sciences.

Today's anthropology is thus no longer indissolubly tied to the West, where it was born, and ethnologists have moved beyond the sorts of biased comparisons that made their society, and their world, seem the measure and the mirror of human progress.[72] The obligation to suspend one's judgment, to deliberately decenter one's values and the representations of self and others, is equally incumbent on thousands of ethnologists around the world, from places as varied as India, Japan, South Korea, Taiwan, South Africa, Indonesia, Sri Lanka, Brazil, Mexico, and Peru. Their ever-growing number is both a testament to the stakes entailed in anthropology, and a promise for its future. Just as the discipline arose by breaking with the improvised ethnography of missionaries, soldiers, traders, and explorers, so too is the process of decentering increasingly important in the larger world. We need only look to China, where the so-called "national" minorities—those who are not as "civilized" as the Han—are allowed to have three children or to obtain aid for economic development precisely to give them a leg up, or to India, where the country's tribes and the lowest castes continue to be listed as "backward classes," and to even demand this classification to guarantee a "quota" of their members a place in the Indian civil service and the universities, to understand what must be changed.

Anthropology is a fragment, one aspect of the process of developing a "rational" knowledge about oneself and others, freely practiced by individuals who do not, or no longer, believe that their thought and work stems from what earthly or divine powers would allow. Understanding the beliefs of others without being obliged to share them, respecting their views without precluding their criticism, and recognizing that by living with and listening to them, one gains a better understanding of oneself—this was, is, and will be the scientific, the ethical, and the political core of anthropology, yesterday, today, and tomorrow, in and out of the West.

1

Some Things One Keeps, Some Things One Gives, Some Things One Sells, and Some Things Must neither Be Sold nor Given but Kept to Pass On

The aim of this chapter is to explore the distinctions between those things one sells, those one gives and, lastly, those that can be neither sold nor given but which must be kept and transmitted. To be sure, these distinctions do not reside in the things themselves. The same object may first be bought as a commodity, then circulated in gift-exchange, and finally hoarded away in a clan treasure as a sacred object and thus withheld for a time from any form of circulation, commercial or noncommercial. Michel Panoff showed this nicely in his study of the seashells used by the Maenge of southern New Britain.[1]

In exploring this theme, my point of reference must be one of the great milestones in this history, Marcel Mauss's indispensable text, "Essai sur le don" (*The Gift*), published in 1924.[2] I will outline the context in which the "Essai" was written, but first I will discuss the ethnographic points that brought me back to the analysis of these problems

The Baruya furnished me with the example of a society that still practiced gift-exchange—the exchange of women, for example—but that did not have the potlatch (the competitive exchanges practiced by such Native American societies as the Kwakiutl and Tlingit). They also produced a sort of "commodity-currency"—salt—which they bartered with neighboring tribes for tools, weapons, feathers, and other goods that they did not produce themselves. But salt was never used as money within Baruya society; there it circulated in the form of gifts. And there were sacred objects, the *kwaimatnie*, which the Baruya treated with the utmost respect; these were used in the boys' initiation ceremonies and presented as gifts from the gods to their ancestors, gifts they must not give to other human beings.

In an era in which the idea that "everything is for sale" (as the title of Robert Kuttner's book indicates[3]) is rapidly gaining worldwide acceptance, we need to reexamine the place of non-commercial relations in market societies in light of what history and anthropology can teach us, and seek to determine whether some realities essential to the life of societies lie beyond the market, and will continue to do so.

But a rereading of Mauss is not necessarily a return to Mauss, for we shall see that many of the facts reported in his book have not been analyzed, either by Mauss himself or by his commentators, and many of the questions he did raise have gone unanswered. But perhaps it would be helpful at this point to recall the climate in which Mauss wrote the "Essai sur le don." This was immediately after the end of the First World War, in which Mauss had lost half of his friends. As a socialist, he had backed Jean Jaurès, one of the leaders of the European socialist movement, who was assassinated for opposing the war. As a renowned academic, Mauss wrote a weekly column for the popular newspaper, *L'Humanité*. And again as a socialist, he had made a postwar visit to Russia, where the communists were building their power structure, but had come back hostile to Bolshevism for two reasons: because the Bolsheviks wanted to create an economy that bypassed the market, and because they systematically used violence to transform society.[4] But Mauss was most critical of liberalism in his "Essai," and did not want society to become progressively imprisoned in what he called the "cold reasoning of the merchant, the banker, and the capitalist." In 1921, fifteen years before the Front Populaire swept to victory in France, he drew up a "social-democratic program" in which he called upon the state to provide workers with material assistance and social protection. But he also appealed to the rich and the powerful to demonstrate the kind of self-interested generosity that was practiced by Melanesian chiefs and Kwakiutl noblemen and, according to Mauss, had formerly been exercised in Europe by ancient Celtic and Germanic noblemen. Furthermore, he observed that, even after centuries of Christianity, charity was, and is, "still wounding for him who has accepted it." There is thus an apparent continuity between our era of the capitalist global world economy and the era that inspired Mauss.

What is gift-giving for Mauss? It is an act that creates a double relationship between donor and recipient. To give is to share of one's own free will what one has or what one is. An obligatory gift is not a gift. A gift freely given brings the giver closer to the receiver. But at the same time, the gift creates a debt, obligations for the one who accepts it. Giving does two things at once, then. It both reduces and creates distance between the two parties. It creates a dissymmetry, a hierarchy between giver and receiver. Thus, from the outset, Mauss set out the analytic principle that gift-giving cannot be studied in isolation. It is part of a set of relations between individuals and groups that arise from the concatenation of three obligations: the obligation to give, the obligation to accept the gift, and the obligation to give in turn once one has accepted.

It was because he thus defined the giving of a gift as the first link in a chain of acts whose structure must be analyzed as a whole that Mauss was celebrated as the precursor of structuralism by Claude Lévi-Strauss, and as his forebear. But he was only a precursor, for according to Lévi-Strauss, somewhere in the course of his "Essai," Mauss had unfortunately lost sight of the methodological principles he had established at the outset, and had mistaken for a general scientific explanation of the obligation to give in turn what was actually a particular, indigenous explanation offered up by an old Maori sage, Tamati Ranapiri. Ranapiri had explained to the anthropologist Elsdon Best the Maori beliefs concerning the existence of a spirit (*hau*) in the thing one gives that compelled the receiver to give back the same thing or something equivalent.[5] In essence, Lévi-Strauss concluded that Mauss had allowed himself to be "mystified" by a subtle and complex indigenous ideology; this was not the first time, in his estimation, that an anthropologist had stumbled into such a trap.[6]

There was indeed a flaw in Mauss's reasoning, and Lévi-Strauss lost no time in seizing upon it. In its place, he proposed another explanation of the notions of *hau* or *mana*, which he interpreted as "signifiers in their pure state" or "floating signifiers," because they are "empty of meaning." For Lévi-Strauss, whenever the human mind is confronted with something it cannot explain, it invents empty concepts that are not manifestations of some property of the thing given but which directly manifest the unconscious structures of the mind and attest to the symbolic origin of society. In short, Lévi-Strauss notes that the notions of *mana*, *hau*, and *manitou* demonstrate the primacy of language and, on a deeper level, the primacy of the symbolic over the imaginary and the real. For Lévi-Strauss, symbols are ultimately even more real than the reality they symbolize.[7]

With this in mind, I will demonstrate that, if primacy had to be assigned, the imaginary would hold sway over the symbolic rather than the other way around. For sacred objects and valuables are first and foremost objects of belief, and their nature is imaginary before it is symbolic because these beliefs concern the nature and the sources of power and wealth, whose content has always and everywhere been in part imaginary. The shells exchanged for a woman or given to compensate the death of a warrior are symbolic substitutes for human beings—the imaginary equivalents of an individual life, and of life in general.

But where exactly is the flaw in Mauss's theory? Let us go back over his reasoning. In explaining the first two obligations, that of giving and that of accepting gifts, Mauss advanced sociological rationale. One is obligated to give because giving creates obligations, and one is obligated to accept because to refuse a gift threatens to create a conflict with the giver. But when he came to the third obligation, that of reciprocating (or more accurately, giving in turn), Mauss offered another type of explanation, which relied primarily on ideology and, in the case at hand, on mystical-religious beliefs. What compels the receiver of a gift to reciprocate, he argued, is a force, the action of a "spirit" present in the thing received which compels it to return to its original owner.[8] A closer reading of Mauss shows that he seems to think that the objects given are inhabited by not one but two spirits. The first is the spirit of the original owner who gave it. But the thing itself would seem to have a soul as well—a second spirit—and therefore to exist as a person with the power to act on other persons.[9] In short, in espousing these Maori beliefs, Mauss seems above all to be trying to say that the thing given was not completely alienated, that it remained attached to its owner and was therefore at the same time both inalienable and alienated. How can this duality be explained?

Lévi-Strauss appealed to the unconscious structures of the mind, and Mauss to the religious representations of societies. Perhaps the explanation does not lie in either, but in the fact that the thing given is invested with two legal principles at the same time: an inalienable right of ownership and an alienable right of use. This very interpretation, as we shall see, is the one advanced by the Trobriand Islanders to explain the workings of their ceremonial exchanges, the legendary *kula*, which Mauss analyzed as the Melanesian counterpart of the American Indian potlatch. But Bronislaw Malinowski had not discovered this explanation of the kula mechanism, and Mauss could therefore not have known about it. We owe this discovery to Fred Damon, Nancy Munn, Annette Weiner, and others, who conducted fieldwork on Woodlark and other islands in the Massim starting in the 1960s, documenting the other parts of the kula ring, the set of exchange routes that connects this series of islands and societies (to which I will return shortly).

Before going on, I want to reiterate that Mauss was not interested in all forms of gift-exchange. He was concerned primarily with what he called "total prestations," those exchanges involving whole groups or persons acting as representatives of these groups. He was not interested in the gifts a friend might make to a friend, nor was he interested in the (imaginary) gift a god might make of his life to save mankind. He was interested in gifts that are socially necessary for producing and reproducing social relationships—kinship relations, ritual relations, power relations—in short, a certain number of the social conditions of the existence of the individuals and groups in a given society. He cites gifts of women between clans, rites performed by one moiety of a society for the benefit of the other moiety, and so forth as examples of such "total prestations," a term he uses to designate two things whose difference is usually ignored by those who have written on the subject: either the fact that gift-giving has *multiple dimensions*—economic, political, religious, artistic—and therefore the act subsumes within itself many aspects of the society; or the fact that, by engendering a constant flow of counter-gifts, gift-exchange mobilizes the wealth and energy of numerous groups and individuals, drawing the whole society into the movement and thereby constituting a mechanism and a moment that are essential to the reproduction of the society as a whole.[10]

But Mauss emphasized something we have forgotten: that there are in fact two types of total prestations, one of which he called "non-agonistic" and the other "agonistic" (from the Greek αγων, meaning "combat"). Each type has its own logic. However, he says almost nothing about the logic of non-agonistic prestations, and privileges the analysis of agonistic gift-exchange—which he designated in a general way by the term *potlatch*, a term borrowed from the Chinook language—in the "Essai."[11]

Manifestly equivalent, non-agonistic gift-giving did not interest Mauss. And yet he clearly indicated (something usually passed over in silence) that the starting point of his analysis of agonistic gifts was non-agonistic gift-exchange. This point of departure is not to be found in his "Essai," however, but in his 1947 *Manuel d'ethnographie*. There he cites the examples of the exchange of goods, rituals, names, and so forth between the groups and individuals of the two moieties of dualist societies. He mentions in passing the names of several Australian and

North American tribes, but does not discuss the particular logic of these gift-exchanges. Because I personally had the occasion to observe the exchange of women between the lineages and clans that make up Baruya society during the course of my fieldwork in New Guinea, I will attempt to fill in this gap.[12]

The basic principle is simple: One lineage gives a woman to another lineage, a man gives one of his real or classificatory sisters to another man, who in turn gives him one of his own real or classificatory sisters. To all appearances, these reciprocal gifts should cancel the debt each incurred. But this is not the case. When one lineage gives a woman to another, it creates a debt and finds itself in a relationship of superiority with respect to the receiving lineage. But when this first lineage in turn receives a woman, it becomes indebted and assumes inferior status. At the close of these reciprocal exchanges, each lineage finds itself both superior as givers and inferior as receivers. Both are therefore once more on an equal footing, since each is at the same time in a superior and an inferior position with regard to the other. Thus counter-gifts do not cancel the debts created by gifts, but create new debts that counterbalance the earlier ones. According to this logic, the exchange of gifts constantly feeds obligations and debts, thereby ensuring a flow of services, mutual assistance, and reciprocal obligations of solidarity. The debts are never cancelled or extinguished in one fell swoop, but they do gradually die out over time.

These examples show that to give in turn does not mean to repay, a distinction that is hard for the Western mind to grasp. They also demonstrate how absurd it would be for a man to give two women for the one he had received. The end result of such non-agonistic, equivalent gift-exchanges is a relatively egalitarian redistribution of the resources—human beings (women and children), goods, labor, and services—available to the groups that make up the society. By this logic, a woman equals a woman, the death of one warrior is compensated by the death of another warrior, and so on. The sphere of equivalencies between objects and subjects, between material wealth and human beings—living or dead—is limited. It is no use amassing wealth to get women, or women to accumulate wealth. Accumulating wealth and women does not enhance one's name, nor one's influence or power. That is why this type of gift-giving is often associated with Great Man societies rather than with Big Man societies in New Guinea.[13] In the latter—as the work of Andrew Strathern,[14] Daryl Feil,[15] and many others has taught us—the fame of a Big Man and his group depends on their continued success in a cycle of such competitive ceremonial exchanges as *moka* and *tee*.

✕ ✕ ✕

The potlatch (and agonistic gift-exchange in general), by contrast, operates on an entirely different logic. Mauss emphasizes that the potlatch is a veritable "war of wealth" waged for the purpose of winning or keeping titles, ranks, and power, in which the spirit of competition outweighs that of generosity. Here we are dealing, as he observes, with another type of "economy and moral code dominated by gift-giving." Using descriptions taken from Franz Boas[16] and prior Russian and Canadian authors, Mauss shows that the Northwest Coast Indians held potlatches in order to legitimize, in the eyes of all present, the possession and transmission of a title.[17] The potlatch is therefore an exercise in power, which entails accumulating massive quantities of valuables and subsistence goods in order to redistribute them in a splurge of ceremonial feasting and competition, or to destroy them with ostentation. At the outset, several rival clans and their chiefs compete for a title, but at the finish there is only one winner—at least for the time being, for as long as it takes another clan to mount a challenge with an even bigger potlatch. Here we do not find the logic of non-agonistic gift-exchanges, which end in the relatively equal distribution of the resources necessary for the reproduction of the social groups involved. And a potlatch debt can be offset by a counter-gift (which is not the case in equivalent gift-exchange), since a debt is cancelled when a man gives more than he has received, and the ideal is for a clan ultimately to give so much that no one can reciprocate, so that it stands alone, unrivaled.[18] Once again we find that debt is an essential component of the logic of gift-exchange, and in the potlatch, crushing the other with one's gifts is even the main goal. But as a debt can be cancelled by a greater counter-gift, which in turn creates a new debt, a whirlpool movement is set up that produces a relentless escalation of gifts and counter-gifts, thereby drawing the entire society into the spiral.

This was a rough outline of Mauss's analysis of the potlatch. However, there are in his text some facts he did not investigate and which his commentators have not mentioned. For instance, he observes in a footnote that the best Kwakiutl coppers, like their greatest titles, "at the very least remain unchanged within the clans and tribes,"[19] and were never entered in pot-latch. They were kept in the treasure of the clan, whereas the other coppers—the greater proportion—that circulated in the potlatches had less value and seemed to "serve as satellites for the first kind."[20] Of all those who have discussed this text, only Annette Weiner, in her book *Inalienable Possessions*, has noted the importance of these observations. This point, which no one else deemed a problem, has in fact altered the whole outlook on those things that could be given or sold, since it introduced the category of things that could neither be sold nor given, but which must be kept—the domain of inalienable possessions.[21]

Before analyzing this category of objects, though, let us come back to Mauss's theory about things having a spirit, which pre-supposes the absence of a clear-cut distinction between things and persons. According to Mauss, this belief characterized the social and mental worlds of many non-Western societies, and was the key to understanding the ancient Greek and Roman legal systems and ancient Chinese and Hindu law, which did not draw a distinction between a law pertaining to persons and a law pertaining to things. As we have seen, Mauss was trying to understand why a thing that has been given must be returned to the donor or must prompt a gift in return. In 1921, while praising the richness of Malinowski's ethnographic material,[22] Mauss regretted that it did not cast much light on the gifts and counter-gifts exchanged in the kula: "Sociologically, it is once again the mixture of things, values, contracts, and men that is so expressed. Unfortunately, our knowledge of the legal rule that governs these transactions is defective. It is either an unconscious rule, imperfectly formulated by the Kiriwina people, Malinowski's informants; or, if it is clear for the Trobriand people, it should be the subject of a fresh enquiry. We only possess details."[23]

It is not certain that Mauss believed things were really clear for the Trobrianders, for he speaks of their mixed categories. But his formulation of the problem was prophetic. The answer came only with the new research undertaken in the 1970s by such anthropologists as Frederick Damon, Nancy Munn, Annette Weiner, Jerry Leach, John Liep, and others who conducted fieldwork in a dozen societies in the kula ring.[24]

To understand the importance of the discoveries made about the kula half a century after Malinowski, we need a brief summary of the way kula is conducted. In essence, a shell armband is circulated in the hope of obtaining a shell necklace of the same rank in exchange, or vice versa. Note that, in this game, the same object or kind of object never takes the place of the object given. Thus, we cannot assert, in the case of kula, that a spirit present in the thing compels the receiver of the gift to give it back to the original owner. This was a source of some frustration for Mauss, who wrote that "Malinowski has not found any mythical or other reasons for the direction of this circulation of the *vaygu'a* [i.e. the valuables which circulate in the kula]. It would be very important to discover them. For if there was any reason for the orientation of these objects, so that they tended to return to their point of origin . . . the fact would be miraculously identical to . . . the Maori *hau*."[25]

Unfortunately, this is not what was found. Malinowski had missed two key indigenous concepts that illuminate the kula exchanges and explain why the owner appears to remain present in the object, even after it has been given: *kitoum* and *keda*. *Kitoum* are valuables owned by a lineage or even an individual—such as canoes, polished shells, stone axe-blades, and the like—

that can be used by their owners in various contexts and for distinct purposes. They can be given as compensation for the killing of an enemy, or as bridewealth, to obtain a wife; they can be exchanged for a large canoe, or sold to an American tourist; and so forth. But they can also be launched on a kula exchange path, a *keda*. Once a necklace is sent along a kula path and has left its owner's hands and come into the possession of the first recipient, it becomes a *vaygu'a*, an object that can no longer be used for any purpose other than kula exchanges. It continues to belong to the original giver, who can ask the temporary possessor to give it back, thus taking it out of kula. This practically never happens, but the fact that it is theoretically possible clearly indicates the relationship between the owner and original donor and the object he has given. What he ceded when he gave the object was not in fact its ownership but the right *to use it for making other gifts*. Therefore none of those individuals through whose hands the object will pass may use it as a *kitoum* and thus for such purposes as to compensate a killing or to procure a wife. And yet the object given never returns to its original owner, for what comes back to him in place of a necklace is always an armband of equivalent rank, which has been ceded by someone who owned it and chose to exchange it for a necklace. The armband, which has also become a *vaygu'a*, travels back along the chain of intermediaries until it finally reaches the necklace owner, who will appropriate it once again as a *kitoum*, which closes that particular exchange path (*keda*).

So there is indeed a legal rule that explains how valuables circulating in gift-exchanges can be alienated and still be the inalienable property of their original donor. But what this rule does not explain is why it applies to valuables but not to sacred objects—rare shells or very old coppers, for example—which are often of the same nature as the valuables. And yet, like sacred objects, valuables are endowed with an imaginary value not to be confused with the labor invested in locating or manufacturing them, or with their relative scarcity. This imaginary value reflects the fact that they can be exchanged for a life, that they are made equivalent to human beings. The time has come, therefore, for us to cross the line that Mauss did not cross.

But before taking this step, I will conclude my analysis of the potlatch and other forms of agonistic gift-exchanges by proposing the following hypothesis, which Mauss did not suggest: namely that such forms of competition emerge historically only if two sociological and ideological conditions are present and combined.[26] First, marriage must no longer be based primarily on the direct exchange of women; this practice must have yielded to the generalized use of bridewealth (the exchange of wealth for women). Second, some of the positions of power and prestige characteristic of a society, and therefore part of its political-religious field, must be achievable through the redistribution—in the form of ceremonial gift-exchanges—of wealth accumulated by the groups and individuals that vie with each other to appropriate such positions. When these two types of social relationships are combined within the same society, it seems that the conditions are present for the emergence of potlatch practices. Moreover, potlatch societies are not as numerous as Mauss imagined. He saw this as a widespread form of transitional economic system situated between primitive societies practicing non-agonistic gift-exchange and market societies. To be sure, we now know of many more examples of ceremonial gift-exchange than did Mauss—as in New Guinea, Asia, and other places—but the number is still low and cannot be compared with the much more frequent practice of the non-agonistic giving of gifts and counter-gifts.

This brings us to the things, such as sacred objects, that must not be sold or given but which must be kept. Sacred objects are often presented as gifts, but gifts that the gods or the spirits are supposed to have given to the ancestors of men, which their present-day descendants must keep safely stored away and must neither sell nor give. Consequently they are presented and experienced as an essential component of the identities of the groups and the individuals who have received them into their care. These groups and individuals may use them on their own behalf or for the benefit of all other members of the society, but they can also use them to inflict harm. Sacred objects are thus a source of power within and over society and, unlike valuables, are presented as being both inalienable and unalienated.

My fieldwork in New Guinea afforded me numerous occasions to see the uses to which a sacred object might be put. Among the Baruya, a certain number of clans own *kwaimatnie*.[27] These are bundles, containing objects that are never seen, which are wrapped in strips of red bark that are the color of the sun. The Baruya call themselves the "sons of the Sun." The word *kwaimatnie* comes from *kwala*, "men," and *ñimatnie*, "to cause to grow." The *kwaimatnie* are kept in a secret place in the house of the masters of the boys' initiations. These men represent the clans responsible for the different stages of the initiation, which takes place over a period of more than ten years, ending with the boys' marriage. At around the age of nine, the boys are (literally) torn away from their mothers and the world of women, and are sequestered in the Men's House at the top of the village. There they are introduced to various sacred objects: the flutes, the bull-roarers, and the *kwaimatnie*. Later they learn that the flutes were originally owned by the women and that an ancestor of the men stole them. These flutes contained, and still contain, the powers women have to make babies, with and without men.[28] What is inside a *kwaimatnie*? I had the honor and the joy one day of being shown the contents of a *kwaimatnie* by a master of the initiations. When he unwrapped the strips of bark, I saw a black stone and a pointed bone from the eagle, the Sun's bird. The man did not say anything, but I knew—having been partially initiated myself—that for the Baruya this stone contained some of the powers of Venus. For them, Venus is the metamorphosis of a Baruya woman whom their "Dreamtime" ancestors offered up in order to appease the Python, the god of rain and thunder. As for the bull-roarers, they are said to be objects that the *Yimaka*, the forest spirits, formerly gave to an ancestor of the Baruya and which are supposed to contain powers of death—the power to kill game or enemy warriors.

Thus in the sacred objects—the exclusive property of certain clans which only a few men may touch or handle—are conjoined *two* types of powers: *female* powers, the powers of life which the men are supposed (imaginarily) to have expropriated; and *male* powers, the powers of death and war received directly from the forest spirits. But in the eyes of the Baruya, women still own the powers of which they were dispossessed by the men, even if they are no longer able to use them. This is why men must resort to violence in order to separate the boys from the women's world, and initiate them into the secrets of the powers they have appropriated from women. Baruya men justify this expropriation by telling how the first women did not use their powers for the good of society. They killed too much game, for instance, and caused many kinds of disorder. The men had to intervene and dispossess them of their powers so that society and the cosmos might be restored to order.

In essence, a sacred object is a material object that represents the nonrepresentable, which refers men to the origin of things and attests to the legitimacy of the cosmic and social order that replaced the primal time and its events. A sacred object does not have to be beautiful. A splinter of the "True Cross" is not beautiful—it is more than beautiful; it is sublime.[29] A sacred object places man in the presence of the forces that command the invisible order of the world. For those who handle and exhibit them, sacred objects are not symbols. They are experienced and thought of as the real presence of forces that are the source of the powers that reside in them.

It is important to note that, in the stories relating the circumstances in which certain objects were given to the mythic ancestors of today's real men and women, these ancestors appear as being at the same time both more and less powerful than their descendants. They are more powerful because they were able to communicate *directly* with the gods at any time and to receive gifts from them; they are less powerful because these first humans did not know how to do any of the things that modern-day humans know how to do—hunt, work the land, marry, initiate their children—knowledge they received from the gods. The sacred object, then, is a "material" synthesis of the imaginary and symbolic components present in the relations that organize real societies. The interests at stake in the imaginary and in the symbolic always have a real social impact. For instance, when the rites have been performed, and in the name of their myths, Baruya women are really—and not merely symbolically or imaginarily—dispossessed of land ownership, the use of weapons, and access to the gods, but they are also deprived of the use of their bodies and their desires.

From this standpoint, one might postulate that the monopoly of sacred objects, rites, and other imaginary means of access to the forces that control the cosmos and society must have sociologically and chronologically preceded the development of the various forms of exclusive control of the material conditions of social existence and production of wealth—namely the land and its resources, or the individuals and their labor. One might cite here the example of the Australian Aboriginal rites for multiplying the living species and the initiated men's monopoly of the sacred objects, the *tjuringas*.

I am not saying that religion is the source of the caste or class relations that have arisen in many parts of the world since Neolithic times. But it does seem to me that religion may have furnished ready-made models for representing and legitimizing the new forms of power in places where certain social groups and their representatives were beginning to raise themselves high above the others and thus sought to legitimize their place in this now different society by means of a different origin. Did not the Inca present himself as the son of the Sun? And the pharaoh as a god dwelling among men?

To better discern the nature of sacred objects, we would need to go even further and understand that they are an ultimate testimonial to the opacity necessary for the production and reproduction of societies. In the sacred object, the men who manufactured it are at once present and absent. They are present, but in a form that dissimulates the fact that men themselves are at the origin of the forces that dominate them and that they worship. This is the very same relationship men have with money when it functions as capital, as money that makes money, which appears capable of reproducing itself unaided, of generating money independently of the men who produced it.

It is not true, then, even in highly developed capitalist societies, that "everything is for sale." Let us consider the constitution of a Western democracy. It is a fact that votes can be and frequently are bought in democratic societies, but it is not yet possible to run down to the supermarket and buy a constitution. Democracy means that each person—however rich or poor, whatever their gender or social function—possesses an equal share of political sovereignty. To be sure, a democratic constitution is not a god-given set of commandments. It is a set of principles that people give to themselves as a means of organizing their life together and that they oblige themselves to respect. A democratic constitution is a common good that, by its very essence, is not the product of market relations but of political relations and negotiation. For this reason, in a democracy, the political power of each person is an inalienable possession.

But let us go one step further. The expansion of the market has its limits, and some of these are absolute. Can one imagine, for instance, a child making a contract with his or her parents to be born? The very idea is absurd, and its absurdity demonstrates that the first bond among humans—namely birth—is not "negotiated" between the parties concerned. From its inception, life is established as a gift and a debt, in whatever society it may appear.

✕ ✕ ✕

By way of conclusion, I would like to present a sort of general hypothesis concerning the conditions of existence and production of human societies. As I have already noted, people not only live in society, like the other primates and social animals, but also produce society in order to live. And it seems to me that, in order to produce society, three operations and three principles must be combined. There must be certain things that are given, others that are sold or bartered, and still others that must be kept. In our societies, buying and selling has become the main activity. Selling means completely separating the thing from the person. Giving means maintaining something of the giver in the thing given. And keeping means not separating the thing from the person, because in this union resides the affirmation of a historical identity that must be passed on, at least until such time as it can no longer be reproduced. It is because these three operations—selling, giving, and keeping-to-transmit—are not the same that objects in these contexts are presented respectively as alienable and alienated (commodities), as inalienable but alienated (gift objects), and as inalienable and unalienated (sacred objects, democratic constitutions, and the like).

✕ ✕ ✕

Today the global economy encompassing societies like the Baruya, but also those of France and many other countries, is no longer a regional globality, as it was in the two or three mountain valleys of New Guinea before the Europeans arrived. It is now a world globality. Local economies are now subsumed by a single system—the capitalist system, the most highly developed form of market economy. Once again this does not mean that all local cultures and forms of social organization are destined to be reduced to pale copies of European and American ways of living and thinking. Not everything is for sale, nor will it ever be; and identities continue on through their own transformations. The time has come, it seems to me, to develop a new focus of economic anthropology, one that, without claiming to exhaust the complexity of local societies, will explore the new linkages between the local and the global.

2

No Society Has Ever Been Based on the Family or on Kinship

The title of this chapter may seem surprising, and perhaps even shocking, for it explicitly challenges one of the major axioms of anthropology—namely that before the appearance of societies divided into castes, orders, or classes toward the end of the Neolithic era, and before the appearance of centralized powers in the context of states, human societies were composed of groups of individuals linked by kinship. Even today this vision of the past is held to be true because, on almost every continent, we still find societies governed by a state whose internal organization does not rest on the existence of castes, orders, or classes, such as the Yanomami in the Amazon.[1]

This was once the case for the Baruya of New Guinea, with whom I lived and worked between 1967 and 1988. The Baruya were "discovered" in 1951 by a young Australian patrol officer, Jim Sinclair, who had mounted an expedition to find the people who were reputed for producing the salt bars used as a currency among the groups in the region he patrolled.[2] He had been vaguely pointed in their direction and told that their name was the "Batia." The Batia were in fact the Baruya. They and their neighbors spoke the same language, one of the 1,500 found on the island of New Guinea, which now encompasses the nation of Papua New Guinea (formerly the Australian eastern half) and Irian Jaya (formerly the Dutch western half, now under Indonesian control). Nowhere in this multitude of societies had anyone found great chiefdoms, as in Polynesia, much less states. In 1960 a second military expedition returned to the

Baruya, this time to build a patrol post and a landing strip for small aircraft to facilitate contact with the local tribes. With this, the Baruya lost both sovereignty over their territory and their cultural autonomy. Until 1965 the region was closed to Europeans, with the exception of those living around the patrol post. Two missions immediately established themselves within a radius of five miles—the Summer Institute of Linguistics and the Lutheran Mission. In 1965 the region was deemed "pacified" and was "derestricted." In 1967 an anthropologist arrived, thus rounding out the Western complement of patrol officers and Australian, European, and American missionaries. Then in December 1975, without having expressed the wish or grasping the concept, the Baruya became citizens of the new independent state of Papua New Guinea, which at the same time became a member of the United Nations.[3]

In the course of my fieldwork, I was to learn that the Baruya— as a group living in a territory whose boundaries are known, if not always respected, by their neighbors—did not exist three or four centuries ago. I got them to explain their history and the conditions in which their society came about, which led me to ask myself some questions of a much more general nature. What is a society in this part of the world? What is the difference between nearby societies if their members share the same language and the same culture—in other words, the same ways of thinking and of organizing themselves? What was the social form of these societies? What does the notion of tribe used to characterize this form of society mean? What roles did kinship relations and kin groups play in the formation of this society and its perpetuation?

The facts I am going to analyze will, I think, show why I was forced to question the idea that such societies as the Baruya were founded on kinship, a theory widespread in anthropology since at least the time of Lewis Henry Morgan, which has spread from anthropology to the social sciences in general. In addition, these facts also undermined another thesis that, at the time, was rather dear to my heart. After the Second World War, under the influence of Marxism and other scholars who focused on similar concerns without sharing Marx's revolutionary conclusions, the thesis had been advanced that the foundations on which a society, any society, rested were the economic relations that existed between the individuals and groups that comprised it—namely, the relations of production and distribution of the means of subsistence and material wealth, but also exchange relations within the society and with neighboring groups.[4]

Today I believe that these theories are not supported by the facts, and moreover that they are analytically ineffective. In the first place, the existence of kin groups and the many kinds of exchanges, and not only matrimonial ones, that develop between these groups are not enough, in New Guinea or elsewhere, to make such groups a society. And in the second, the economic activities and exchanges between the individuals and groups that make up this kind of society never create ties of material and social dependency that extend to *all* of the individuals and *all* of the groups which comprise it. Economic activities cannot be the foundation upon which a society is formed and exists *as a whole*, in the eyes of its members as in the eyes of neighboring territorial groups.

The history of the Baruya and the analysis of their social structures before the Europeans arrived support these assertions.[5] The Baruya claim to descend from clans that once belonged to another tribe, the Yoyue, who lived near Menyamya, a few days' walk from where the Baruya now reside in the mountains around Marawaka, a patrol post created by the Australian administration in the 1960s. One day (according to the Baruya), when most of the men and women of one of the Yoyue villages had gone into the forest on one of the big hunting expeditions that commonly precede the initiation ceremonies, their enemies overran the village, killing those who had stayed behind and destroying the Men's House. In reality this attack had been instigated by other Yoyue clans, who had asked their traditional enemies to liquidate part of the tribe with whom they were at odds. The Baruya clearly remember the place where their ances-

tors used to live—Bravegareubaramandeuc—and at each initiation a few members of the tribe, the masters of the initiations
and the shamans, walk for several days until they come to the de-
serted site of the ancestral village. There they gather sacred plants,
which they then secretly give to the new initiates to ingest.

The Baruya recount that the survivors of the seven Yoyue
clans fled to the forest, crossed a chain of mountains, and found
refuge with the Andje, a tribe that lived in the Marawaka Valley at the foot of Mount Yelia, an extinct volcano that rises to
an altitude of 3,300 meters. There one of the local clans, the
Ndelie, gave them some land and took them into their village.
Women were exchanged, the refugees' children were initiated
along with the Andje children, and the Baruya, who spoke a
language closely related to that of the Andje, quickly adopted
their hosts' language. Two or three generations later, the Yoyue
refugees, abetted by the Ndelie local clan, massacred part of the
Andje, who fled to the other side of Mount Yelia, abandoning
their territory. A new territorial group was then formed, made
up of the descendants of the refugees and a few autochthonous
clans who joined them because they had intermarried. A new
tribe was thus born, which continued to expand until the start of
the twentieth century, conquering the neighboring Wonenara
Valley and driving out its inhabitants, and absorbing a few more
lineages with whom the Baruya had exchanged women along
the way. This new territorial group took the name *Baruya* as
their "big name," from the name of the clan that today holds the
most important of the sacred objects necessary for the initiation
of the boys and young warriors.

The Baruya and their neighbors—friends or enemies who
speak closely related languages[6]—are fully conscious that they
all belong to one set of groups, which they call "those who wear
the same ornaments as us" (the same insignia).[7] This refers to
the array of signs that immediately tell everyone in these groups
that a man has been initiated because he wears a headdress of
black cassowary feathers, or that he is a shaman because there
is a long eagle feather in the middle of the headdress, and so

forth. I use the term *ethnie* to designate this set of local groups who know that they come from the same stock, speak related languages, and share certain principles of social organization, representations of the social and cosmic order, and common values. But the fact of belonging to the same ethnic group does not give its members women or access to land; it gives them a particular identity which goes beyond simply being a member of their society, and it makes them part of a cultural and linguistic community that is far broader than the local group, the tribe to which they belong by birth or by adoption.

I use the word *culture* here to designate the set of representations and principles that consciously organize the different domains of social life, together with the values attaching to these ways of acting and thinking. A culture thus resides first of all in the mind, but does not truly exist until the mental components—principles, rules, representations, values—become associated with concrete social and material practices to which they give meaning. In the Baruya's case, however, sharing the same culture and language does not automatically make one a member of the same society. What else is needed then to make a "society," or more particularly for the Baruya, an organized group distinct from their neighbors—the Wantekia, the Boulakia, the Yuwarrounatche, and other groups—who share the same language and culture? Their history shows that the Baruya became a society distinct from their neighbors the moment they laid claim to and gained control over a territory on which they could reproduce their group, to the exclusion of neighboring groups. It is this connection with a territory, acquired through violence in the Baruya case and then passed on from one generation to the next, added to the language and the shared principles organizing social life, that changed the ties between a certain number of kin groups into something else—a social whole that both encompassed and transcended the kin groups, a local society in the form of a tribe with a name of its own.

But why the need to claim and to control a territory?[8] To guarantee permanent social and material access to a number of natural resources that largely ensure the material continuity of the local group, and therefore of all the clans and lineages that compose it—in other terms, to lay claim, for oneself in the first place, to a portion of the natural environment. A territorial group thus becomes a *society* when a number of groups and individuals decide to reproduce themselves together in the same territory and to designate themselves, for their purposes and for the surrounding groups, by an overarching name that encompasses the individual names of their natal clans and lineages. One is a Baruya for one's neighbors, but when among Baruya, one is an Andavakia or a Bakia (two of the tribe's clans). But we must bear in mind that there is also a clan called the Baruya, which holds the most important sacred objects necessary for initiating men and has given its name to the tribe as a whole.

Once a new territorial group—in this case a tribe—makes its appearance, it must both *reproduce itself as such*, as a whole, and *represent itself* to itself and *present itself* to others as such, as a *whole*. As we will see, the level at which a society like the Baruya thus represents itself belongs to what we in the West refer to as the domain of political-religious relations, a set of institutions and social relations that do not fall into the domain of kinship, but which subsume it and compel these relations to serve the reproduction of the society as a whole. This is why, in practice, individuals and their kin groups are obliged to act in such a way that they not only reproduce themselves, but in so doing reproduce the society with its global logic which, as such, provides them daily with a share of the conditions of their existence.

Now if belonging to a linguistic and cultural community, to an ethnie, does not afford a person access to land or to a spouse, while being a member of a tribe or of one of the kin groups that comprise it does, what then is a *tribe*? A tribe is a local society—*not* a community—composed of a number of kin groups united by the same principles of social organization, the same modes of thought, and the same language, bound together by repeated marriages and associated in the defense and the exploitation of the resources of a common territory. It is precisely this control of a particular territory whose boundaries are known by their neighbors, even if they are not always acknowledged or respected, that both distinguishes and opposes societies. Thus it is not kinship that makes "society," but the shared exercise of a sort of sovereignty over a portion of the natural environment and the beings that populate it, not only the plants and animals but also the humans, and with them the dead, the spirits, and the gods that may reside there and who are supposed to bring people life or death. And their history shows that all these societies which belong to a single cultural and linguistic community, to a single ethnie, do not forego the pleasure of making war on each other and sometimes appropriating their neighbors' territory after having expelled or decimated its population.

This sovereignty over a territory and those that inhabit it is exercised through a number of institutions distinct from kinship among the Baruya, such as the male and female initiations, the age-group system, and the initiation of shamans who protect the group from sickness and attacks by evil spirits or enemy shamans. In sum, by our definition, a tribe is a society, whereas an ethnie is a community. Both are social realities, but they are not of the same order, and they do not have the same impact on the destiny of individuals or on the evolution of their society, which manifests itself as such through an overarching name, a territory, and collective political-religious functions and institutions. The Baruya's very history demonstrates that kinship relations produce kin groups, which on their own cannot make a society. A group of refugee clans became a society when they appropriated their hosts' territory and began to initiate their own children, to erect the great ceremonial house they call *tsimia*. This is why, when you want to ask a Baruya or someone from the neighboring groups what tribe they belong to, you say "what *tsimia* do you belong to (*tsimiyaya*)?" And when you want to ask someone what kin group they belong to, you have the choice of asking either "what tree do you stem from (*yisavaa*)?" or "who are the same as you (*navaalyara*)?"

Before going further, let us leave New Guinea for a moment

and look at a few other facts that seem to substantiate our theoretical propositions concerning the distinction that must be made
between *community* and *society*. A telling, contemporary example
is the state of Israel. For centuries the Diaspora comprised separate communities within the societies of Europe, the Near and
Middle East, North Africa, and other countries. Later, when the
European nations and states emerged, these communities became minorities endowed by the new polities with a variety of
statuses. Today the Jews have returned to the land of Israel and
are building their own society and state, based on a territory of
their own with borders whose recognition they demand from
such neighboring states as Lebanon, Syria, and Egypt. Another
example that has garnered international attention is that of the
Pashtun tribes, which belong to a far-flung ethnie living in Afghanistan and Pakistan.[9] Though some criticize and reject the
notions of tribe or ethnie as inventions of the colonialist West
that have no connection with any reality on the ground,[10] the
wars raging in Afghanistan and Iraq demonstrate that these
notions are not just fabrications. No one can deny that France
and other former colonial powers have manipulated ethnic and
tribal as well as religious differences for their own ends. But for
something to be manipulated, it must already exist.

Let us now return to the Baruya, and to the fact that a society
must assume an overarching name in order to represent itself to
itself and to its neighbors. The English call their country "England," the land of the Angles, who together with the Saxons
were Germanic invaders of an island inhabited by Celtic tribes.
For the Baruya, the choice of an overarching name reflects the
political and ritual importance of the Baruya clan with respect
to the other clans, which is justified by a myth that is essentially
the tribe's political charter. Here is a summary of the story that
was told to me by the master of the initiations, who was from
the Baruya clan:

> In olden times, all people lived in one place on the edge of the sea.
> One day they split up, and our ancestor, the ancestor of the Ba-

ruya Kwarrandariar, rose up into the air and flew away to Bravegareubaramandeuc. Our ancestor's name was Djivaamakwé, and
he flew along a path as red as fire. This path had been built by
the spirit men of the Dreamtime for him and for the Kwaimatnié
the Sun had given him before he flew away. When he touched
ground, the spirit men revealed the Sun's secret name to him and
told him the name he must give the people he would meet: Bara-
gayé [a red-winged insect the Baruya are forbidden to kill]. At
Bravegareubaramandeuc, Djivaamakwé came across some men.
He gave them their clan name, then he explained to them that
they had to initiate their boys, and gave each clan certain tasks to
perform. He told them to build a Tsimia, a big ceremonial house,
and he proclaimed: "I am the center-post of his house, you are
below me, I am the first, and the first name of all of you now will
be mine: Baruya." The others did not object when he raised his
name and lowered theirs. All they had were some little Kwait-
mainé. They said to him: "We are your warriors, we can't let you
be killed by enemies, you won't go to war. The rest of us will go
and you will stay in our midst." Then Djivaamakwé set on their
heads the insignia of the great warriors, and of the shamans; he
saw and marked those who would become great men. Afterwards
there were many wars, and we fled to Marawaka.[11]

This myth begins in legend (the Sun) and ends in history ("we
fled to Marawaka"). Its social function is clear: it legitimizes in
an imaginary (for us) fashion the fact that one of the clans now
has the leading role in the rituals that make boys into warriors—
and with it the general domination of men over women—and
confirms the ascendancy of the Yoyue refugee clans over the
autochthons, who were taken into the tribe but play no role
in the rituals. This story is the Baruya equivalent of a Western
constitution. But let us not forget that before the appearance of
constitutions based on human rights in late-eighteenth-century
Europe, power and institutions derived from a divine, cosmic
order. The king of France proclaimed himself "King by divine
right."

A society is thus a whole, which must reproduce itself as a whole and be so perceived, to show itself to be a whole. In order to represent their society to themselves, the Baruya produced a reality that was both material and symbolic. The symbol is the *tsimia*, a vast edifice they construct every three or four years in order to initiate a new generation of young boys and to promote those already initiated to the next stage. (In effect, Baruya initiations have four stages; when the young adolescents reach the third stage they have the right to go to war, and at the end of the fourth stage they leave the Men's House to take a wife.)

Construction of the *tsimia* brings into play all of the social dimensions and all of the symbols of Baruya society. Let's consider a few essential facts. When the *tsimia* is raised, the father of each new initiate brings a long post, which represents his son. The shaman-master lines the men up around a big circle traced on the ground, which outlines the future initiation house. The men stand side by side, grouped by village but not by lineage, and at a signal given by the master of the initiations (a man from the Baruya Kwarrandariar clan) they plant their posts in the ground at the same time and give a war cry. Each of the posts is regarded as a "bone," a part of the gigantic skeleton of the ceremonial house, which is called "the body of the Baruya." The center post on which the roof rests is considered the symbol of the ancestor who received the first *kwaimatnie* from the Sun. The thatch covering the edifice is brought in bundles by hundreds of women and is described as "the skin" of the body of the Baruya. For the Baruya, this collective action, which unites all of the adult men and women of the tribe in the construction of an edifice where the distinctions between lineages and clans are obliterated to produce a single "body," founds their society anew. And by holding the initiations, they repeatedly reestablish and re-legitimize the two hierarchies that structure this society: the general domination of the men over the women, and the superiority of the clans that own sacred objects and formulas with respect to those that do not.

The reality is obviously far more complex, for it is built on social relations, several of which are a potential source of conflict. For example, when I questioned the clans that did not have *kwaimatnie*, and therefore no master of the initiations among their members, the elders confided to me that when their ancestors agreed to join up with the Baruya, after their tribe had lost a war, they buried their *kwaimatnie* in a secret place. And they told me that, if tomorrow their clan were to enter into conflict with the rest of the Baruya and were forced to leave the tribe, they would dig up their *kwaimatnie* to use them once more in another society. This response suggests the internal tensions generated by the relationship between refugees who appropriated a territory and the local groups that joined them because they had become their allies by marriage and were assured of keeping their lives, their land, and their hunting territories if they united with the Baruya. By contrast, I heard a different story when I asked the masters of the initiations why some clans did not have *kwaimatnie*. They replied that these men had lived in the forest before joining the Baruya, where they were like cassowaries (or, to put it more accurately, they were like "cassowary droppings").[12] One can gauge from these two explanations the continuing disdain of the conquerors and the ongoing ulterior motives of the indigenous inhabitants. All this lurks behind the united front presented by the Baruya when they gather together to initiate their younger generations, a time of truce when feuding is suspended and enemies are invited to come and admire the newest Baruya warriors, against whom their sons will or would later fight.

Kinship relations thus divide as much as they unite the members of a society. And the Baruya explained quite clearly that, by giving women to potentially hostile neighboring groups, they hoped that their brothers-in-law would forsake their original tribe and side with them in the event of war. Such betrayal guarantees that their lives and lands will be spared when the Baruya seize the territory of those they have conquered.

Another example of an institution that transcends kinship is shamanism. Once again only one clan, the Andavakia, holds the *kwaimatnie* necessary for initiating the shamans, those men and women with exceptional spiritual powers who can appear in any clan. The shamans are supposed to afford all the Baruya continual protection against evil spirits sent by the shamans of enemy tribes or by evil forces. The Baruya believe that every night the spirits of male shamans change into eagles or other birds and fly to the tops of the surrounding mountains to keep watch, while the spirits of female shamans become frogs and take up positions along the rivers that enclose or flow through the Baruya territory. The mission of these two groups of spirits is to keep the spirits of ordinary Baruya who leave their sleeping bodies from unwittingly straying beyond the borders of the territory, where they run the risk of being attacked and devoured by the evil spirits wielded by enemy shamans. Shamanism and its representatives thus serve all Baruya, regardless of clan.

Let us turn to one last important fact, which is the Baruya's darkest secret. In the course of the initiations, the young first- and second-stage initiates, who have been taken from their mothers and the world of women, drink the semen of the third- and fourth-stage initiates, who have never had sexual intercourse with a woman. The close young male paternal and maternal relatives of the initiates are prohibited from inseminating them, for this would constitute homosexual incest. The male substance, free of any female pollution, is regarded as the principal source of the Baruya's strength and of their life, since their view of conception holds that it is the man who makes the essential part of the child by means of his semen. Semen—the vital energy that creates life—is thus transmitted from one generation to the next in the Men's House, and the construction of the men's identity and their power is accomplished through practices that recognize but transcend the boundaries drawn by relations of kinship.

Let us now turn to the Baruya kinship system to examine my second thesis, which focuses on the role of economic relations in the formation of this type of society. Baruya society is characterized by patrilineal descent, and marriage is based on the direct exchange of women between two lineages according to two complementary rules: a man must never reproduce his father's marriage (he must never take a wife from his mother's clan), and two brothers must never marry two women from the same lineage. As a result of these prohibitions, every lineage is always allied with several other lineages at once, and after three or four generations the same alliances are contracted again. Nevertheless, despite the plurality and diversity of their alliances, no lineage is materially linked at any given moment to all others. The lineages and the clans generated by the patrilineal descent rule all own a certain number of garden plots and hunting territories in common. These lands are exploited by the families of the men of the lineage, who provide most of their material necessities. Before the Europeans arrived, the Baruya also produced bars of salt which served as a currency they exchanged for bark capes, bows and arrows, stone adzes, and bird-of-paradise feathers— in short, for means of production (tools), means of destruction (weapons), and means of social reproduction (feather ornaments for the initiates and the like). Within the Baruya tribe, however, salt never functioned as a currency. It was redistributed in the form of gifts to members of one's lineage and one's allies. By contract, in exchanges with neighboring tribes, salt became a commodity, and even more than a commodity, a currency.[13]

Each lineage thus produced surpluses in order to acquire from the neighboring tribes those things it did not produce itself. And each time the initiations came around, every three or four years, all the clans would busy themselves producing enough food, sugar cane, new clothes, and ornaments to perform the rites and properly receive the hundreds of guests who normally attend the weeks-long ceremonies. These necessary surpluses fall into two categories: those needed to reproduce the families and lineages, and those needed to reproduce the tribe as it exists in its overarching institutions. Identical phenomena are found in many other societies. Among the Inuit, families split up into small groups during the winter in order to exploit scarce resources, while bands come together in the summer to contract marriages and perform the rituals dedicated to the masters of the animals, who ensure the animals' return the following year (and thus provide new gifts of game). During female initiations among the Mbuti of the Republic of Zaire, bands intensified their hunting and their gathering of forest products to celebrate over a period of several weeks, a time marked by feasting, dancing, and singing, with thanks offered to the Forest goddess for her gifts.[14]

For Baruya individuals, belonging to a kin group was the prerequisite social condition for having access to land, receiving help from others, being given part of the products of their labor and sharing one's own. In modern parlance, kinship relations functioned as economic relations, regulating the production and distribution of the material products necessary for the Baruya's social life. The crucial point here is that the economic activities of production and exchange between Baruya—between individuals as well as between their lineages—*never* constituted a network of material and social ties of dependence linking *all* clans of the tribe at the same time. Just as the exchanges of women that enabled the kin groups to reproduce never bound one clan to *all* the others, so too their economic exchanges never bound everyone together simultaneously, except during initiations, when each lineage contributed, through its labor and its products, to reproducing all of the clans within the framework of the ceremonies.

One could nonetheless argue that, in certain places, kinship relations are truly ties of social dependence that simultaneously bind together all of the individuals who make up a society. One might plausibly assert that this is the case among the Australian Aborigines, whose society is divided into four sections or eight subsections that govern such factors as matrimonial exchanges. In this system, a man from section A must marry a woman from section B. Their children belong to section C and must marry someone from section D. The children of this last marriage once again belong to section A, their father's father's section. But this assertion poses problems, since we now know that the section system is a relatively recent social invention, which seems to have appeared slightly over a thousand years ago in northwest Australia and only gradually to have spread to the middle of the Western Desert by the beginning of the twentieth century. For the more than two centuries before Europeans first arrived, the sections apparently did not govern kinship, but instead organized the rituals necessary to increase animal and plant species and to initiate men and women. In short, we now believe that the sections were a political-religious construct designed to ensure the reproduction of the cosmos and of society, which placed men in a primary role.[15] As this political-religious apparatus spread, it revamped the previously existing kinship structures—which were probably Dravidian and ego-centered—by superimposing sociocentric dimensions on them.[16] This is why one always finds numerous individuals in any section who have no real genealogical tie with an anthropological "Ego" via descent or marriage, and yet are called "fathers," "mothers," "brothers-in-law," or "sons" and "daughters." The general dependence among all members of the society created by its division into sections does not work fundamentally on behalf of kinship but for its overall reproduction and its relations with the entire cosmos, and thus does not refute my thesis.

Baruya kinship and economic relations do not create bonds of general dependence that provide the basis on which to build their society. Rather, as among Aboriginal people, it is the areas of social life concerned with the construction and maintenance of political-religious relations that create a general interdependence of all the clans, through their concern with the production of great warriors and men capable of leading the society, and with the activities of the male and female shamans who protect them from sickness and evil spirits and assist in warfare by casting spells on the enemy. (I will not dwell on this since we have already seen some of the domains that create a general dependence, which of course is in part purely imaginary—not for the Baruya, but for us.)

We could cite other historical examples that would demonstrate how the political-religious institutions subsume and supercede relations of kinship. At the head of ancient Roman kin groups—*gentes*, a word whose root is related to birth—stood the *pater familias*, who held sway over the life and death of his children and could either abandon them or accept them by raising them over his head when they were born. If the child was a boy, this gesture signaled the arrival of a new citizen to the City of Rome.[17] Of course this applied only to freemen, not to slaves, who were part of the city but were excluded from the community of the *populus romanus*.

✕ ✕ ✕

The conclusion here is obvious: In all societies—including ranked societies with castes, orders, or classes, such as ancient Rome—the political-religious relations extend beyond and integrate kinship relations and kin groups into a much broader unit that must be reproduced as such. But things are not so simple when it comes to the role of economic relations in forming a society. This is because societies fall into one of two broadly defined categories: those where there is no social division of labor but where labor is distributed according to gender and generation, with no social group specializing in any particular task, such as agriculture or crafts; and those where there is a true social division of labor such that certain social groups do not participate directly in production but devote themselves entirely to other social functions performed for the benefit of all (such as the Brahman caste in India, who perform the ritual sacrifices, or the Kshatriya warrior caste who served the Raja, or kings). The problem posed by the latter category is that those groups which do not take any part in the production of their own material conditions of existence must rely on others to do it for them.[18] As a consequence, those who work produce twice over—once for themselves and once for those who do not produce—and are therefore obliged regularly to produce more than they need so that the other castes or classes may continue materially to exist. Here we pass beyond the Baruya, for in this circumstance the social relations organizing the production and the distribution of the goods and services underpin the society as a *whole*. If the peasants and the artisan castes were to stop producing for others for a year or two, the material foundations of the social hierarchy would collapse, bringing down the society's overarching framework.

The roles of the economy thus differ greatly between a society like the Baruya and those that are caste or clan based. Among the Baruya, a clan can sever its ties with one tribe and join another—where it will survive if is given land and hunting territories in addition to protection—and its departure does not threaten the existence of the society as a whole. But if a peasant caste should stop producing for others, the overall reproduction of society would be jeopardized. Of course the social redistribution of the products of labor can take place without commercial exchanges, through such actions as direct deductions or payment of tribute, for example. For this to happen, the governing castes must control the conditions of production—the land, the labor of others, and, of course, redistribution of the fruits of this labor—without taking part in the labor process. In this manner, we have witnessed the emergence and development of "global" economies in the past where commercial exchanges did not play a predominant role.

With these points in mind, let me advance a somewhat oddly formulated hypothesis. Economic relations in societies like the Baruya are in a way "narrower" than the society as a whole, since they do not connect all individuals and all groups. Commercial exchanges are one-off occurrences, serving to procure what the lineages do not produce, and thus concern the lineages alone, and not the entire society. This is not the case when a market economy develops and encompasses the better part of production and the services useful to the society's reproduction. With the development of international trade and colonial Western expansion in sixteenth-century Europe, the economy created both a national and an international market in order to sustain its growth.[19] In effect, the capitalist mode of production required the elimination of internal customs barriers, such as those which existed between the provinces of a state, by way of example. Its development demanded that the entire national space be conquered and opened up to the circulation and distribution of commodities. There was thus once a time in Europe, now rapidly drawing to a close, when the national economies were largely congruent with the national borders, and provided each society with its material base. This is no longer the case; all or nearly all production is now aimed at a global market, and firms target markets that extend beyond national boundaries. One could conclude that the Baruya economy was too narrow to support the whole society, while today's multinational economy is too broad to be the basis of a single society. It is obvious that, today, in the "Western" part of our planet, kinship is even less important for the reproduction of society than it was—and still is—for the Baruya, who remain at the periphery of the capitalist world system.

✕ ✕ ✕

Let me turn to a last, essential point of theory. The historical evolution of a kinship system always produces another kinship system. Kinship begets kinship, and never anything else—not, for instance, overall political and religious relations. When such new forms of social organization as castes, orders, and classes appeared, and when such new forms of power as states or empires arose, they were the product of the evolution of the political and ritual relations they replaced, not the outcome of the evolution of the kinship relations and systems that went before. This is not to say that kinship systems do not change over historical time, but that we should not look to kinship relations to find the social forces and contradictions which alter the overall configurations of societies.

✕ ✕ ✕

But, I repeat, humans do not merely live in society, like other social animals, but also produce society in order to live. And producing new forms of society does not mean merely adapting to the market, for the simple reason that "not everything is for sale."[20]

3

It Always Takes More Than a Man and a Woman to Make a Child

The different cultures that distinguish human societies are responses to fundamental existential questions encountered by all peoples and in every time—concerns that can be divided into five thematic axes which intersect and overlap at many points:

1. What relations do humans entertain with the invisible, the ancestors, the spirits, and the gods?
2. What are the forms and figures of the power and powers exercised in societies?
3. What does it mean to be born, to live, and to die?
4. What forms of wealth and exchange (and eventually currency) exist in each society?
5. How does each society see its natural environment and act upon it?

Each axis represents a chain of human events and relations that poses a problem every society must resolve, and allows us to compare the answers worked out by the people of different societies at different times. This comparison is the object of anthropology.

Though one of these axes concerns being born, living, and dying, before a human being can be born, he or she must be conceived. In this chapter we will explore the various representations of the process by which a child is made that are found in a range of human societies. I have compared ethnographic material from 26 such societies—13 from Oceania (which is not surprising in light of my fieldwork), 4 from Asia, 4 from Native North America, 3 from Africa, and 2 from Europe—and was surprised to find that no one, in any of these groups, thought that a man and a woman were sufficient to make a child, be it an ordinary human, an extraordinary human, a headman, or a human god. In every society, whatever the kinship system or the political-religious structures, a man and a woman make a fetus. But for this fetus to become a complete human child, it needs the help of agents more powerful than humans—the intervention of ancestors, spirits, or gods. By way of example, I will compare the conception theories of seven of these societies in the pages that follow.

The first society I have chosen to discuss is the Inuit, who were still hunter-gatherers at the start of the twentieth century. Their kinship system, like that of the English, French, and other European and Euro-American societies, was undifferentiated, or cognatic, where neither the maternal nor the paternal side prevails; anthropologists thus classify this type of kin terminology as "Eskimo."

Given this kinship system, how is an Inuit child created?[1] According to their beliefs, a man and a woman must engage in sexual intercourse to make a child. The man's sperm forms the child's bones and skeleton, while the woman's blood makes its flesh and skin. The fetus takes shape in the woman's womb, and will look like either its father or its mother depending on the relative strength of their respective life forces. The child's body—which at this stage of intrauterine life is a soulless fetus and not yet a human being—feeds on the meat of the game supplied by the father and ingested by the mother, and becomes a true human only when it is born and Sila, the master of the universe, gives it a bubble of air, which will become its breath. This breath of life, which connects the child with the cosmic breath animating the universe, contains a soul that grows along with the body to become a double that eventually separates from the body when life ends and it travels to the world of the dead.

This soul is endowed with intelligence and shares certain features with Sila, who is the mind of the universe. And so a human child is born.

But this newborn child is still not a social being. It becomes an Inuit when it receives one or several names from its parents in the course of a ceremony attended by all of its relatives as well as the parents' friends and neighbors. In this society, names are not labels,[2] but *are* themselves souls, in that they contain the identity and the life experience of those who have previously borne them. Unlike the inner soul, which imparts life to the body and grows along with it, the name-soul envelops the child entirely and suffuses it with the identities of all those who have carried the name.

But what are these name-souls, and who chooses them? They are typically the names of friends or close relatives of the child's father or mother, people who died during the time that the mother was pregnant—or before—whom the parents want to keep with them by thus reembodying them.[3]

These imaginary representations of the child's conception and the make-up of its innermost identity explain the Inuit practice of occasionally raising a boy as a girl, or a girl as a boy, depending on the sex of the person whose name was given to the child at birth. Such practices, which separate gender and sex, end at puberty, when a child is called upon to take part in the process of reproducing life and the society by assuming the role that its original sex dictates: the son reverts to being a boy, and the daughter ceases to be one.

⋊ ⋊ ⋊

What are the underlying theories implicit in the Inuit representations of conception?

For the Inuit, sexual intercourse between a man and a woman is needed in order to make a fetus, *but it is not enough to make a child.* As the child's genitors, the father and the mother make distinct and complementary contributions to producing the body of the fetus and shaping it; both thus contribute to their child by giving it substance and form. In this regard, it is indeed "their" child, and belongs to "their" kindred. But the man and the woman do *not* give the child *life*.

Life begins when Sila, a supernatural power, introduces some of his breath into the child's body, thereby linking it to the thread and movement of the world it has just entered and where it will grow up, and giving it a soul that enables it to learn from its own experiences.

Then, by receiving one or more names after birth, the child is connected to a chain of its eponymous predecessors, and gives new life through its own body, and a new future, to members of its kindred and those who have gone before. These name-souls, which exist before and will continue living through the child, are thus spiritual components of his or her identity. An Inuit individual is therefore never an absolute starting point; he or she sets out in life equipped with his or her personal experiences, and those of all so-named who have gone before.

✕ ✕ ✕

My second example comes from the Baruya, a New Guinea society among whom I lived and worked for many years. The Baruya are horticulturalists and hunters who are divided into patrilineal clans, with no central authority. Marriage is accomplished by the direct exchange of women between two clans, and the central feature of their political-religious structures are large-scale male initiations where boys are gradually rid of all things female and reborn wholly masculinized through the practice of ritualized homosexuality. For the Baruya, the process of making a child begins with a man and a woman having sexual intercourse. The man's semen makes the bones as well as the flesh and blood of the fetus, which grows in the woman's womb, a simple receptacle that contributes nothing to the child. As soon as the woman senses the first signs of pregnancy, the couple increases the frequency of their sexual relations to nourish the fetus with the man's semen. The father thus both engenders and nourishes the child-to-be. Nonetheless, it takes more than a man and a woman to make the fetus developing in its mother's womb—which has no nose, mouth, fingers, or toes—

into a child. The Sun, the father of the Baruya, completes the body and animates it with his breath.

At birth, the child breathes and has a human body, but does not yet have a soul. A spirit-soul enters the child's body later, when the father gives it a name that previously belonged to a male or female ancestor in his lineage. But unlike a newly named Inuit, the Baruya child possesses no memory of the life of the ancestor it embodies. In this instance, then, it is the man who plays the more active role in making the child's body and connects the child with his own ancestors by giving it a name; the Baruya beliefs about conception are thus linked to the patrilineal descent rule that organizes their kinship relations and contributes to legitimize the domination of men over women. This is all the more apparent for boys, who must be born twice: first from their mother's womb and then from the men's body during male initiations, when at the age of nine or ten they are separated from their mothers and the women's world and ritually fed the semen of the oldest group of initiates, young men who have not yet had sexual relations with women. The ingestion of this substance free of any female defilement causes the boys' bodies to become wholly masculinized. Through this male rebirth, Baruya men give themselves the right to represent their society on their own and to govern it without the aid of women (a point which is discussed and developed in chapter 4).[4]

✕ ✕ ✕

A young man is no longer allowed to inseminate young initiates after marriage, when his penis has entered a woman's body and is thus polluted and polluting, for menstrual blood, which acts as an "anti-sperm," defiles the social and cosmic order and saps men's strength. A man's nurturing role begins as soon as he marries (and even before he has children), since the Baruya believe that the semen ingested by married women turns into milk, which swells their breasts when they suckle their children. Each time his wife gives birth her husband will provide her with his life-giving substance. A Baruya man thus distributes the male life force to young initiates before marriage, and engenders and nourishes his children thereafter.

Here too, it takes more than a man and a woman to make a child. The intervention of a god, the Sun, is needed, together with the ancestors, who return to live in Baruya children through their names. The Sun is a kind of superhuman father common to all Baruya, whatever their clan and regardless of their sex, a cosmic power and a tribal god who confers a human form and the breath of life to them all.

✕ ✕ ✕

Our third example is that of the Trobriand Islanders, who are one of the most famous societies in academic anthropology, known from the work of Bronislaw Malinowski[5] and Annette Weiner, as well as other anthropologists—such as Fred Damon, Nancy Munn, and Shirley Campbell—who have worked in the kula ring[6] (a far-flung network of gifts and countergifts that circulate among the dozens of islands lying to the east of New Guinea). The Trobrianders, also known as the Kiriwina, are a matrilineal, ranked society in which children belong to their mother's clan and are placed under the authority of their mother's brother. Residence after marriage is virilocal, however, and children live with their father, save for the eldest son, who, upon reaching puberty, goes to live with his mother's brother, whom he will succeed. How is a child conceived in the Trobriands? Malinowski won fame by, among other things, claiming that the islanders believed semen had nothing to do with the conception of a child.

For Trobrianders, conception is not the result of sexual union between a man and a woman. To be sure, this act is needed to "open" the woman so that she will be capable of becoming a mother, but it is *not* done to engender a child. According to their beliefs, a fetus is formed in a woman's womb when a spirit-child and the woman's menstrual blood meet and mingle. Spirit-children are spirits of the dead (*Baloma*) who wish to return in the body of one of their descendants. The dead live on Tuma, a little island off the coast of Kiriwina, under the authority of a god, Tupileta, who rules the world of the dead. When one of the dead wishes to be reborn, he or she turns into a spirit-child (*wai waya*) and is carried across to Kiriwina by the sea. There the *wai waya* makes its way to the body of a clanswoman, but only if guided by the spirit of a living member of the woman's clan. All children are thus the reincarnation of someone deceased, but they have no memory of the life led by the ancestor who has reincarnated him- or herself in them.

For Trobrianders, the woman must be pierced in order to become pregnant. She must therefore make love, and hence young people engage in sexual relations at an early age and have a very active premarital sex life. But lovemaking does not suffice to form a child, for a woman is not made a mother by the semen a man deposits in her, but through the intervention of the *Baloma*, who introduce the spirit of a clan ancestor into her body. The spirit mingles with the menstrual blood and becomes a fetus—a runny, shapeless mass that is not yet a child—whose flesh, bones, and skin derive from the mother's substance. She alone engenders the child. As soon as the woman tells her husband she is pregnant, he increases his sexual attentions, to make a plug that will keep the woman's blood from flowing out of the womb, to give the shapeless mass of coagulated blood a form that resembles its father, and to nourish the fetus at regular intervals during the pregnancy. The man thus pierces and plugs the woman, and shapes and nourishes the fetus.

As in the previous examples, here too it takes more than a man and a woman to make a child. In the Trobriands, the man does not engender the child, but rather shapes it, nourishes it, and later gives it a name. Agents more powerful than humans— a god, spirits of the dead, and spirits of living clansmen—must intervene to help give birth to a child. These representations fit the logic of a matrilineal system, since the child's inner substance is entirely female and is made of the mother's blood, *dala*, a blood that has flowed in the bodies of all of her clansmen from the founding female ancestor on. In fact the term for clan is also *dala*, "blood."

✕ ✕ ✕

With the Trobriand beliefs in mind, let us turn to two examples of matrilineal societies in which the representations of conception evolved in opposite directions. For the Na—an ethnic minority living in the mountains that form the border with Yunnan province whose livelihood comes from agriculture and animal husbandry—semen also plays no role in making a child. But unlike Trobriand society, the Na have no marriage and no term in the language for husband or father. Alternatively, for the Maenge, a matrilineal society in New Britain, it is semen alone—and therefore the father—that forms the body of the fetus.

Na kin groups are matrilines composed of all the descendants through women of a common female ancestor.[7] The "domestic" unit, or household, is made up of groups of brothers and sisters who live together and collectively raise the children produced by the women in the household. Aside from the rare exception (which we will not consider here), there is no marriage. At night the brothers leave their sisters to visit women who are their temporary or sometimes more permanent lovers in other households. There is thus a general circulation of men among women, and generalized exchanges of semen among the households. These sexual unions do not result in marriage, though in some cases the couple may live together for prolonged periods. Children are raised by their mother and her brothers, and any allusion to sex is forbidden in the home.

How is a child conceived in Na society? Though sexual intercourse is indispensable to conception, semen—which is called "penis water," a term also used for urine—does not create the child. Its function is the same as that of rain, without which, the Na say, grass would not grow from the ground. So where do fetuses come from? They are present in their mothers' wombs from the start, waiting for semen to water them so they can grow. Their existence thus precedes sexual coupling; they were placed in the woman's womb before she was born, while she was still an embryo, by a benevolent goddess, Abaogdu, who later nourishes them in the womb when she becomes pregnant.

In the case of the Na, then, the man does not engender the child and he does not nourish the fetus. He is merely the waterer-catalyst who triggers its growth and birth. A child is in reality the co-product of a woman and a goddess. The woman gives the child its flesh and its bones, and thus the descendants of the same ancestor, who form a matriline, are called "people of the same bone." It is interesting to note that this representation of the woman's role is the exact opposite of that commonly found in the neighboring Tibetan populations, who have a patrilineal kinship system and believe that the man's semen makes the child's bones and skeleton, while the woman's blood forms its flesh and skin.[8]

Na representations of procreation are thus also directly linked with the rule that organizes their kin system—in this instance, matrilineal descent, together with a belief in the intervention of agents more powerful than humans. Here, though, the goddess does more than complete the fetus; she creates the embryo and deposits it in the woman's womb, and it is she who completes it.

Among the Na, there is exchange of sexual partners between domestic units which does not create alliances. Na society thus understands and exploits the advantages of consanguinity but does not make use of affinity. With regard to power relations, it is important to note that each matriline and each household is run by twö individuals—a headwoman and a headman. The headwoman organizes the fieldwork and the household chores, manages the foodstocks and distributes the meals, and makes daily offerings to the ancestors. The headman takes care of all external relations concerning the land, livestock, and mutual help between neighbors, and represents his line vis-à-vis other lines. But every major decision having to do with a matriline or a household, such as ceding or renting land, is discussed by all members of the line, men and women alike, before any conclusion is reached.

The Na example stands in stark contrast to another matrilineal society, the horticulturalist Maenge of New Britain,[9] who are divided into two exogamous moieties that are in turn divided into exogamous clans and subclans. Neither the moieties nor the clans function as true social groups; with neither a chief nor a leader, they simply serve as categories for classifying those one can and cannot marry. The true political, economic, and ceremonial units are the lineages, whose members live in the same village. Each village is led by a headman, who comes from the matriline of the village founder and is called the "father of the village." In addition to matrilineal descent, there is another rule for classifying kin, known as "relatives by the rod." These groups include all children who have the same father but different mothers, as well as the children of full brothers. All of these people belong to different matrilineal clans but are united by their common descent through men, or patrifiliation. Though the patrifiliation groups have a name and are exogamous, and their members help each other in all manner of contexts—including war, trading expeditions, and the like—the ownership and use of the land are entirely derived through the matrilineal group. There is, nonetheless, a tendency in this society for the village headman to pass his functions and powers on to his own son, who does not belong to his own clan.

How is a child conceived in the Maenge society? Here the man's semen alone makes the child's body, bones, flesh, and blood, and endows it with movement and breath. The woman, by contrast, does not share any substance with her child, but holds the fetus in her uterus and provides it with its inner soul, which lives in the blood transmitted by the father and pervades the whole body to give it strength and beauty. But each person also has an outer soul, the invisible form of the body that becomes the person's double and can detach itself at night. At the time of death, both souls leave the body together; the inner soul, which then rids itself of the outer soul, travels to the ancestral dwelling place of the deceased's matrilineal clan, beneath the sea.[10]

In the Maenge case, we have a matrilineal society in which the mother's blood is inconsequential, and the father's semen predominates. The preeminent role of male substance can be related to the crucial role played by patrifiliation, which provides the society with a complementary organization that competes with the rule of matrifiliation. But regardless of this logic, a woman gives a child its soul, which connects it with the deceased but immortal ancestors, and through this link provides individuals with the access to the land that is the basis of their economy. The Maenge, a matrilineal society where semen plays a preeminent role, thus caution us not look for a straightforward, mechanical link between indigenous theories of procreation and the nature of kinship rules.

✕ ✕ ✕

Before drawing theoretical conclusions from these comparisons, I stress that a society may have several procreation theories, something that stems from power issues. Two examples—the Telefolmin, who live in the New Guinea Highlands near the headwaters of the Sepik River and practice intensive horticulture and hunting, and the Kingdom of Tonga in the southern Pacific—are particularly relevant here. The Telefolmin have two coexisting models of conception: an "official" account shared publicly by men and women, and a "secret" explanation known only to the women that partly contradicts the men's model.[11] The Telefolmin kinship system is cognatic, with neither clans or lineages; the villages are highly endogamous and organized around a large men's house, which holds the sacred relics, the bones of famous male ancestors that only the men may see and worship. The cult of the men's house is marked by a series of initiations reserved exclusively for boys, responsibility for which is shared between two ritual moieties—the "taro" people and the "arrow" people. The taro rites concern the power to give life, grow fine crops, raise pigs, and feed people; the arrow rites concern the power to take life, kill, and thus to be successful in hunting and war. The defining color for taro is white, and for arrow is red.

In the "official" model of conception—which the men stress is not really very interesting—children are formed when the "penis water" and the vaginal fluids combine in the women's womb during the course of lovemaking. A couple must have intercourse often so as to accumulate enough semen and vaginal fluids to make the fetal body, which becomes a child only when a soul has been added, and the child grows and takes on a form that will distinguish it from other people. This is the task of the *sinik*, a power whose origins the Telefolmin admit they do not know. Nonetheless, the male account of procreation corresponds to their cognatic system, with its lack of lineages or clans, where kinship is based as much on caring for the child as on descent.

When the anthropologist Dan Jorgensen turned to the women to understand why the men considered menstrual blood so dangerous, he discovered the existence of a second account of procreation. The women agreed that the fetus was formed by mixing vaginal fluids and semen, but focused on something that the men hadn't mentioned—namely, the role of menstrual blood in making a child. According to the women, though semen and vaginal fluids do indeed play an equal role in making the child's flesh and blood, its bones are formed from women's blood. What was at stake in this difference of interpretation? We must turn to the power relations between men and women, and the religious practices for which men are responsible and from which women are excluded, to find an explanation.

One of the fundamental objectives of these religious practices is to slow the gradual drift of the universe towards nothingness through the performance of certain rites. This is a key aspect of the cosmology of the populations in the Mountain Ok region of New Guinea. In order to slow this drift, the men must ritually manipulate the bones of the most prominent male ancestors in each village, which are stored as sacred relics inside the "spirit houses." However, according to the women's account of conception, the sacred relics at the heart of the male practices from which they are systematically excluded come from menstrual blood, the very substance that the men most abhor. The women's theory thus extends beyond the sphere of kinship and domestic life, which is the focus of the men's account, while the men reserve for themselves the leading role in the political-religious sphere that encompasses kinship and serves society as a whole.

Jorgensen went on to discover that the men were partially aware of and even a party to the women's theory, of which they nonetheless feigned ignorance. At the heart of the initiation rituals is a rite in which the men smear the young initiates' bodies with yellow clay. The secret name for this clay is "menstrual blood," and, unbeknownst to the initiates, blood from a woman who is menstruating at the start of the male initiations is secretly mixed into it.

⨯ ⨯ ⨯

Our final example from Oceania is one in which we also find two models of procreation coexisting within the same society. The Kingdom of Tonga stretches over 169 islands and, together with Hawaii and Tahiti, was one of the most highly stratified societies in Polynesia.[12] Before the Europeans arrived, there was a complete separation between the *tu'a*, the mass of commoners without rank or titles, and the *eiki*, who had titles and ranks and made up a sort of aristocracy around the royal family, that of the *Tu'i Tonga*. Only the Tu'i Tonga and the *eiki* possessed *mana*, a power contained in their bodies that attested to their divine birth. Those carrying these titles had authority over part of the territory and the people who lived there; this authority was always delegated, however, and ultimately flowed from the person of the paramount chief, the Tu'i Tonga, who was a direct descendant of the gods. The Tongan kinship system is cognatic, with a preference for links through women.

With these sociological features noted by way of background, what were the two coexisting theories of procreation found in Tonga before the Europeans arrived and introduced Christianity? According to the first theory, which is likely very old, the man makes the child's bones and its skeleton with his semen, which mixes with the woman's menstrual blood and forms a clot. The woman's blood then makes the child's flesh and blood, and the embryo becomes a fetus. At this point, the fetus is possessed by a soul, which is a gift not only from the ancestors but also from the gods, such that even today the hair of a newborn child is called "hair of the god." In this account, the female substances—blood and a fluid called "water of life" (perhaps the amniotic fluid)—were believed to be endowed with life-creating capacities, something that men did not possess.

But a second model also existed in which the child's entire substance—flesh, blood, bones, skin, and so on—derived from the woman. In this account, the man's semen merely keeps the woman's menstrual blood in the uterus; this then forms a clot that becomes an embryo and then a fetus with the help of the gods and of the Tu'i Tonga. In this model, the man is no longer the genitor, but merely the woman's sexual partner whose role is to prepare her for impregnation by a god or by a human god, the Tu'i Tonga. The paramount chief thus impregnates all the women with his seed, which dematerializes to become an impregnating breath or *sperma pneumatikon*. The latter account is clearly a transformation of the former, effected by two mental processes working in opposite but complementary directions. The woman's role, prominent in the first model, is enhanced in the second, where her blood makes up the entire substance of the fetus, while the man's place as impregnator is supplanted by the power of the Tu'i Tonga. This altered account fit quite nicely into an aristocratic society with ranks and titles, since a Tongan woman transmitted not only her blood but also her rank. The child of a high-ranking man and a common woman was a commoner, but the child of a commoner and a noble woman was a noble.[13]

We can therefore presume that the second model was conceived not merely to extol the procreative capacities of women but also to formally exclude ordinary men from the process of creating life and to glorify the *mana* of the supreme *eiki*, the Tu'i Tonga. By appearing as the one who impregnates all the women without actually inseminating them, and as the one who fertilizes all the lands without actually working them, the Tu'i Tonga appears as the "Father" of all Tongans, a Father whose ancestors link him to the gods. It seems reasonable to assume that this account of procreation is connected with deep-seated political and ideological changes that took place in Tongan society several centuries ago, when it was coming to grips with the growth of an aristocracy increasingly divorced from the rest of society and was governed by one of the royal families that was aiming to corner power and, contrary to tradition, wanted to transmit its function and rank from father to eldest son.

This change in the account of conception was accompanied by a shift in the representations of death. Deprived of their own ancestors, whose place had been taken by the Tu'i Tonga, commoners were also deprived of an afterlife in their human form. Their souls were thought to leave their corpses and change into insects, which were ever in danger of being swallowed—as much by an animal as by a god—since animals, chiefs, and gods in Tonga were cannibals.

✕ ✕ ✕

I will end my survey with a brief allusion to the West and its system of kinship. Christian theologians see the sexual union between a man and a woman united by the sacrament of marriage as making one flesh of the two, *una caro*. It is this flesh born of the mingling of their substances that is transmitted to their children. And it is because the man's and the woman's substances mingle that a man cannot have sexual relations with his wife's sister, because she has essentially become his own sister. In a very particular way, the Western Christian kinship system has made affines into consanguines in the eyes of Christ, and applies the same sexual taboos to both. But here too it takes more than a man and a woman to make a child. A husband and wife create a fetus (which has no breath) to which God, who brings it to life in its mother's womb, supplies a soul. But how is this soul seen? Let us consider the words of the twelfth-century nun, Hildegard of Bingen, a great mystic who describes how God imparts life to human bodies in her book, the *Liber Civias*.[14] She depicts the fetus as "a completely formed person"—a homunculus—a miniature human being who, "by the secret order and hidden will of God receives the spirit in its mother's womb at the right moment precisely fixed by God." But what does this soul look like? According to her account, "It has the appearance of a ball of fire that has not one feature of the human body and takes possession of the heart of this form [the fetus]." By this logic, are we thus far removed from the Trobriand Islands, where an ancestor's spirit gives life to the fetus, or from the human god, the Tu'i Tonga, whose spermatic breath impregnates the women of his kingdom?

But let us not forget that Christianity has a small peculiarity. When a man and a woman unite sexually to become one flesh and engender a child, they involuntarily transmit the transgression of Adam and Eve, known as "original sin," which has ever since been carried by the flesh. Like the Baruya Sun, the Christian God completes the fetus made by humans, in this case by giving it a soul together with the promise of eternal life. But this soul must be cleansed of the original sin which was transmitted by its parents. It is the role of baptism to wash this soul of sin and to introduce the child into the community that will attend to its salvation. Christian kinship is thus one of several cultural views that associate birth and defilement, and attribute the defilement to sex.

✕ ✕ ✕

As we conclude our voyage through these seven societies, attempting to discern and understand what they think about the way that human beings are conceived (or recently thought, before their conversion to Christianity and their subjection to the Western world order), we must acknowledge that there is no society in which a man and a woman suffice, on their own, to make a child. What they create—with contributions that vary

from one group to the next and with different substances, such
as semen, menstrual blood, and the like—is a fetus, but never
a complete, viable human child. For this, other agents who are
more powerful than humans and who add what is lacking—be it
a soul, a spirit, a breath, a nose, or fingers and toes—must come
into play.

Two kinds of agents collaborate with humans to make
children—ancestors and gods—and sometimes both are needed.
Of course ancestors are human, but they live another life after
death, and sometimes come back in the body of a child. The
child is usually a descendant, but it can also be the child of a
neighbor or a friend, as among the Inuit. Generally speaking,
such an ancestor is manifested in the name given to the child,
though the child who receives an ancestor's name usually has
no memory of the existences and experiences of those who have
come before.

In short, in many societies, the birth of a human being is not
an absolute beginning, just as death is never an absolute end.
But it takes more than just ancestors; powers of an order other
than human—the Sun for the Baruya, God for Christians, Sila
for the Inuit—are also necessary. Nowhere, then, is a child born
as the outcome merely of sexual intercourse and kinship; it takes
its place in a cosmic and social whole that extends beyond and
encompasses the sphere of kinship.

Another theoretical conclusion we can draw from this comparison is that, in all societies (even those where semen does not
play a role in conceiving a child), the appearance of a fetus in
a woman's womb normally implies that the woman and a man
have had intercourse. Whether it is for the purpose of stopping
up the womb with semen to retain the menstrual blood, or opening the way for a spirit-child, or nourishing the fetus, men and
women expect one possible consequence of sexual intercourse
to be a child, whatever the real or imaginary role the society may
ascribe to the male or female substances in conception and gestation. This observation, in my opinion, puts an end to the long-
running polemic that has raged among anthropologists from

Malinowski to Edmund Leach[15] over whether or not Australian Aborigines or other societies know about the role the sexes play in procreation. Everyone knows that, for Australian Aboriginal people as for Trobrianders and the Na, children exist even before they are conceived, as spirit-children or fetuses deposited in a womb. But no society believes that children are born of ordinary humans without their having had sexual intercourse.

Nonetheless, all societies do acknowledge that in some circumstances women can be impregnated by supernatural beings and give birth to children without coming in contact with a man's penis. In fact, this describes the very mystery of Jesus's birth and the role of the Virgin Mary. According to Catholic dogma, Mary, who was born by the grace of God without the original sin that parents transmit when engendering a child—this is known as the "Immaculate Conception"—did not "know" her husband, Joseph, in the biblical sense, when she received Jesus in her womb.

It is perhaps useful to remember that these cultural representations of the process of procreation are imaginary constructions, and that the powers that are ascribed to or denied the various bodily substances—such as semen and menstrual blood—are the product of fantasies. No fetus has ever been nourished by semen, nor has menstrual blood ever turned into a fetus. No one has ever actually seen a ball of fire enter the heart of an embryo and bring it to life.

But what is at stake in these imaginary representations is neither imaginary nor merely symbolic, for two reasons. First, they legitimize the rules that organize kinship relations, and the transmission of goods, statuses, and powers through men or through women or both, depending on whether the system is patrilineal, matrilineal, bilineal, or nonlineal. Second, even before a child's birth, they implant in its body the superior/ subordinate relations that prevail between the genders, as well as the political, economic, and ritual power relations that exist between the groups that make up a given society. After all, isn't it by virtue of the man's predominant role in procreation that

Baruya women are barred from owing land, using weapons, or worshiping the Sun and other gods? In short, these representations are not merely mental facts with conceptual results, they are social facts with real consequences. In order for there to be domination, the bodies of the dominators must be disjoined from those of the dominated, and their substances altered. The Baruya practice of ritual homosexuality produces both this disjunction and this transmutation. And as a substance does not exist in isolation, the positive overvaluing of semen finds its counterpart in the negative undervaluing of menstrual blood. Thus, if Baruya women believe that their bodies constitute a threat to men because they bleed, and therefore to the social and cosmic order, they may well feel responsible for the disorder that might result were they to fail to properly manage their bodily components, which are capable of detaching themselves and attacking other bodies.

But such is not always the case. In certain circumstances, members of the dominated group can break out of the mental and social mold that prompts them to accept the kind of life they lead because of what they "are." This explains why, in 1978 and 1979, some Telefolmin women who converted to Christianity when they heard Fundamentalist preachers proclaiming the second coming of Christ and the "revival" of humankind destroyed the relics central to the male rituals from which they were excluded.

As we've seen, all of our analyses revolve around one basic phenomenon—namely, the uses of the sexes and of gendered bodies to manufacture life and social, and even cosmic, order. But it is also apparent that, in every society, the gendered body is pressed into the service of a number of realities—economic, political, religious, and the like—that have no direct connection with gender or sexual reproduction. It is within kinship relations, starting with a child's birth, that society exercises its first direct control over the person's sexuality, and attraction to persons of the opposite and the same sex. The subordination of the individual's sexuality is not that of one gender to the other, but of one aspect of social life to the conditions of reproduction of other social relations, and thus the positioning of this area within the *structure* of society. This impersonal subordination of sexuality is the basis of a mechanism that stamps into a person's innermost subjectivity and embeds in the person's body the order or orders that reign in a given society and must be respected if it is to be reproduced. This mechanism operates through the interplay of representations of the body and the individual, and the role assigned to each of the genders as well as to other agents, in the process that brings a child, or life, into the world. It is by means of these representations that the appropriation of the child by those adults regarded as its kin and its place in society marked out by its gender are legitimized. Through representations of the gendered body and the process of making children, sexuality not only bears witness to the prevailing social order, but declares that this order *must* continue to prevail, and testifies not only *to*, but *for*, and occasionally *against*, the order that prevails in society and in the universe, since the universe, too, is divided into male and female worlds.[16]

× × ×

In short, bodies and gender work like those ventriloquist's dummies which are hard to muzzle and relay to an audience they cannot see words they themselves do not utter. Sexuality, too, cannot speak, but speaking occurs within it, and someone speaks through it. But who speaks? And why in this guise? It is precisely to the extent that sexuality is forced, beforehand, to serve as a language and to legitimize realities other than itself that it becomes a source of fantasies and imaginary worlds. But it is not sexuality that fantasizes about society, but rather society that fantasizes about sexuality. It is not sexuality that does the alienating, but sexuality that is alienated.

Here we touch on an essential point of social logics. These fantasized representations of the body are usually *ideas and images*, shared by both genders, that sum up and encode the social order and inscribe its norms in each and every body. It is the sharing of the same representations and their embodiment that, beyond language, inscribe a way of thinking and a given society into the body of each individual, thus making the body a source of assumptions about the social and cosmic orders. From being alienated, sexuality goes on to become an instrument of alienation. Ultimately, when a Baruya woman sees the blood running between her thighs, she can no longer object to her fate; she knows she is guilty, she feels her guilt and, as a consequence, feels responsible for whatever happens to her. This is why sexuality is experienced as something that can, at any time, challenge and subvert the order of society and the universe, and why it is hedged about with so many taboos.

In each society, representations of the body thus draw a kind of *ring of social and cultural constraints* around the individual, which constitutes the social form that is paradoxically shared by the other members of the society, who are imbued with the same representations of their inner being. It is inside this impersonal form, as it were, of the individual's intimate inner subjectivity— which is imposed at birth and organizes the child's social encounters—that he or she will begin to experience desires for others. Whereas the child has already been appropriated by others—its kin, social group, and the like—he or she will spontaneously want to appropriate them in turn. This is when the child will discover that not everyone can be appropriated, as some—such as father, mother, sisters, and brothers—are off-limits to desire. Sexuality as a "desiring machine" is thus confronted by its role as a "talking machine."[17]

Thus, even if it takes more than a man and a woman to make a child in all societies, the child is not allowed to direct its desire towards its parents. Between them stands the taboo on heterosexual as well as homosexual incest, but that's another story . . .[18]

4

Human Sexuality Is Fundamentally A-social: The Example of the Baruya of Papua New Guinea

When anthropologists and psychoanalysts are asked to define what constitutes a sexual act on the basis of their professional experience, they appear to find themselves in distinct yet similar situations. Though neither are in the habit of *observing* sexual acts *directly* in the course of their respective practices, and it seems that their experience consists of how people do or don't talk about sex, they most likely do not elicit the same discourse and thus do not interpret the same realities.

There are exceptions of course. The eighteenth-century accounts of the voyages of Captain James Cook or Louis-Antoine de Bougainville, which describe Polynesians making love in full view of an audience that applauded or jeered their techniques, or hospitably offering the European crewmen young women for their pleasure, were proof for such philosophers as Diderot that peoples "closer than we are" to nature saw no harm or sin in lovemaking. It may have been with the "progress" of "Civilization" that we began to feel uneasy and ashamed about sexual activity.[1]

We have come a long way from such philosophical debates, and with much more detailed knowledge of the cultures and societies of the Central and South Pacific we no longer see Polynesians as exempt from sexual taboos and conflicts. In using the terms cultures and societies, I am not referring to separate realities that somehow stand in opposition. By *culture*, I mean the set of representations and principles that consciously organize the different aspects of social life, together with the positive and negative norms and the values connected with these ways of acting and thinking. By *society*, I mean a set of individuals and groups that interact with reference to common rules and values that govern their acting and thinking, and who regard themselves as belonging to the same "whole," which they must (or are supposed to) reproduce while they act in their own self-interests.[2] The society and the culture are always already there, extant and active, at the birth of each individual.

Consistent with the object of study, it is the work of an anthropologist to go into the field and systematically collect, through "participant observation," a body of information on how the individuals and groups that make up a society of a given culture represent "sexual" relations between individuals of the same or opposite sexes. This, by necessity, should lead the anthropologist to extend his or her observations to all social relations between the genders—not only sexual relations, but those involving power, wealth, the material division of labor, rituals, and so on.

Unlike the psychoanalyst, perhaps, anthropologists do not simply listen to what people say, directly or indirectly, about sex and the sexes. Fieldwork requires that they immerse themselves, for months and years on end, in local groups whose actions and interactions they attempt to observe and to understand. It goes without saying that, during these months of immersion, a great deal of activity occurs, most of which happens independently of the anthropologist; nonetheless, through systematic investigation, he or she will discern the logic that underpins such events, and the causes and meaning people attribute to them, and thus discover the effects they entail for individuals and the society, and the comments they inspire. While all of this has to do with discourse, it embraces much more. The anthropologist's ear is attuned to more than the individuals he or she questions; it must also listen to the concerts of harmonious or inharmonious voices all expressing themselves at the same time in a given social context. He or she then collates these solo or polyphonic discourses with the contexts that inspired them—such as births, marriages, initiations, murders, adulteries, and feuds—in an attempt to lay bare the logics behind the representations and behaviors of individuals and groups, and those underlying the social relations upon which these individuals and groups reflect and act.

There is another difference between the relationship that develops between the analyst and the analysand and that which forms between the anthropologist and the people he or she lives with, some of whom become official "informants." The analysand goes to the psychoanalyst in order to talk and to be heard, in order to get a better sense of him- or herself. The anthropologist, in contrast, usually moves in with a group without having been invited, and while keen to listen, he or she does not refrain from speaking, asking both direct and indirect questions and interpreting the answers received and the happenings observed. And, in the beginning at least, the anthropologist does so by using concepts and models that are for the most part largely alien to the conscious awareness and the culture of the people he or she is living with and whose life he or she shares, for a time. Nevertheless, anthropologists and psychoanalysts are alike in that they must never—either in public or in private— take a stand on what they are told or what they see. They cannot side with one part of the society against another or espouse and promote the interests of some to the detriment of others, but must strive to discover and to understand the source and the nature of the antagonisms that divide the parties.

What Is a Sexual Act for a Baruya?

The Baruya, with whom I lived and worked for a total of nearly seven years, have two kinds of sexual practices: heterosexual relations between adult men and women, and homosexual relations between young male initiates. There is some evidence to suggest the existence of homosexual practices between young women as well, but there is insufficient information to analyze and interpret this.

Let us start with the domain of heterosexual relations. In principle, a man and a woman should not have intercourse unless they are married. But the Baruya do not forbid the rape of enemy women, which is an act of war. Newlyweds are not supposed to have sexual intercourse for several weeks. They must wait until the walls of the house that has been built for them have become blackened with soot from the fire. A wife must never step over the fireplace, which is made of flat stones and clay by the husband's kinsmen, as her vagina would open over the fire that cooks the food that goes into her husband's mouth.

When their house is finished and the fireplace is made, the couple does not immediately sleep together there. On the first night the young husband sleeps in the house one last time with the boys of the village, while on the second the wife sleeps there with the village girls. Only then can the couple can sleep together alone. Even so, they may not have sexual intercourse for the first few weeks, but can only exchange caresses. The man strokes the woman's breasts, and she drinks his semen. There is, of course, an erotic side to these caresses and to this act, but the drinking of semen is designed first and foremost to build up the woman's bodily strength and to create a sort of reservoir of male substance, which according to the Baruya will become the milk she feeds her children when they are born. *Fellatio* is thus an erotic physical act whose symbolic logic is clear: women's milk is transformed semen. And the social import of this act is equally clear: men are the true source of strength and life. Fellatio and the ingestion of semen are thus part of the arsenal by which men's domination of women is established and expressed. By way of further evidence, cunnilingus, the reciprocal act, is strictly forbidden, so much so that Baruya men are scandalized at the very suggestion that a man might touch a woman's vagina with his mouth, and will scream and shout and may even vomit at the thought.

Once a few weeks have passed, and soot from the fire has blackened the walls, the couple can make love. They will lie on the ground in the women's part of the house, the side nearest the door; the other side, at the far reach of the hearth, is reserved for the man, who sleeps there alone or with his male guests.

The woman lies on her back under her husband, for a woman may not straddle a man for fear that the "juices from her sex," her vaginal secretions, might run out onto his belly and spoil his strength. Sodomy is not practiced (not even in the homosexual relations between boys, a point we will consider later).

Just as certain positions are prohibited, couples are forbidden from making love in cultivated gardens and in certain parts of the forest—especially mountaintops and marshy places— reputed to be inhabited by evil spirits, hostile beings who can attack people through their bodies. The semen and the vaginal fluids that spill onto the ground could be carried down into the depths of the earth by worms and snakes to the *chthonian* spirits, who are usually hostile to humans. This is why the Baruya believe that adulterous relations, which usually take place in the secrecy of the forest, are even more dangerous for the individuals concerned and for society as a whole than legitimate sexual relations.

There are also strict rules governing the time when sexual relations can occur. The Baruya forbid lovemaking when it is time to clear the forest for new gardens or to filter and evaporate salt. The Baruya use salt as a currency, as well as in all of their rites, and associate it with semen and the strength it holds; if people were to make love when salt was being produced, it might turn to water and thus could not be exchanged with neighboring tribes. Nor are couples permitted to make love when one of the family pigs is to be killed, as this might make the meat watery, too. And it is unthinkable to have intercourse when a woman has her period, since menstrual blood is the most dangerous substance of all for men. In fact, at the start of a woman's period, she leaves the house and goes a hut situated well away from all dwellings, where she spends several days. Here she is not allowed to cook because her hands are polluted, and must rely on other women to bring her food. When she returns home, her husband goes hunting and leaves one or several birds he has killed on the doorstep of the house before departing. When the woman arrives, she picks the birds up one at a time, sets fire to the feathers, and runs the flames over her hands and her body, especially around her genitals and her armpits, so that the pungent smell of the burning feathers and sizzling skin "depollutes" her. Once this is done, she can once again touch and cook food and resume marital life with her husband. The same "decontamination" rites are performed each time she gives birth, which takes place in a shelter made of branches erected downhill from the village. This space, which is totally forbidden to men, is the counterpart of the Men's House that stands uphill from the village, the home of the young initiates that is off-limits to women and children.

This list of prohibitions that limit, and therefore delimit, the spaces and circumstances in which heterosexual intercourse can *legitimately* be performed attests to the fact that coitus is an act that implicates the order both of Baruya society and the cosmos. As a result, the Baruya feel an overwhelming sense of responsibility whenever they make love, and they approach this act with a mixture of apprehension and anxiety—sentiments that seem to be shared by both sexes, though the men exhibit more anxiety than the women. (The reason for this will become apparent when we analyze male homosexual practices.)

The Baruya believe that children are usually begotten by making love. But they also think that woman can be made pregnant by a supernatural being (not an immaterial being, but simply one that is not visible or not recognizable). In their origin myth, the first woman became pregnant by eating the fruit of a male tree.

Kurumbingac lived on her own, without a man, and with her lived a wild dog, Djoué. One day she ate some fruit from a very straight tree and became pregnant. The dog that was with her saw she was pregnant; and one night it entered her womb through her sex and devoured the head of the fetus. The woman gave birth to a headless child. It was a girl. She continued her journey and once again ate some fruit from the same tree. Once again she became pregnant; the dog realized she was pregnant and, one night, entered her womb and this time devoured the arms and legs of the fetus. The woman gave birth to a dead child. It was a boy. Noticing blood stains on the dog's body, she guessed the culprit. The dog ran away, and she set out in pursuit, up and down the mountains, seeking vengeance. At last the dog found refuge at the back of a cave. The woman spotted its footprints, and her spirit made trees grow up around the cave and block the mouth. Then she turned away, leaving the dog to die.

However the dog had magical strength, and it split open the cave and its spirit escaped, changing into an eagle, the bird of Sun, father of all the Baruya. The dog's skin and bones were left to rot in the cave, where they changed into various kinds of animals, which today are the game hunted by the Baruya in the forest and along the streams, and which are eaten at initiations. Nevertheless, the dog went on living as a dog, keeping its distance from men; today it lives on the slopes of Mount Yelia, a volcano dominating the Baruya's mountains. The dog also became the secret companion of shamans, and its spirit joins them whenever they perform the war rites or intervene in cases of difficult childbirth.

Twice in this account we find mention of a sexual act that occurs between a woman and a tree—a "male" reality that predates the time when there were any real men, when the world was first shaped (which the Baruya call the time of the *wandjinia* or "dream men"). While this is both an imaginary and a real world for the Baruya, for us it is imaginary but unreal. We regard this story as a "myth," which is not the case for the Baruya because they "believe" in it; it has repercussions in the way they organize their society, and gives rise to (what we consider) the symbolic practices that are performed in male and female initiations.

Thus, when the Baruya hold the first-stage initiation ceremonies for their boys—children of nine or ten who have just been torn away from their mothers and the world of women—one of the most secret rites takes place deep in the forest, at the foot of a tall, straight tree decked with feathers and necklaces similar to those worn by the men. The small boys are lined up facing the tree while their sponsors, young unmarried fourth-stage initiates who have not yet had sexual intercourse with a woman, fill their mouths with the sap of a tree that grows nearby and transfer it into the mouths of the younger boys. For the Baruya, this sap is the tree's semen, analogous to the semen the fourth-stage initiates will later give the younger initiates to ingest. These ritual acts form a chain through which life forces and powers flow from the Sun, the father of all Baruya, to the tree, to the young virgin men, and finally to the young boys who have been separated from their mothers and removed from the female world for years to come. The sap is therefore both the (imaginary) semen of the tree and the (symbolic) substitute for real male semen.

Here we need to pause for a moment and consider the Baruya representations of the gender roles and the bodily substances necessary for the conception of a child. According to their beliefs, a child is made primarily from the man's semen.[3] The woman is a receptacle, and her uterus is seen as something akin to a netbag, into which male semen is deposited to become the fetus. In order to grow inside the womb, the fetus needs to be fed at regular intervals with more of the man's semen; when a Baruya woman notices the first signs of pregnancy, the couple increases the frequency of their sexual relations, to nourish the fetus.

Though a man's semen constitutes the bones and the flesh of the fetus, it does not form its nose, eyes, mouth, fingers, or toes, which are created by the Sun. From a certain point of view, every person therefore has one mother and two fathers: the social father who is the mother's husband, and the Sun, a super-father who is the source of the sacred objects and the social and cosmic orders. Note that in the Baruya origin myth, the wild dog that lived with the first woman and devoured the head and then the arms and legs of the children she conceived after eating fruit from the tree fills the role of an anti-Sun, the force that twice undid what the Sun accomplished. The opposition between the Sun and the wild dog is one of the deep structures of Baruya thought and mythic discourse.

For the Baruya, not only does the Sun complete the body of the child in the woman's womb, but—and this is very important in their worldview—it is he who enabled human beings to have sexual intercourse and to conceive children in the first place. According to one of their myths, in the beginning the first man's and first woman's sexual organs and anus were closed. The Sun threw a flint-stone into the fire, and the stone exploded, piercing the man's penis and the woman's vagina, as well as their anuses, and ever since humans have been able to copulate and defecate. This is why, in the opening ceremony of the large-scale male initiations, all fires were extinguished in all villages and in the secrecy of the big ceremonial house, the primordial fire was rekindled from a spark produced by striking together two sacred flint-stones.

But there is another version of this myth, which ascribes the opening of the sexual organs not to the Sun but to the primordial woman. Seeing that the man's and woman's genitals were walled up, the primordial woman stuck a sharpened bone from the wing of a bat into the trunk of a banana tree. The man, not noticing the bone, impaled his penis on it and cut himself open. Mad with rage and pain, he snatched up a sharp piece of bamboo and with one swipe sliced open the woman's vagina. In this account, the woman indirectly opens the man's sexual organ, whereupon he opens hers directly. The Sun is nowhere to be found. Despite these differences, both versions of the myth emphasize that violence must be done to male and female bodies in order for them to function as sexual beings.

⋉ ⋉ ⋉

We have briefly reviewed where, when, and how the Baruya make love, but have not yet considered with whom this is permitted or forbidden. To learn this, we must turn to the Baruya kinship system. At the center of this system, which is patrilineal and uses the Iroquois terminology, there is a zone where sexual relations must not occur, where to make love would be to commit incest. A

Baruya man cannot have intercourse with his sister, his mother, or his daughter; and a Baruya woman cannot have intercourse with her father, her brother, or her son. We must, however, bear in mind that the Baruya terms for father, brother, mother, and sister do not mean the same thing as in the West, where the kinship system is cognatic (one's ties with father's and with mother's ascendants are recognized as equivalent), where the terminology is of the Eskimo type (the father's brother has the same status as the mother's brother and both are called by the same term, "uncle"), and where the edifice of kinship links together nuclear families but not broader groups such as lineages or clans.

For the Baruya, by contrast, a man's father's brothers are also his fathers, and all of their daughters are his sisters, with whom he cannot have intercourse or marry. Likewise, all of his mother's sisters are his mothers, and their daughters are also his sisters, to whom he can neither make love nor marry. But a Baruya man can marry his father's sisters' daughters—his patrilateral cross cousins—because they have been begotten by men belonging to different clans and therefore do not share the same sperm, as is the case for his patrilateral parallel cousins. Likewise, he may not marry his mother's brothers' daughters—his matrilateral cross cousins—because he is not allowed to reproduce his father's marriage by taking a woman from the clan his mother came from and for which his clan has given a woman in return. But though a Baruya man cannot marry them, he is allowed to make sexual innuendoes toward or bold-faced obscene jokes with them, and can even tease them by grabbing at their breasts in public. All of this goes on amid general hilarity, and no onlooker is shocked.

⋇ ⋇ ⋇

I have offered these details to forestall any temptation to project our Western images of father, mother, sister, brother, husband, or wife onto what seem to be the equivalent Baruya terms. With this point in mind, let me add that the Baruya normally refrain from talking about sex and alluding to certain parts of the body. When men do mention these, they use a coded language; for example, to talk about the penis, they use a word that designates a flat-tipped arrow that is used to kill birds without damaging their plumage. Married couples must never touch each other in public, and are forbidden to kiss, even though women may smother babies in kisses. In addition to this physical reserve, a married couple must also curtail their speech and never show intimacy in public, to the point that they cannot call each other by name. The wife uses "man" when she addresses her husband, and the husband uses "woman" to address his wife. Custom also used to dictate that any woman—whether alone or in a group—who met a man or a group of men coming the other way had to stop and avert her face by hiding it under her bark cape. Before the arrival of Europeans, Baruya territory was crosshatched by a system of split-level paths, the higher ones reserved for the men and the lower ones for the women.

✕ ✕ ✕

Before turning to Baruya homosexual practices, let us address the issue of incest, a practice on which human society was, according to Lévi-Strauss, founded and from whence it resulted, and which, for the Baruya, today is strictly forbidden. We have here a double view of incest, which engenders a fundamental ambiguity about this taboo. To understand this duality, we need to turn once more to the Baruya's "myths." Their most secret story, which I have already started to relate, tells of the first woman's adventures. After Kurumbingac walled the wild dog, Djoué, in the cave, intending for him to die, she

> continued on her way and once again ate fruit from the tree, and gave birth, this time with no problem, to a boy. The child grew up and later made love with his mother, and from their intercourse a boy was born and then a girl. Later the brother and sister made love, and from their intercourse were born the ancestors of the Baruya and all the people who live in New Guinea.

Humankind (which for the pre-contact Baruya meant their neighbors and a few other inhabitants of New Guinea) thus came into being as the result of two episodes of incest—between a mother and her son, and between a brother and his sister. (Note that there is no mention of father-daughter incest in this account.)

In sum, the myth tells us that women existed before men (but not before the masculine-gendered tree), and that the first humans were engendered through incest, but that subsequently this practice was forbidden and the social and cosmic order that now governs Baruya life was set in place. This order exists first and foremost between the genders, a sexual order that only thereafter governs the relations between the lineages, villages, and tribes. It also exists between humans and supernatural powers. All of these orders are embedded in the body, which explains the Baruya's fascination with incest, as well as the paradoxical condition of human beings, who are a result of incest but have renounced the practice and now take husbands and wives from outside their own lineage. It is interesting to note that the Baruya express their ambivalence about this state of affairs openly, and say that anyone who dared to marry his "sister" would be like a dog (which couples with its sister). In such a circumstance, the man and the woman would have to be killed, something that would fall to their brothers to do, so as to avoid calls for vengeance. But at the same time they express regret that a man cannot marry his sister, with whom he is familiar and comfortable, rather the woman who is fated to become his wife, an outsider for whom he exchanges his sister, and who always represents a threat.

⨯ ⨯ ⨯

We now leave our analysis of sexual relations between men and women and move on to an essential element needed to complete our picture of Baruya society: specifically, homosexual relations between men. Strictly speaking, these practices do not take place between "men" at all, but between pubescent adolescents and small boys who have just been separated from their mother. A Baruya man must be married, and a married man cannot have homosexual relations with a boy. There are no bachelors by choice. Some men live alone because they were married and are now widowers. There are also very rare cases of men who never marry because they are hermaphrodites; these individuals entered the Men's House as boys and took part in the secret rituals of male initiations, but because they did not mature and their penises did not develop, they were obliged to stay in the Men's House and thereafter were known as "women-men." But a normal man gets married, and once his penis enters a woman's vagina, it can no longer enter a boy's mouth.

Male homosexuality is thus strictly confined to the world of boys and adolescents, and these sexual relations are never symmetrical among the Baruya. The third- and fourth-stage initiates, young men between the ages of fifteen and twenty who have reached puberty, give their semen to the younger initates to drink. Yet sometimes—and this is a closely guarded secret—these younger boys give their semen to a member of their cohort if his body has become very weak and he seems on the verge of losing his strength and his life. Several points are worth noting here. Though fellatio is permitted in the context of these one-way initiation rites, sodomy is completely excluded. According to the Baruya, they discovered that the practice existed only after the arrival of Europeans. Bursting with laughter, they recounted that a soldier from one of the northern tribes, where sodomy was part of ritual homosexual practices, had once offered money to a young Baruya, explaining what he wanted him to do. Afterwards, the Baruya man went around the tribe, explaining in each village's Men's House what he had just done in exchange for money, and remarking that it had hurt and was not a pleasant experience. Since then people talk about it, but no one does it, either in the context of homosexual or heterosexual relations.

Homosexuality in the Baruya culture is thus the basis for the formulation and affirmation of power relations between the genders and the generations. In a way, though it is erotic, the act is overwhelmingly political; the young boys cannot refuse the semen they are given, and should one try to do so, his neck is broken and his death disguised as a hunting accident or as the unfortunate result of a fall from a tall tree, so that his mothers and sisters harbor no suspicions. Thus, from one generation to the next there circulates a male substance that issues from the bodies of young men who for years have had no contact with the world of women. And this substance, free of any female pollution, is at once the source of the men's superiority over women, the basis of human life, and the strength men give women to overcome the original weakness of their bodies and carry out their tasks, such as bringing children into the world, working in the garden, and carrying heavy loads on their heads. The fact that the Baruya forbid and repress masturbation is also telling: A man's semen does not belong to him but to others, just as the semen of others belongs to him, save for certain kin categories.

But who, among the occupants of the Men's House, are the partners in these homosexual relationships? The donor must not belong to the lineage of the boy's father or mother, and semen thus comes from beyond the circle of consanguines. The circle closed to homosexual relations corresponds in part to the space forbidden to heterosexual relations characterized as incestuous. Sperm, like women, must come from outside. The couples in the Men's House consist of an older boy and a younger boy, with the older boy choosing his partner. Between them, there are many expressions of tenderness, gestures that are delicate, reserved, modest. Here there is room for desire, eroticism, and affection, but also for submission, as the young partners are forced to do many chores for the older boys, and are treated in some respects as though they were wives.[4]

Bear in mind that, from the age of nine until the age of twenty or twenty-two, Baruya boys are no longer under the direct authority of their father, who has practically no more say in their day-do-day upbringing, but in the collective charge of the older boys. The children are raised, educated, and beaten by the group of older boys, and quite often their mothers, recognizing their children's cries, will urge their husbands to go up to the Men's House and intervene. The father usually does not heed his wife, though if he finally gives in to her insistent pressure, he is insulted, ridiculed, and even physically threatened by the twenty-year-old warriors: "We are treating your son just like you and your co-initiates treated us when we were in his place. So go away!"

A Baruya boy loves his mother, loves his mother's brother because he cannot say no to him, and sometimes loves his father's brothers because he can always go to them for help and protection, but seems to have less love for his father. The Baruya admire Great Men, great warriors, great shamans, and above all the masters of initiations. One gets the impression that the machinery of their male initiations and the group of young initiates take over the father's role in the everyday socialization of the boys. This all-male group is supervised by Great Men who, in exceptional ways, fulfill such functions as warfare and shamanism, and thus embody forces serving the general interest.

Nevertheless, the female world is not completely absent from the circle of the Men's House, since two young men, usually bachelors from the mother's clan, act as an initiate's sponsors. One of these sponsors takes the child on his back when he is torn from his mother at the beginning of the initiations, and carries him, under a hail of blows, the two or three hundred meters that symbolically separate the group of mothers and sisters who bring the small boys to this spot from the group of men waiting for them. This is a moment fraught with intense emotion, as it is last time the mother touches or sees her child at close range for the next ten years or so. This protective sponsor looks after the initiate during all of the subsequent rites, through the rest of his childhood and adolescence until the third-stage initiations. But at the start he calms the boy's fears, takes care of him when he is hurt, and holds him on his lap—in short, acts as a mother within this world of men. A female function thus moves out of the women's world and is reproduced in the world of men.

× × ×

These details afford a better sense of what all of these ritual (and for us symbolic) practices mean, and the role they play in the construction of the social order that prevails in Baruya society. What the men aspire to do is clearly to *re-engender* the boys independently of the world of women, erasing the fact that they were born from the womb of a woman. From a certain standpoint, these rituals constitute a male reappropriation of the process of reproducing life, whose essential stages take place in the female body. And in the course of the initiations, the men's group, via the masters of the *kwaimatnie* (the sacred objects that cause bodies to grow), drum into the boys the idea that they are superior to women, that they must protect themselves from women, that they must stop thinking about their mother's loving touch, and so on. In short, they manufacture a male personality that amplifies the boys' image of themselves in their imagination even as the image of women is derided, belittled, and humiliated. But to see the opposition between men and women as a simple opposition between two components—one positive and the other negative—of social and cosmic reality would be to thoroughly misunderstand Baruya society.

The Baruya's deepest secret is that woman preceded man on earth. It is the women who invented the sacred flutes (whose secret name, as revealed to the initiates, means "vagina"). It is the women who invented such things as the bow and clothing. In short, the Baruya worldview recognizes that women originally had infinitely greater creative powers than men. But it also asserts that this creativity was a constant source of disorder from the start—that the women turned the bows the wrong way around, and killed too much game, and so on—and the men had to step in and establish some kind of order so as to save society. They did this through violence. A myth tells how the men became aware of the power contained in the women's sacred flutes and decided to get hold of them:

> One day, while the women were away, the men sent one of their group, a young man, to steal the flutes that were hidden under some skirts stained with menstrual blood. [The man thus broke a major taboo in order to capture the flutes.] He put one of the flutes to his lips and drew forth a wonderful sound. Then he

put them back where he had found them. When the women
returned, one of them wanted to play the flute, but no sound
came out. So the women gave the flutes to the men, who brought
forth their sacred music.

In another version, the women threw the now mute and useless
flutes to the ground. The men picked them up, and the flutes
have played for the men ever since.

In another narrative we are told that cultivated plants sprang
from the body of a woman who was murdered by her husband
and secretly buried in the forest.

> From her corpse came forth the first cultivated plants [such as
> taro]. The man ate some, and his body, which had been black and
> ugly, became shiny and fine-skinned. Later, assailed by people
> wanting to know how he had got such fine skin, he led the men
> and the women into the forest and told them to take cuttings
> from these cultivated plants *that had grown out of the dead woman's
> body*, and shoots of bamboo to make knives, etc. That is how hor-
> ticulture came into being.

All of these accounts say the same thing: women are more creative than men, but for the good of society men have resorted to
violence to deal with them, by stealing the flutes and by "mentally" killing them.[5] These acts of violence inflicted on women
in the mythic accounts, in thought and by means of thought,
are consistent with and legitimize a series of violent acts that are
far more tangible. Baruya women do not inherit land, the main
means of production. They are not allowed to carry weapons,
the main means of destruction and repression. They do not have
access to the sacred objects or the sacred knowledge that give
men a monopoly on the (imaginary) power to act on the conditions that reproduce society and the cosmos. And they do not
dispose of their own person and body at the time of marriage,
or pass their name on to their children.

The imaginary violence inflicted on women in the myths
and the rites thus goes hand in hand with real psychological,

physical, symbolic, political, and material violence perpetrated on a daily basis, as women are regularly ridiculed, insulted, and beaten. The Baruya stress that this curb must not be removed, for the women's powers did not disappear after the men made off with them, and might be recaptured by them at any time. That is why it is necessary, generation after generation, to initiate the boys and to circulate among them the male force that is contained in their semen, unsullied by intercourse with a woman. In the Baruya worldview, the cassowary is the wild woman, who roams the forest alone and sets upon men; this is why the great cassowary hunters are Great Men. But a cassowary hunter is not allowed to spill the blood of his prey; instead he must catch it in a noose trap, where it strangles to death, and give the meat to the initiates to be devoured in the Men's House. One can imagine the unresolved issues present in the male representation of women—admiration and jealousy of their powers, and contempt for their weakness—but this contempt can never be total.

The ambivalence is particularly apparent in their representation of menstrual blood, for which there is a special word, to distinguish it from the blood shared by men and women. The possibility that even a few drops of this blood could fall onto a man's belly or drop into his food terrifies the Baruya. But they are also aware that a woman who does not menstruate will not have children, something that raises the man's standing as well as that of the woman who bears them.

✕ ✕ ✕

In these accounts, the imaginary is caught in the act; its work consists of adding to one side of the real that which has been subtracted from the other side, with both operations accomplished by means of thought. Thus, the Baruya's imaginary male ancestors, the duplicates of the Baruya who lived in the beginning, robbed the original women of their powers, which were stronger than theirs, and added them to their own. And they went on to steal the flutes, which are vaginas, and added them to the men's bull-roarers, which are whirled overhead during the ceremonies and produce the voices of the *yimaka*, the forest spirits. The Baruya believe that the *yimaka* shot magic arrows at some men during the time of the *wandjinia* (the ancestors living during the Dreamtime), and that these arrows became the bull-roarers, the musical instruments that resound with the flutes during initiations. But these arrows also gave men powers of death, the power to kill enemies in war and game while hunting. Today's men thus see themselves as masters of two distinct sets of powers, which they cumulate and combine: the life-giving powers that originally belonged to the women, and the powers of death that they received directly from the *yimaka*. This mental arithmetic of addition and subtraction occurs against the backdrop of the belief that the powers stolen from the women could be taken back *at any time*, a belief that encompasses an imaginary fear and the apprehension of a possible reality.

It would be a mistake to think that this social order, which continually presupposes and reproduces the domination of one gender (men) over the other (women), is devoid of conflicts or resistance, as I have seen women refuse to submit to all of these constraints. A woman can "forget" to cook food for her husband for several days, or refuse to make love for weeks on end, even if there is a risk of being insulted and thrashed. In such instances, a man must be discreet, because everything can be heard in a Baruya village and the neighbors might laugh at such circumstances, thus humiliating the man. But a wife can do worse. Sometimes a woman will make love to her husband in order to collect the semen running down her thighs and fling it into the fire with a curse. When this happens, the man will usually commit suicide because he believes he has been bewitched and is doomed to die. I heard about an even more serious situation, when an initiate's mother, traumatized by the screams she heard when her son was being beaten, set fire to the roof of the *tsimia*, the big initiation house. According to the Baruya, she was killed either by the members of her lineage or through sorcery performed by the shamans.

Nonetheless, such acts of resistance do not mean that the

women, as a group or as individuals, had envisioned a different social order or had some counter-model in mind before the Europeans arrived. The very idea of a son not being initiated horrifies them, for no girl would want to marry him. We have thus come full circle. Men's greatest strength does not lie in the types of violence they inflict on women, but in the fact that men and women both share the same representations of the body, of life, and of the cosmic order. In short, their strength lies in their belief—in different forms to be sure—in shared imaginary and fantasy worlds, which result in the women's paradoxical consent to their own subordination. With such representations in her head, how can a Baruya woman watch the menstrual blood run between her thighs and not believe she is responsible for the circumstances that vicitimize her? In the end, these representations of the body ultimately impose silence. A woman has only to see and thus experience herself through this imaginary to realize that there is no alternative but to keep quiet and accept the social and cosmic order to which she is subjected.

✕ ✕ ✕

These various ethnographic points having been noted, let me conclude with a number of more general propositions. All of our analyses lead back to one basic point: in all societies, sexuality is pressed into the service of many realities—economic, political, and the like—that have no direct connection with sex or gender. In Baruya culture, being born a woman and not a man bars you from inheriting land, or carrying weapons, or having access to sacred objects, and deprives you of the social, material, psychic, or symbolic capacity to represent the society and to define the common good. Thus, above and beyond the personal, individual, and collective subordination of women to men, we see the general subordination of one aspect of life, sexuality in both its forms—that is, sexuality-as-desire and sexuality-for-reproduction—to the necessities dictated by the reproduction of other social relations, be they economic, political, or the like. What is apparent here, then, is the place of sexuality within the structure of a society, which lies within but also beyond any *per-*

sonal relationship between individuals who relate to each other as father, mother, son, daughter, husband, brother, sister, wife, friend, enemy, or something else.

This general subordination of sexuality is brought about in part by the elaboration and implementation of a set of imaginary and symbolic representations of the body and the sexes. From the start it is one's sex that gives the body its identity, that makes it like or unlike other bodies and—at least externally—either a woman or a man. And in addition to the flesh, blood, and bones that everyone has, regardless of sex, there are differences in the organs and substances men and women possess. One has or does not have a penis or a clitoris; one secretes semen, or milk, or menstrual blood.

Among the Baruya, as we have seen, semen is thought of as the source of life, as a force in itself, and as a food that gives life its force. It is the opposite of menstrual blood, which endangers this force and thus the source of men's strength, constantly threatening to make the cultivated fields barren, to turn the salt to water, to cause the group to meet with defeat in war, and other equally dire prospects. But this blood is not merely the negation of semen, since the Baruya know that a woman must have menstruated in order to be fertilized. Thus life, children, men's status, and the strength of their lineages all, in some way, depend on women's periods, and hence the ambiguity of these representations and oppositions, and the ambivalence of the Baruya's attitudes toward them. And through these representations, sexuality is constantly enlisted to testify to the order that reigns, or should reign, in society.

So it is not only sexuality and desire that fantasize in relations between individuals and within society; it is society itself that fantasizes in sexuality. For the body extends well beyond the domain of language, and, as the prevailing social order and the even more imaginary, purportedly cosmic order become embedded in the body, they take on different guises and conceal their original nature, ultimately reducing individuals to silence. And, as I have observed, these cultural and social representations of the body, shared by most if not all members of the society, form something like a ring of constraints within and around each person, restrictions that from the start dictate the way he or she experiences and/or appropriates the self and others. These shared cultural representations, the positive or negative norms that continually act upon the body and the individual's conscious and "unconscious" mind, operate much like an impersonal cultural sheath surrounding the individual's intimate being, an anonymous mental ego shared with all other egos of the same sex, a common cultural and social ego incised into the singular ego—the innermost personal ego—from birth, if not before.

Sexuality-as-desire always springs from an ego that contains others, not only those of the same or the opposite sex, but all others insofar as they are the source of the shared norms, representations, and values to which each individual is subjected from birth in the forms preordained by his or her sex. And sexuality-for-reproduction is similarly subjugated in advance. We must be wary here, however, of misinterpreting the notion of reproduction. It is not their "species" that individuals strive to reproduce; for the Baruya, it is the social group to which they belong, the social relationships within which each new person engendered will take his or her place. When Sigmund Freud declared that the characteristically aggressive behavior of the male, and thus of men, served to ensure the reproduction of our species because it made it possible to overcome female passivity and resistance, he was advancing a biological and ideological view of sexuality, something that does not seem to be the goal human beings are pursuing when they reproduce.

This observation provides a good opportunity for us to recall that in most extant societies, and in practically all of those that have gone before, desire is and was not recognized as the fundamental starting point for a legitimate union between the sexes. A man marries a woman because she is a cross cousin, or because she is from the same caste or village, and this is what society tells him to do. Though this does not necessarily preclude desire or affection—even between people who did not know or crave each other before the marriage—spontaneous desire is seen in such societies as a potential threat to its legitimate unions and to its norms, customs, and law.

When a young Baruya girl menstruates for the first time, she is allowed in theory to refuse the game and the gifts sent by her fiancé, who hunts with his kinsmen to provide these to her. If she rejects the gifts, she rejects the marriage—a right she is permitted once in her life. Thereafter she can never break the tie, except by dying. Once she is married, she can be put to death or forced to hang herself if her desire draws her to other men. Desire is thus systematically repressed, and directed to reproducing the social order, perpetuating the lineages, and producing their alliances. Only with the development of Western societies has the weighty responsibility of choosing the other to reproduce oneself and society been entrusted to individual desires; this is the reason that the question of desire has of late become paramount.

This detailed analysis of aspects of Baruya culture supports two conclusions of a more general nature. Society is inevitably built on the foundations of the sacrifice of something that is deeply ingrained in human sexuality—its fundamentally "a-social" character. Humankind is obliged to make social material out of sexual matter, and thus, as Jacques Lacan observes, there is little sex in a sexual act.[6] But this assertion runs the risk of obscuring an irreducible fact—namely, that pleasure, *jouissance*, enables sexuality to comply with the metamorphoses imposed on it by all societies and all cultures. The sexual organs permit the individual to pleasure him- or herself, and to be pleasured by others and pleasure them. This is a fundamental fact and a force that can either serve society or be turned against it.

But sex brings an equal amount of suffering and frustration, as well as pleasure, and it is these bodily experiences, all together, one after the other and at any moment, into which society, like the individual, with all its states and fantasies, can burrow and take root. Sexuality is the privileged site wherein the logic of the individual melds with the logic of society, and thus where ideas, images, symbols, and conflicting interests are "em-bodied." It is also along this suture line that the two forms of repression which enable the individual and society to exist and subsist, and that engender the unconscious life of the mind, organize themselves: repression as the dressing up as something else of everything in sexuality that is not compatible with peoples' conscious activities, and repression as the disguising of everything in the content of these social relations that wounds, that by way of their inequalities affects individuals and the groups to which they belong by virtue of their occupation, their function, their culture, their caste, or their clan.

It is by no means certain that psychoanalysts know how to untangle the intertwined but distinct effects of these kinds of repression in the discourse of those who seek them out. Nor can we be completely sure that anthropologists are capable, through "participant observation," of fully accessing the inner alchemy that transforms collective fantasies into individual fantasies, and vice versa.

5

How an Individual Becomes
a Social Subject

How does an individual come to be a social subject? What are the roles played respectively by conscious and unconscious mental activity in the emergence of the social subject? Though these are questions of prime interest to psychoanalysts and to anthropologists, my contribution here will be strictly that of an anthropologist, as, not having been analyzed myself, my only acquaintance with psychoanalysis comes from books.

Let me start with a few words about the occupation of the anthropologist, who deals in getting to know the "other." To do this, one must choose to hold oneself "at a distance," the better to approach the subject of study. One also has a choice between studying societies other than one's own or focusing on parts of one's own society distinct from those from which one comes or in which one works or lives.

Once the field has been chosen, a paradox arises. As the anthropologist usually turns up without having been invited, he or she must win over a community, building relations of trust and open dialogue with individuals who will choose to talk about themselves and their social relationships or become go-betweens to facilitate the observation and interpretion of events that occur in their society (and thus become the anthropologist's "informants"). A fieldworker therefore begins by establishing one-to-one relationships to observe individuals and groups as they interact, but paradoxically tries to determine what in their actions is not explained by their individual characters, to identify and understand the nature of the social relations—such as kinship, power, and friendship—that these interactions presuppose or create between individuals. And each time he or she comprehends the logic of their social relations a bit better, the individuals will appear in a new light.

But what actually is a social relationship? It is a set of relations having many dimensions—material, emotional, social, mental—produced by the interactions between the individuals involved and, often through them, between the groups to which they belong. These relationships form aspects of everyday life and are named according to the nature of their various domains, such as kinship or politics. The term *mental* (a working if inadequate gloss of *idéel*) refers to more than concepts; it is the set of representations, rules of conduct, positive or negative values and feelings attached through the content and logic of a culture to the beings, and actions and events that surround the individuals, which they experience or originate. For example, a person cannot get married unless he or she has some idea of what marriage is, and a vague or a clear notion whom they can or (depending on the nature of the kinship system found in the society) must marry. These mental and emotional aspects of the relationships that characterize a particular society are the subjective part of social relations, a set of representations, values, and feelings that exist as much within individuals as in the relations they entertain with others, which give the relations meaning.

Thus we see that social relations exist not only *between* individuals but at the same time *within* them. They reside in the individual in various forms, insofar as their very content affects the individual on several planes: mental, to be sure, but also material, emotional, cognitive, political, and so forth. And if certain relations exist not only *between* people but *within* them as well, they can be produced or reproduced only *by* those individuals, whereas the relations specific to their society existed before their birth and will probably endure after their death. The individual, single and singular, cannot be the source of his or her society; he or she is born and grows up in a web of structured relationships and institutions whose content is every bit as "imaginary" as it is "real," and whose signs are symbols.

The anthropologist thus begins by focusing on specific individuals, who gradually slip behind the relationships that he or she analyzes to discover either their overarching logic or their local, partial principles (those that cause the actions of the individuals to converge and/or diverge, but that always *coalesce* in a cultural field where they *have meaning* for the actors). Here the anthropologist faces another challenge: how to get back to the individuals, or to the individual, and bring the meaning that he or she has reconstructed face-to-face with the meaning gleaned from the actors themselves. This shift in focus is constant, and is more like two poles of a single approach than two distinct, sequential stages of research.

✕ ✕ ✕

Thus far we have touched on the mental and emotional aspects of social life, but have made no mention of the unconscious. Though the meanings of acts as collected from the actors are explicit and conscious, if we understand the relations of power, interest, hostility, or complicity between individuals, we may also come to comprehend their unspoken messages, what the actors *do not* say about themselves and about others.

With these preliminary remarks in mind, we can now define the social subject as an individual embedded in a network of relationships that have meaning for him or her and the others involved, who is able to sustain or transform these relationships or even to break free from them but incapable of altering the overall structure of the society. Though the network of relationships that originates from or terminates with the individual defines the various aspects of his or her social identity, individual relationships are themselves encompassed by those that connect the other members of the community or society.

By way of example, the identity of a Baruya—an individual, male or female, who belongs to a local tribe in New Guinea which exercises a sovereignty of sorts over a defined territory and the individuals and groups living there—is thus both over-arching and multifaceted. As a member of the tribe, he or she is a "Baruya"—as one is a "Frenchman" or an "Englishman"—but also a member of one of the kin groups that constitute it, such as a "Bakia." But this identity can never be reduced to merely the enveloping identities of tribesman and clansman. A Baruya has as many identities as the different social groups to which he or she simultaneously belongs by virtue of one or another aspect of him- or herself. A male co-initiate . . . a female co-initiate . . . a shaman . . . a master of the initiations . . . son of . . . brother of . . . sister of . . . mother of . . . all these identities are crys-tallizations of various relationships with others, of functions and statuses that either terminate in the individual and imprint themselves there or originate in the individual and imprint themselves in others. The content and the form of these identi-ties stem from the specific relations and culture that character-ize a particular society, drawn from the special features of its structures and functioning, and these form the concrete multi-plicity of the individual's social identity, which is never a simple tally of distinct identities and particular relationships. Personal identity is always the product of a singular, unique history, one that is never reproduced anywhere else and develops in life cir-cumstances that are never the same for any two people, be they brothers, sisters, or brother and sister.

⋊ ⋊ ⋊

Given this brief précis of the social subject, it seems obvious that psychoanalysis and the psychological sciences cannot teach us anything about the reasons why different forms of society—such as tribes, states, castes, and classes—appeared and disap-peared over time. And these approaches are even less adept at explaining the forces, causes, and events that drove the evolu-tion of such societies through their often irreversible transfor-mation into other forms of social life, and thus into other forms of social identity, other types of social actors, and, in short, other historical kinds of social subjects.

Yet it seems to me that using another approach, which repudiates nothing of the aforementioned critique, might make it possible to reach a place where psychoanalysis, and other disciplines that consider the intimate relations a subject entertains with his or her body and mind, could help us understand how individuals emerge who are capable of becoming social actors and subjects within every society, regardless of its form or its particular logics or the time in which it exists.

In the simplest and therefore the roughest terms, I would say that in every society, an individual becomes a subject responsible for his or her own acts when he or she has made a significant break with the world in which he or she was first socialized without experiencing the sort of trauma that leads to social paralysis and isolation or down the path of forbidden or marginal practices. The world from which this break occurs is that of the family and kinship relations, but it is also a place in which the individual discovers the body and learns about the differences between the sexes and the generations, where the incest taboo, among many other prohibitions both sexual and nonsexual, holds sway. To put this in the language of psychoanalysis, for the individual to become a subject, he must ultimately have resolved his Oedipus complex, without coming to serious harm, to successfully identify with those of his or her own sex. (In contrast to many psychoanalysts, however, I do not believe that this means that a person will be heterosexual.)

This opens the vast question of the relationship between the individual and his or her sexuality, and more particularly between sexuality and society. In contrast to that of other primates, human sexuality is "generalized," since the absence of the *visible* signs of estrous in the human female means that sex is no longer directly subject to the rhythms of the natural world,[1] and there is no special mating season followed by periods of calm and playful eroticism. Men and women can potentially make love at any time, all year round, engaging in behaviors ranging from homosexuality to heterosexuality, and in a masculine or a feminine way, without this being a direct consequence of the individual's physiological sex.

This has been the human condition for thousands of years, ever since human sexuality was emancipated from the cycle of natural reproduction. No biologist has been able to explain when and how the visible signs of estrous disappeared in the human female (if indeed they ever existed), though Jean-Didier Vincent suggests that this "loss" was linked to the development of the brain and to the cerebralization of all of the bodily functions.[2] Human beings are "brain driven," in that they respond to internal representations and are therefore more susceptible to internal than to external stimuli. Because of this, human sexuality responds more readily to representations and fantasies than to "reality."

But the specific and unique nature of human sexuality is not due to its generalized, polymorphous, and polytropic character alone. It is also set apart by the fact that the two forms it necessarily takes—sexuality-as-desire and sexuality-for-reproduction—can potentially be disjoined and even opposed. But whereas sexuality-for-reproduction has social meaning insofar as it enables individuals to produce other individuals, and thus reproduce the groups that make up a society and ultimately the society itself, sexuality-as-desire can work equally to reinforce the social order or to destroy it, since every social order is at once a sexual order and an order between the sexes. Because desire does not have a "social sense," properly speaking, the threat it poses to the social order is most pronounced when it is incestuous. If this is so, then the evolution of human sexuality would have ultimately produced a permanent danger and a threat to the reproduction of society (and more specifically to the relations of cooperation, responsibility, and authority instituted between the sexes and the generations).

It was probably this line of thought that Sigmund Freud was pursuing when he stressed that sexual desire "isolates" individuals more than it brings them together, and that love is a "selfish passion."[3] He took a broader view of desire in *Civilisation and Its Discontents*, linking the emergence of such major institutions as religion and ethics with the need to control and repress sexuality. Seen in this light, it is understandable that a generalized, polymorphous, and polytropic sexuality cannot be lived entirely at the level of a social subject's conscious acts, as some aspects of desire (libido) must be repressed from the conscious mind. But as Freud has taught us, what is repressed never disappears, but continues to exist in different and unconscious forms that resurface in the conscious mind cloaked in ways that make it partially undetectable. This phenomenon, which cuts across historical periods and cultures and acts on the conditions of an individual's emergence as a social subject, is evident in each society's need to control the exercise of sexuality, beginning with the earliest kin relationships into which an individual is born and socialized. To control means both to allow and to forbid; to forbid does not mean to eliminate, however, but to suppress and therefore to repress from the conscious mind, from the place where intent is met by the decision to do or not to do.

To state this ontological fact in another way, I would assert that no society—and therefore no social subject, no actor, no individual capable of producing and reproducing it—is possible without a social sacrifice of one kind or another, without metaphorically giving up, individually and collectively, a part of human sexuality. This sacrifice is necessary, and is codified as law in all societies and all periods of time. Here I depart from Freud, in that the sacrifice that "becomes law" should not be confused with the necessity of "murdering the father." It is a law that lies behind all human laws and has no gender; in fact, human society proper began, as I see it, not with the mythical murder of the father but, among others, with the amputation of the "a-social" character of sexuality. By this, I mean that sexual desire, a person's libido, can *spontaneously* direct itself toward persons who are socially forbidden, such as the mother, father, sister, and the like. Nature does not dictate the direction that desire takes, nor does the body. This sacrifice, this amputation, simultaneously mutilated humans and promoted them to a position of co-responsibility with nature for their own existence. Humans are not merely beings who live in society and adapt to it like the other primates; they need, instead, to produce society in order to go on living. Society is thus erected on the foundations not of murder but of conscious amputation, the waking negation of something that belongs to humans and is part of them, the a-social character of their desire. This negation and amputation are simultaneously conscious and unconscious acts that repress, suppress, and subordinate, for humans cannot divide up their being, but must repress part of it into the unconscious, where it continues to exist in other forms.

What I am attempting to address here is an *ontological* reality, the necessity for all societies to subordinate sexuality to the conditions of their production and reproduction. This is not the same as the social arrangement that becomes established between individuals of opposite sexes; it is basically the subordination of homo-, hetero-, or other sexualities to the reproduction of the social, political, and economic relations that draw society into a structured totality imposed by various means on all of its members. Though this structural subordination of sexuality to other social relations also penetrates and articulates itself with—while remaining distinct from—the concrete forms of subordination that exist between the sexes, it does not completely account for their content.

It is when the subordination of sexuality that lies at the heart of a social order (which is always a sexual order as well) is stamped into the innermost recesses of individuals that they emerge as social subjects. But in order to do so, other fundamental conditions must exist—namely, access to spoken language and to consciousness of relations, reciprocal or not, with persons other than oneself. This occurs through a process that marks the individual's body and his or her innermost subjectivity, and presupposes the existence of a twofold metamorphosis present in all societies, which occurs at the intersection of kinship and other social relations. In the first metamorphosis, economic, political, and religious relations that have nothing to do with kinship, so far as their origins and meanings are concerned, become "aspects of kinship relations." Then, with the second metamorphosis, everything that comes under the heading of kinship ultimately changes to become "sexual and gender relations," and imbed themselves in the individual accordingly. Thus social relations become kinship, and kinship relations become gender.

Let us consider a few concrete examples. In many societies, land is inherited by sons to the exclusion of daughters, and sometimes by only the eldest or the youngest son to the exclusion of the others. An economic relationship—a component of social wealth, in this instance ownership of land—is thus transmitted exclusively through men and is bequeathed along kinship lines from father to eldest or youngest son. In almost all societies we know of, women are barred from the use of weapons, and cannot employ armed violence in power relations. In these instances, the economic (land ownership) and the political (exercise of armed violence) become attributes of kinship, which implies a relation of domination, of gender inequality.

It is no small matter that this twofold metamorphosis occurs precisely in the field of kinship relations, where the individual is born and initially socialized, and that the results of this impersonal transformation are always embedded in the *body*, in the person of the individual. And so every culture constructs for the individual—before they are born and because they are *already* awaited as a boy or a girl—an intimacy with the self that is initially impersonal. Thus the body is summoned to testify not only *about* a particular culture, but above all *for* or *against* the prevailing order—between generations, clans, castes or classes, or countless other systems of rank—that characterize a society and *reign* therein.

× × ×

Let us return to the process of the inscription of a social order in the innermost intimacy of the body. We have already noted, in chapter 3, that every society has one or more theories of what constitutes a child and how babies are made, and that these are not based on universal biological "facts" (which, until the advent of embryo transplants, were presumably the same everywhere and at all times), but instead on widely variable cultural models.

In a patrilineal society like the Baruya, people believe that a child is formed from a man's semen, which constitutes the bones, the flesh, and the blood of the fetus, and a woman is regarded as a mere vessel. But the fetus is not complete until the Sun puts the finishing touches on the body by making the nose (which is the seat of intelligence), the arms, and the legs. Though a Baruya child thus belongs to its father's lineage, it also claims the Sun—who the Baruya call *Noumwe*, or Father—as a parent. The Sun is the source of life and of the cosmic order, together with either his younger brother, the Moon (according to an esoteric version of one of their myths), or his wife (in the exoteric version known by the women and the noninitiated boys).

For the Trobriand Islanders, a matrilineal society found to the east of New Guinea who were superbly analyzed by Bronislaw Malinowski (and more recently by Annette Weiner), a child does not belong to its father's clan but to that of its mother and her brothers. Given this kinship arrangement, the Trobrianders believe that the child is the result of an encounter with a maternal spirit, which lives with other spirits on a small island at a sacred site belonging to the mother's clan. This spirit-child enters the woman's vagina, mixes with her menstrual blood, and becomes an embryo. What does it mean, then, to be a "father" in this society? A child's father does not engender it, but *pierces* the woman and opens the way for the spirit-child. He is thus not a genitor, but a nurturer, who nourishes the fetus with his semen and shapes its features. A couple thus increases the frequency of intercourse at the first signs of pregnancy (in stark contrast with other societies where intercourse during pregnancy is strictly forbidden), and children are believed to look like their fathers, who do not engender them and to whom they do not belong.

These views of conception are "social ways" of making babies, and variants of the twofold metamorphosis that helps to create the impersonal, cultural form of intimacy which is imprinted in each newborn child and conditions how he or she will experience his or her body and encounter the other.

⨯ ⨯ ⨯

The body is thus the place where the unconscious—which is not, or not necessarily, "a subject"—is stitched to the social subject, the individual who carries a name and an identity. As such, it is akin to a ventriloquist's dummy, in that it lends its voice both to the social domain and to the forces and desires that make up the unconscious. The language of the body is therefore both a shout and a murmur—influenced, reclothed, disguised—that sometimes ends in silence. For the body is always summoned in advance to testify for or rise up against the social order that dwells in it, by a subject who thus expresses either acceptance or rejection of the particular order of his or her society.

This twin metamorphosis, an essential part of the process of constructing the individual as a social subject, is a cross-cultural phenomenon that stems from the fact that humans not only live in society but produce society in order to live. And this trans-cultural point explains the cultural diversity exhibited by the human species. It is therefore not sufficient for us to observe and understand the many ways that humans *adapt* to the various situations they have invented or to which they have been subjected, since they are also adept at inventing themselves in these circumstances. In essence, humans cannot live in society without endowing themselves or being endowed at birth with the capacity to *produce society in order to live.* The social subject is therefore not a second-order subject, because its unconscious component does not precede it, either ontologically or historically. (There is no justification for characterizing the unconscious as a subject in itself.) And yet the social subject cannot be reduced to just its conscious activities, its conscious state, the conscious part of its self and its various egos. This is evident when a social subject speaks; using a language that he or she did not invent and whose origin is not known, the subject finds all other speakers present within him- or herself, and thus is no longer alone. The other is present in me before I learn to speak, and talks to me before I utter a word.

⨯ ⨯ ⨯

Let me make one further remark on the awakening of the social subject. We know that every individual begins life by being compelled to live and internalize a cultural vision of the "self," which the subject neither created nor chose. This is an aspect of what Pierre Bourdieu refers to as the *habitus*, which bury themselves in the individual and give his or her thoughts and actions meaning and direction.[4] We also know that the child begins life having already been *appropriated, claimed* by a set of adults, and that these "others" have rights over and obligations to him or her because they call themselves the child's parents and kin and/or are recognized as such by society. But the child must *in turn appropriate* these individuals—father, mother, and so forth—and ultimately *let go of them*, on pain of never becoming fully adult.

⨯ ⨯ ⨯

We thus return, full circle, to the likely universality of the Oedipus complex, which an individual must resolve to emerge as a social subject who is capable of adapting to the preexisting, imprinted social order essential to human life. But we must also bear in mind that a social subject is also capable of changing and sometimes overthrowing the order that dominates him or her.

On this thought I will conclude this brief discussion, and urge anthropologists and historians to begin a dialogue with psychoanalysts and other social scientists who deal with the human psyche, instead of drawing apart as we did when we found ourselves confronted with the diversity of the known forms of society and the irreversibility of their histories, but with the caveat that the probable universality of the Oedipus complex does not imply the universal necessity of the paternal dogma and the Law of the Father for its resolution.[5]

6

What Is a Society?

This chapter continues the analysis of the problems raised in chapter 2, which concluded that no society has ever been based on the family or on kinship. Here my aim is to go beyond the limits set by my focus on the Baruya, to see whether I can enrich and generalize my theoretical conclusions.

Having learned from the Baruya that their society did not exist a few centuries ago, I found myself faced with two obvious tasks: to determine the conditions that produced this now-identifiable group, and to discover the social foundation on which it was originally constructed and through which it continues to exist today. I soon discovered that the Baruya appeared in the wake of two episodes of killings and violence that occurred two or three generations apart. The initial players were a group of men, women, and children from various clans and lineages of the Yoyue tribe, which lived near Menyamya, a few days march from the mountains now occupied by the Baruya. These men and women had left their village, Bravegareubaramandeuc, some weeks earlier and had gone deep into the forest to hunt and bring back a large quantity of game for the upcoming male initiations. While they were away, the news reached them that all those who had stayed behind, including the young boys who were to be initiated, had been massacred by warriors from an enemy tribe, the Tapache, and that this had been done at the behest of members of their own Yoyue tribe.

Terrified and unable to return to their village for fear of also being killed, the survivors sought refuge with other tribes that were willing to accept them. And so a number of refugees arrived in the Marawaka Valley at the foot of volcanic Mount Yelia, to ask for asylum with the Andje tribe. The Andje agreed, and one of their clans, the Ndelie, let the newcomers settle on their lands. A few generations later, the descendants of these refugees had exchanged women with their hosts, and their children had been initiated alongside the children of the Andje, whose language they now spoke. It was then that the Yoyue made a secret pact with the Ndelie and laid an ambush for the other clans of the tribe, inviting them to take part in a ceremony and killing many of those who attended. The survivors fled and went to live on the other slope of Mount Yelia, leaving their lands to the conspirators.[1] After these massacres, which were perpetrated on and by Yoyue groups, a new society arose that took the name— *Baruya*—of one of the refugee clans. This particular clan was chosen because it plays a key role in the male initiation rites.

Having usurped part of their hosts' territory and expanded it by warring with their neighbors, how did the Baruya go about making a new society? I raised this question in a number of ways with my informants, but not until I had spent several years with them and learned about the way the group functioned and how its members thought and acted did I begin to formulate an answer. I did so in light of all the field data I had gathered: the genealogies of all the members of the tribe; the demographic makeup of all the villages and hamlets; information about who owned and used the more than 700 gardens; the notes and films documenting the initiations of boys, men, girls, and shamans; and other ethnographic observations that I'd recorded.

I analyzed all this to address an all-encompassing question: Among all the social relations that characterize Baruya life, which had and still have the capacity to create ties of dependence, reciprocal or not, regardless of sex, age, lineage, or village? That is, which relations create an overarching shared identity to which individual Baruya feel they belong, a *whole* that enables them to exist and reproduce and that they in turn must help reproduce, as well?

It was from this vantage point that I examined Baruya kinship relations, not just to understand their abstract, underlying principles but to determine how they really function. Here I drew on hundreds of genealogies, which clearly document the alliances contracted among the various lineages and clans over four or five generations. I ended up concluding that producing and reproducing kinship relations between lineages did not bind everyone with everyone else, either through direct or indirect ties.

I next turned to the ties created by material cooperation, mutual aid, and the sharing of resources between individuals and lineages, which were established in the course of producing the material means that ensured social existence. This includes both daily subsistence and the surplus that is exchanged with neighboring tribes to procure whatever the Baruya do not produce, or for which they create insufficient quantities, such as bark capes, weapons, tools, and featherwork insignia of rank. Here too I was obliged to conclude that these social ties—which we in the West refer to as economic relations—did not create a common material basis such that everyone was socially dependent on everyone else, and thus united through and for its production and reproduction.

I thus concluded that neither kinship nor economic relations had the capacity, in the past or at the time I observed them, to draw all of the Baruya lineages and individuals into an overarching whole. This was hardly in line with the views of Confucius (551–479 BCE) or Aristotle (384–322 BCE), for whom the family and kinship were the foundations of the city or the state.[2] Nor would it suit Karl Marx, for whom the relations that shed light on the way a society works are "the mode of production and redistribution" of the material goods and services existing between the groups that make up a society, or the neoliberal economists who assert that the "true" economic relations—the market economy, which should result in the development of democracy, respect for human rights, and so forth—fashion a society's structure.

Where was I to find what made the Baruya regard themselves, and be regarded by neighboring friendly or hostile tribes, as belonging to a single society, one that set them apart from surrounding groups, many of which spoke the same language?

I found, through my analysis of their economic activities, a trail leading to an area I had yet to explore: the political-religious relations, which indeed concerned and simultaneously involved all lineages and all individuals, but in different ways depending on age, sex, and clan. My focal point was the production of a surplus of food, clothing, and other goods that occurred when the tribe decided to carry out a new round of initiations every three or four years; this surplus was not intended to reproduce each lineage as such, but as a material contribution to the performance of rites and ceremonies that lasted for weeks. Initiations were attended by hundreds of visitors from neighboring tribes, scores of friends and enemies who had to be appropriately fed and received, since all warfare was then suspended or banned.

I have explained the nature and meaning of these initiations elsewhere, and so I will simply recall here a single moment that expresses their overall meaning: the construction of the *tsimia*, the large ceremonial house where part of the boys' initiation as well as the passage of the older initiates to new stages take place. For the Baruya, the *tsimia* represents their "body" and testifies that they are a single body, whose skeleton is made of the poles that hold up the building, and whose "skin" is the bundles of grass, gathered and carried back by hundreds of girls and women of the tribe, that are used to thatch the roof. The huge center pole that supports the roof is called *tsimie* and represents the Baruya clan ancestor, to whom the Sun gave the sacred objects necessary for the initiation of the future warriors and shamans, and who is said to have assigned distinct positions and functions in the performance of the initiation rites to the other clans.

During my stay, I observed that each of the poles for the walls of the *tsimia* had been cut in the forest and carried back by the father of one of the future initiates. When they reached the place where the *tsimia* was to be erected, the men lined up at an equal distance from one another, forming a circle that traced the circumference of the structure. At a signal from the master of the initiations (who belonged to the Baruya clan, and at whose side stood the great shaman, Inamwe, from the Andavakia clan responsible for initiating the shamans), all of the fathers suddenly and simultaneously lifted their poles, planted them in the ground and raised the Baruya war cry, which was echoed by all of the men standing around the site. It is important to note that the men who planted their poles in the ground were not grouped by kinship, clan by clan, but rather village by village, according to ties of coresidence and daily cooperation.

From these facts, whose meaning was explained to me by the Baruya themselves, I deduced that the male and female initiations accomplished several things at once. First, they divided the whole population into distinct, socially ranked categories, each of which encompassed all individuals of the same age and sex, and in so doing reproduced the division of the population into age-grades. Second, since the masters of the initiations and the shamans, aided by the spirits and the ancestors, were able to determine which new initiates would become great warriors, shamans, or cassowary hunters, the rites identified those exceptional individuals the society would be able to count on.

But there was also a third aspect of the initiations: the reproduction of the hierarchical relations that existed between those clans that exercised ritual functions and possessed sacred objects and the secret formulas indispensable to their use, and those that did not have or no longer had these. It just so happened that the clans that possessed these objects and functions were descended from the Yoyue refugees and the Ndelie, the clan that had betrayed the Andje when the refugees decided to kill their hosts and appropriate their territory.

The conclusion was clear: the relations that had enabled the Baruya to make themselves into a new society and ensured its reproduction through to the present were political-religious in nature. What was at stake in the initiations was how the society was to be run—by whom and why—and the order and hierarchy that was to prevail there; this meant assigning everyone

(male and female[3]) a place in the workings of society according
to sex, age, and clan, but also with regard to individual abilities.
But the Baruya also believed that this society could not function and endure without the helping hand of normally invisible
beings—glorious ancestors, nature spirits, and gods like the Sun
or the Moon or the rain god (a huge python that dwells in the
sky) among them. Through this cooperation between humans
and spirits, a society is reproduced and a cosmic order is made
manifest that assists in human endeavors. The social order is
inscribed in a cosmic order—of this the Baruya are perfectly
conscious.[4]

But does this hold for other societies? For all societies?
To validate or invalidate this hypothesis, we must take leave of
the Baruya and turn our attention to other examples. We will
thus shift from Melanesia to Polynesia, and then, enlightened
by what we have discovered in the Central and South Pacific,
we will rapidly review Pharaonic Egypt, ancient China, and the
Indian caste system.

✕ ✕ ✕

In essence, the question I am posing is as follows: *What are the
connections—political, religious, economic, kinship, or other—that
have the capacity to bring together groups and individuals who thereby
form a "society" (with borders that are known if not recognized by the
neighboring societies) and so fuse them into an all-encompassing whole
that endows them with an additional, overarching, shared identity?*

These human groups—clans, "houses," orders, castes, classes,
and ethnic or religious groups among them—are often highly
diverse in nature, and an individual usually belongs to several of
them, each of which provides him or her with one or a number
of specific identities. To these particular identities is added the
overarching "oneness" attaching to all individuals who belong
to the same "society," the same Whole.

This question is thus not only central for the social sciences,
but stands at the heart of contemporary world affairs. Faced
with the globalization of the capitalist market economy, many
people in Europe and on other continents wonder what is to

become of their particular nationality, and of the tribal, ethnic, and religious identities inherited from an often distant past.

Because of the globalization of the capitalist economy (and the collapse of the so-called "socialist" system), for the first time in human history all local as well as national societies have found themselves forced to become cogs in a single economic system, which encompasses nearly the whole world (save for a few pockets of resistance, like Cuba and North Korea).[5] But integration of all societies into the world market means that they now engage in power struggles, competition, and self-interested behavior, all of which have not only economic but political and cultural consequences as well, since the world market is currently dominated by the United States, Western Europe, and Japan, and will likely remain so for some time to come.

Yet the many tensions, and even open conflicts, that have characterized such opposing forces as India and Pakistan, Iraq and Iran, and Israel and the Palestinians do not originate in economic competition but in rivalries of another order. In the case of India and Pakistan, there are territorial conflicts as well as political and religious confrontations, since the latter is a Muslim country run by a military regime and the former is a predominantly Hindu democracy. The issue of territory is obviously at the forefront of the conflict between Israel and the Palestinians (who want a territory and their own state), and is also a source of tension between China, Taiwan, Japan, and Vietnam. In short, the fears harbored by some—that the borders between societies and between states will disappear and their members will lose their identity, and that the resulting world civilization, where hundreds of millions of multicultural hybrids swim in the many flows of material and immaterial exchanges, will lead a life in the diasporas, drawn to those places where money and capital accumulate—have, sociologically speaking, no chance of being realized. Hence the importance of analyzing the political and religious relations that make up an essential part of both social and individual identity.

⊁ ⊁ ⊁

Resuming our ethnographic analysis, we must first stress that political and religious relations have the capacity to create new societies only when they serve, in particular sociological and therefore political contexts, to establish and legitimize the *sovereignty* of a number of human groups over one or several territories to whose resources they lay claim.

This sovereignty can take many forms. In ancient Greece, for example, it was shared exclusively by freemen (and not freewomen), who by birth belonged to a city-state such as Athens or Sparta. Such freemen enjoyed the right to possess and to exploit a piece of the territory in their city, either personally or through the labor of slaves and dependents; in addition, they had not only the right but the duty to exercise the political and religious functions necessary to reproduce the city as such and, if need be, to defend it. They alone had the right to worship the gods of the city, to sit in judgment, and to bear arms. The rest of the populace—the freemen of other cities who lived in Athens, men born in other countries, and of course slaves—did not enjoy these rights or share these duties, even though they made up a slightly larger proportion of the city's population.

In Western Europe, the nation-state gradually took hold after the Middle Ages, in part following the disintegration of such political powers as the Austro-Hungarian Empire. By contrast, great empires grew out of the military expansion of a group of tribes in pre-Columbian America, some from the same ethnic group and others not, that deprived other tribes and ethnic groups of sovereignty over their territory and granted them use of their lands in exchange for labor and tribute. This was the case of the Aztecs and the Incas when Hernán Cortés and Francisco Pizarro arrived. By contrast, the most widespread form of sovereignty found by the Europeans when they arrived in New Guinea and other parts of the world was that exercised by the members of a tribe over their territory, whether they were organized into a chiefdom or not.[6]

These examples also shed some light on what it means for a

society, with or without a state, to be "colonized," to lose sovereignty over its territory (and autonomy for social and cultural development) through transfer to or appropriation by a colonizing power. Such was the case in 1960, when an Australian patrol led by Jim Sinclair[7] "discovered" the Baruya and immediately imposed the "white man's peace" and the laws of a colonial state of which the Baruya had hitherto been unaware. From that point on, the development of their society and culture was dependent on the interventions of the British Empire, as administered by Australia. And their religion and rites of initiation were subject to the criticism and pressures of various Protestant missionaries from Europe or America, who made the long journey to convert the Baruya to the only "true" religion, founded by Jesus of Nazareth two thousand years ago.

Though Papua New Guinea became an independent country in December 1975, the Baruya did not recover their sovereignty over their territory. As citizens who had neither demanded nor wished to be part of an independent state and an emerging nation, they had of course acquired new rights and new duties, but were not permitted to settle their own disputes or to attack their neighbors and seize their territory. In the years since independence, Baruya society has not disappeared; indeed, their population has grown. But they have gone from being an autonomous society in the years before the Europeans arrived to a "local tribal group" that is part of a broader "ethnic" group—the Anga—who themselves are one of the hundreds of linguistic and ethnic groups that have had to forge themselves into the nation of Papua New Guinea. When they lost sovereignty over their mountains and their rivers, and over their own persons, the Baruya ceased to be a society, and became a local "tribal community" under the authority of a state, an institution totally alien to their history and their ways of thinking and acting.[8]

We thus see what it means to have a territory, a set of natural elements—lands, rivers, mountains, lakes, sometimes a sea—that provide human groups with resources for their livelihood and development. A territory can be conquered, or inherited from ancestors who conquered it or appropriated it without a fight (if they settled uninhabited regions). The territorial borders must be known, if not recognized, by the societies that occupy and exploit the neighboring spaces. In all cases, a territory must be defended by force, through the use of arms and organized violence, but also through rites that appeal to the gods and other invisible powers to weaken or annihilate the enemy. Thus, before the Baruya undertake any act of warfare, their shamans spend several days and nights calling upon their helping spirits to sap the enemy's strength and make them unable to draw their bows and hit their target, or blind them when an *aoulatta*, a Baruya great warrior, challenges them in close combat.

✕ ✕ ✕

This Baruya example reminds us that, for thousands of years, the social relations which facilitated communication with such powerful, invisible beings constituted an essential component of the exercise of sovereignty over a territory, over the resources found and exploited and often the human groups living there. Did the Inca not declare himself to be the son of the Sun, to whom he forced the peoples of his empire to build temples and pay worship? And was Athena not the patron goddess of Athens? As late as the nineteenth century, according to the 1833 Code of Laws, the czar of all the Russias presented himself as the sole source of law and of the Law, to whom all of his subjects must submit "not only out of fear, but in conscience, as God himself commands." After all, the czar was "the defender and guardian of the dogmas . . . of the true religion of the Slavic peoples"—Orthodox Christianity—according to this code.

The separation between the political and religious spheres is a recent development, and remains altogether unthinkable or unacceptable in many societies. In Europe, the notion of separating politics and religion took on meaning and gained strength only with the Enlightenment and the French Revolution,[9] when the secularization of the state (or of states) began. With this change, a process evident from earliest recorded history beginning with Sumer—namely the union, if not the fusion, of many forms of the political and religious domains—ceased to be the rule.

A religion is the set of all relations that the members of a society entertain with entities that are usually invisible but active in daily life, such as ancestors' souls, nature spirits, and various gods represented in the beliefs, which give proof of their existence and their powers. But human relations with spirits and gods also imply the particular relations between the humans themselves that permit communication with these entities, to beg them to act or not to act. Because of this, a religion endows certain individuals (shamans among the Baruya) or groups (priests or monks in Christianity) with a particular social status that derives from their place and role in human relations with those forces and beings that are supposed to act on the workings of the universe and the fate of humankind. But a religion is not merely a set of beliefs, rites, and social statuses attached to certain individuals and/or groups. It also constitutes certain ways of thinking and behaving, obligations and prohibitions that are obeyed more or less strictly by its followers. Beliefs, rites, distinct social statuses, and norms of thought and behavior that are more or less shared are, in my estimation, the components of all religions, whether they are purely local like that of the Baruya, or entertain claims to universality like the religions of salvation.

How then can religious beliefs and rites contribute to establishing the sovereignty of a human group over a territory, and thus be one of the conditions for the emergence of a new society? There are several ways. First, the myths and stories that comprise the content of the beliefs usually offer an explanation of the origin of the universe and humankind and the relations that, following a course of imaginary events, were set in place between such components as gods, humans, plants, animals, mountains, and the sea. Religions thus offer a cosmic foundation for a social order. Second, through its collective rites and individual conduct that adheres to its dogmas, a religion strives to associate with human powers those other, more powerful forces whose aid must be sought. As such, religion will play a minor or major role, depending on the form of sovereignty a human group exercises over a territory and the peoples living there, and is essential when the sovereignty is embodied and exercised by an individual who is viewed and celebrated as a god living among mortals; that is, when there is a veritable fusion between the political and the religious in the person of the sovereign, as well as in the social relations and institutions of which he or she is the lynchpin and the (apparent) source. This was perhaps most evident in the position of the pharaoh in ancient Egypt, but it was also true of other power figures regarded as gods living among humans, such as the Inca-Inti, or the Sun-Inca. Though they were not seen as gods, the kings of ancient China, and the line of emperors down through the ages from the foundation of the empire (221 BCE) to the dawn of the twentieth century, were believed to be the only humans that received Heaven's mandate to govern humankind and the universe. For this reason the Wang, the king, was called the "Unique Man," who was closer to the heavenly powers than anyone else, and whose person was sacred until Heaven withdrew its mandate, and the dynasty represented by the emperor disappeared.

Having thus mapped the limits of the particular features of Baruya society and history as well as their tribal form of sovereignty, we now turn to several Polynesian societies—Tikopia, Tonga, and Hawaii—whose features return us to the realm of gods living among mortals, or unique men living in the company of the gods.

× × ×

Passing from Melanesia to Polynesia, we will first stop at Tikopia, whose society was documented nearly as it stood just before the Europeans arrived in the remarkable work of Raymond Firth (1901–2001), one of the great names in the discipline of anthropology.

In 1928, when Firth first went into the field, Tikopia's political and religious organization was still nearly intact, as the missionary who arrived in 1924 had not yet made much of an impression. The society was divided into four nonexogamous clans, ranked according to their role in the cycle of rites that ensured the fertility of the land, the sea, and the people, with the Kafika clan and its chief, the *Te Ariki Kafika*, ranked highest. Through these rites, *and the intermediary of their chiefs*, the clans participated in what Firth called "the work of the gods," who granted or withheld plentiful harvests, abundant fish catches, or numerous, sturdy children.[10]

Perhaps one of the most significant facts, however, is that this society and this form of organization *did not exist* a few centuries before Firth's arrival. The four clans actually descended from groups that had arrived on Tikopia at different times from different islands, such as Pukapuka, Anuta, and Rotuma. These groups initally fought with each other before expanding and taking their place in the political-religious hierarchy connected with the "work of the gods" under the ultimate authority of the *Te Ariki Kafika*. What formed the basis of this hierarchical arrangement? According to a Tikopia myth, the ancestor of the Kafika clan was an exceptional being who had given the different feuding groups living on the island the principles and rules for organizing a common society. (This is not unlike the story of how the Sun god gave Kanaamakwe, the purported ancestor of the Kwarrandariar Baruya clan, the sacred objects and secret formulas that enabled them to initiate their men and to assign each clan a role in the rites.) The Kafika clan ancestor was later murdered by a jealous rival, but when he got to heaven, the paramount heavenly god breathed a "mana" into him and made him an *atua*, a god, and gave him authority over all the island's other gods. This is what gave his descendants, the chiefs of his clan, primacy over all other chiefs.[11]

Here we find an example of the aforementioned sociological and historical process: the political-religious relations integrated distinct, hostile human groups to form a whole and ensure its reproduction. And at the heart of these relations, we once again find cores of imaginary representations, foundation myths whose function is to legitimize the power structure and the place of each group in the social hierarchy by attributing a divine origin to some among them. And these imaginary (for us) representations became the source and the raison d'être of real social relations through the implementation of the symbolic practices that formed the annual cycle of the rites comprising the "work of the gods."

Let us compare this form of social organization with the one we observed in the Baruya society. With the exception of making salt money, the only division of labor among the Baruya was that between the sexes.[12] A man derived prestige and authority as the representative of a clan and by playing an important role in initiating the warriors or shamans, but nothing more. Once the ceremonies were over, the masters of the initiations returned to the same tasks as all the other Baruya, cutting down trees to clear forest gardens, going off hunting, building houses, and so forth. They refrained only from engaging in combat, for fear they would be killed and take with them the secret formulas that instilled their powers into the sacred objects, the *kwaimat-nie*, used in the initiations.

This was not the case in Tikopia. The chiefs, who were responsible for the rituals, were treated with great respect, and their persons were protected by a range of taboos. They cultivated their gardens, but were spared the heaviest work. They alone held rights to the land, and thus gave families permission to work it, and at harvest time they were offered the first fruits. And it was the chiefs—the *Te Ariki Kafika* in particular—who exercised control over the productive activities of the whole population, opening and closing the cycle of agricultural work and fishing through the imposition and suspension of various taboos. All such activities essential to the life of individuals and clans were thus incorporated into the cycle of rituals performed by the chiefs working *with* the gods to ensure their success,[13] and the Tikopia believed their productivity depended more on the effectiveness of the rites, through the combined action of the chiefs and the gods, than on their own efforts.

It is sometimes hard for those of us accustomed to thinking in monotheistic terms to imagine this direct cooperation between key individuals and gods in the performance of rites. In a number of societies, nonetheless, the belief that some individuals are descended from gods leads to divine cooperation in the performance of the rites. For the Tikopia, such rites are not "the work *of* the gods," but "the work [of the chiefs] *with* the gods."[14]

Compared with the Baruya, we see here a fundamental change in Tikopian society, which is comprised of clans that are cross-cut by two other social groups: the chiefs and their descendants, and the commoners. As Firth noted, the difference between these groups, in terms of political and religious organization, was one of nature, and it was irreducible because it was based on the proximity of one group to, and the distance of the other group from, the divinized ancestors and the gods. By contrast, in the economic sphere—the domain of the production and possession of the means of subsistence and the material forms of wealth (such as shells)—the inequalities between the two groups were merely a matter of degree.

Even more radical changes occurred in the great "chiefdoms" of Tonga, Samoa, and Tahiti well before the Europeans arrived. In eighteenth-century Hawaii, a sort of state developed from the chiefdoms that had been vying for control of the island chain.[15] These societies were no longer divided, as in Tikopia, solely between chiefs and their families and commoners; in Tonga, by way of example, an aristocracy that included men and women, the *eiki*, was distinguished from the rest of the population. Here, as among the Tikopia, an absolute barrier separated the noble men and noble women, who were believed to possess *mana* (powers that testified to their proximity to the gods), from the rest of society; and the *Tu'i Tonga*, the paramount chief of Tonga, as well as his sister, the *Tu'i Tonga Fefine*, claimed to descend directly from the highest god in the Polynesian pantheon, Tangaloa.[16]

Unlike the Tikopia chiefs, though, the Tongan *eiki* wielded almost absolute power over the persons, the labor, and the goods of the commoners who lived on their lands and belonged to their *kainga* ("estate" or "house"). But these lands, and this power of life and death over the men and women who were in a sense their subjects, were always delegated to the chiefs by the *Tu'i Tonga*. Each year he received from the heads of the *kainga* the first fruits of their harvests or the best fish that had been caught. Thus, in contrast to Tikopia, where the chiefs continued to take part in the various tasks that produced the material conditions of their social existence, the Tongan *eiki* do not work. Instead, they make war or assist the *Tu'i Tonga* in the complex rites addressed to the gods, and exercise over all other groups the political-religious powers that bind them into a whole, governed and reproduced under the sovereignty of the *Tu'i Tonga*.

✕ ✕ ✕

With these additional examples from Polynesia, we have passed beyond the limits of our analysis of the Baruya. Though there is a sexual division of labor between men's work and women's work in both New Guinea and Tonga, the latter is also divided between the majority of members who produce the material goods for all, and the nobles who do not engage in productive labor but devote their lives to performing rites, making war, and pursuing leisure.

Comparison of these ethnographic and historical examples from several Melanesian and Polynesian societies has thus brought us face-to-face with two fundamental changes that occurred in relations between the chiefs and their direct descendants, and the rest of the populations. The changes, which deeply altered both the social and economic dynamics that existed between the groups, were directly linked, although they worked in opposite directions.

By the same sociological and historical process, the chiefs and their descendants detached themselves, first partially and then completely, from carrying out the productive activities that ensured the material conditions of their *own* social existence and that of *their* family line. But at the same time, *as they progressively detached themselves from the concrete process of labor, they attached to their own persons and functions the exclusive right to access the mate-*

rial conditions of production—the land and resources of the sea—as well as the use of the labor, and products, of the rest of the population. Ultimately, the entire material basis of the society came to be controlled by one social group, the aristocracy, and hence was at their service, oriented first and foremost toward the production of their conditions of existence and the material means of conducting their social functions and upholding their rank. Thus, unlike the Baruya, in these circumstances the economic relations between all the groups comprising a society constitute a material and social foundation that *binds* everyone to everyone else. Does this mean that the mode of production and redistribution of goods and services, and not political-religious relations, unite all of the social groups and make them into a society? I will demonstrate that this is not the case, and so conclude this brief discussion of the social relations that make societies, and not of what constitutes the "basis" of human society.[17]

✕ ✕ ✕

What then are the causes that brought about this twofold transformation, and with it the appearance of new forms of social organization that divided society not only into clans and lineages but into groups whose distinct functions afforded them specific rights and duties, and a particular place within an overarching hierarchy, from which one or more groups govern and dominate all others?

Throughout the history of European thought, depending on the period and the realities being described, various words have been used to designate those groups of men and women who occupied different positions in a hierarchy, wherein some governed and others were governed. In ancient Rome and in the Middle Ages, people spoke of distinct "orders," which later became entities such as the Third Estate in France. In the eighteenth century, prompted by the changes induced by the agricultural and industrial revolutions, and inspired by the Physiocrate François Quesnay in France and Adam Smith in England, people began talking about "classes."[18] Before this, when Europeans discovered India, they used the term "castes" to describe the groups that performed distinct and mutually exclusive tasks and were ranked according to the degree of purity or impurity that these activities entailed. Castes are not classes, because they reproduce themselves through kinship relations, by the obligation to marry within one's caste. Nonetheless, the words *estates*, *classes*, and *castes* matter less than understanding the social realities they designate and are used to conceptualize.

✕ ✕ ✕

Our ethnographic journey has thus led us, at last, to address the classic question of the origin of orders, castes, and classes. This question should ideally lead to another, which I will not attempt to answer here: the origin of the state, which is found not only in societies that are divided into orders or classes or castes but also in empires compounded of various tribes and ethnic groups, and is the instrument whereby some of them, but not all, exercise their sovereignty—an institution that until recently was unknown throughout much of Africa, Asia, and Oceania, and parts of pre-Colombian America.[19]

The answer to the first question was already there, under our nose. What profoundly transformed certain societies and altered the course of their history was the appearance, in different places and at different times, of human groups that began to devote themselves entirely to the performance of the social functions that legitimized their right to (1) opt out of personally producing the concrete bases of existence, (2) control the access of the other members of the society to the conditions necessary for the production of the material means of their social existence, and (3) appropriate the labor of others as well as some of the goods and services they produced.

What, then, are these social functions whose exercise both engendered and legitimized the inequalities between groups and individuals that were unknown in tribal societies devoid of classes or a state? The answer is clear: they are religious and political functions. Religious functions entail the celebration of rites and sacrifices that are designed to act together with the gods, the spirits, and ancestors to ensure the well-being of humankind. Political functions have to do with governing society, maintaining a social order that is seen as grounded in the natural and cosmic order, but they also include defending its sovereignty over territory against neighboring groups. In short, political relations are always associated with the right to exercise violence inside or outside the society, a need that has sometimes given rise to warriors, who specialize in such pursuits.

Here we find ourselves on ground familiar to anthropologists, historians, and archeologists. Let us recall the organization of Indian society into four overarching categories, or *varna*, in Vedic times. At the top were the *Brahmans*, specialists in sacrifices to the gods and the ancestors. Just below them were the *Kshatriya*, the warriors who were called upon to spill human blood. The Raja, or king, alone among the warriors could participate in rites performed by the Brahmans and take part in combat on the battlefield. Lower still were the *Vaishya*, those who worked the land and fed all the castes. And below them were the *Shudra*, the "last of men," at the greatest conceivable distance from the Brahmans (who were sometimes called "gods living on earth"). Between these two extremes lay a multitude of castes (*jati*), each of which specialized in a task that endowed them with a recognizable degree of purity or impurity, and thus separated them, excluded them, and ranked them with respect to each other.[20]

In Indian society, each social group therefore depends, materially and socially, on the castes engaged in agricultural and craft production in order to reproduce itself. But though economic relations create a material basis shared by all of the social groups—which was not the case for the Baruya or in Tikopia—these did not engender the caste system; it was the castes, the political and religious organization of the society, that lent economic activities both their material content and their social and religious form and dimension.

✕ ✕ ✕

These points are evident in other historical examples. Consider the Egyptian pharaoh, a God living among humans, who was born of the union of two gods, Isis and Osiris, a brother and a sister, and who reproduced this union by marrying his own sister; whose breath—*khâ*—was believed to animate all living beings down to the smallest gnat; who sailed his sacred boat up the Nile every year to ask the river god to bring back the silt-rich waters to fertilize the fields and guarantee the peasants bountiful harvests. Or remember the emperor of China, the *Wang* (Unique Man), who alone was qualified to perform the rites and serve as the link between Earth and Heaven, and who had received the mandate that authorized and obliged him to govern the world and its inhabitants, both human and nonhuman. The emperor was the pillar of China, and China was the center of the universe.[21]

Suffice it to say that the exercise of these religious and political functions has occurred throughout history and in many societies *with more import* for *all* their members than lesser activities with more clearly visible results, such as those that provide the material conditions of social existence. After all, was not the "work *with* the gods" performed by the chiefs and priests supposed to bring prosperity to all and protect them against misfortune? It is for these fundamental reasons that the commoners, who were neither priests nor powerful, felt themselves to be irrevocably *indebted*—for their existence, their subsistence, and the survival of their children—to those who ensured the favors of the gods and governed them. They felt so deeply indebted that in turn they gave their labor, their goods, and their very lives to those who governed them (gifts that appear to us today as "forced labor," "tribute," or in short "acts of violence"), because they believed themselves unequal to what they received, and would continue to receive, if they knew their place and fulfilled their obligations. This is the fundamental paradox of hierarchical social relations between human groups, orders, or classes, where the dominant groups appear to give much more than that which is given in turn by those they dominate.

✕ ✕ ✕

My analysis thus leads me to conclude that the emergence of orders, castes, or classes was a sociological and historical process that involved *at the same time* the consent and the resistance of the very individuals who, little by little, lost their status and were relegated to the "bottom" of society and the cosmic order by these new, dominant groups. *Consent,* because sharing a world of imaginary representations of the forces that govern the universe offered all hope for prosperity and protection, through the ritual activities and governance of a minority that was henceforth divorced from any form of material activity. *Resistance,* because the price paid by the vast majority of individuals was the progressive loss of control of the very conditions of their existence and of their own persons. And when their resistance prevented any form of consent, the process of class or order formation ground to a halt, or continued instead through recourse to violence by the dominant governing groups to crush the opposition. Consent and violence, then, are the two forces at work in the emergence and development of orders, castes, and classes, and of the two, consent must have often supplanted violence.

I believe I have shown that, of all the relations that exist and make up the historical content of our social existence, only those that we in the West characterize as political-religious—which draw together, through sovereignty, groups and individuals that separately or collectively exploit the resources of a recognized territory—have the capacity to create societies. Neither kinship relations nor economic relations in themselves can accomplish this.

But in a world dominated by globalization, no society, large or small, can produce the material conditions it needs to exist unless it participates, more and more, in the world capitalist system, and all societies must henceforth depend materially and socially on each other to reproduce themselves. But the global conditions of reproduction of this world system are beyond the control that any local society, however powerful, can exert over the world market. It is with this confrontation between local and global, between the political (or more precisely the political-religious) and the economic, that all societies are therefore obliged to come to terms.

7

Social Anthropology Is Not Indissolubly Tied to the West, Its Birthplace

Social anthropology—or ethnology, as it was called in the second half of the nineteenth century—had already experienced several births before it was finally reborn as social science. During the first centuries that witnessed the political and commercial expansion of a number of European nations, ethnology was recast each time travelers, missionaries, soldiers, or colonial administrators set about learning the languages and recording the customs of the local populations, to govern or to evangelize them, or simply for the sake of curiosity. In its initial, spontaneous guises, ethnology thus took the form of narratives and testimonies that were inevitably marked by domination of non-Europeans by Europeans. In short, it produced ethnography,[1] a record of accumulated material that made it possible to compare the ways of living and thinking that typified hundreds of non-Western societies, each with their respective histories. Western imperial expansion was thus one of the conditions—the most important one—that made social anthropology possible. The presence of distinct local groups or diverse villages, or other communities within the countries of Europe (such as the Basques, Catalans, Castilians, and Gypsies in nineteenth- and twentieth-century Spain) were too narrow a basis for the development of a discipline that sought to compare all forms of society. (Indeed, this narrow national basis was and is the object of such nationalist movements as the Spanish and French Basques, who want an autonomous Basque state.) Anthropology was thus a product of the Western empires that were hewn from the rest of the world, but paradoxically only emerged as a "scientific" discipline when it was finally "decentered" from the West.

This decentering means that, each time an anthropologist compares the modes of life and thought of a number of societies dispersed over the globe, his or her professed forms of thought and social action are not used as the basis of the comparison. This was the approach initially followed by both Lewis Henry Morgan and Edward Tylor, who founded the discipline in the mid-nineteenth century and to whom anthropology owes the place it today occupies alongside history, sociology, law, and the rest of the social sciences. To offer a glimpse of how they broke from the spontaneous ethnography of their predecessors, I will briefly consider Morgan's work and the two major currents which run through it: first, how Morgan distanced himself from the West, and second, how he drew upon his scientific investigations to formulate a theory of the evolution of the human family that placed the West, and specifically the American democratic republic, at the apex of human progress, as its mirror and measure.

Morgan, a lawyer in Rochester, New York, began his legal career representing the interests of the railroads that were advancing across the continent, expropriating the land on either side of the tracks. But he was also a friend and defender of Native Americans, most of whom were already living on reservations, and after he secured his fortune, he gave up his career to study their ways and customs. He focused first on the Seneca, noting that they referred to both father and father's brother by the same term, which he translated as "father," and that they likewise used a single term for mother and mother's sisters, which he translated as "mother" (whereas Europeans used different terms). He thus discovered that the Seneca classify their relatives differently from us, and that these classifications follow a logic of their own that applies to the whole range of their kin terms. Children of the father's brothers (who are "fathers" for an individual designated as "Ego" in a genealogical diagram) and of the mother's sisters (who are "mothers" for Ego) are therefore automatically brothers and sisters for Ego, rather than cousins on the father's or the mother's side as they are in our reckoning. Morgan also observed that a couple's children do not belong to their father but to their mother and her brothers among the Seneca, who thus follow a descent rule unknown in Europe, which he called "matrilineal." This rule is the basis of kin groups that he referred to by the Latin word *gens*, which today are called "matrilineal clans." (As we shall see, his choice of terminology was no accident.) Morgan also observed that, after marriage, a man went to live with his wife's people, on her clan lands, and that the couple's residence was therefore uxorilocal.

From his study of the Seneca, Morgan concluded that their kinship terminology, their descent principle, and their residential rule formed a sort of "system," which was different from our own but nonetheless had its own logic. He then began a large-scale study of eighty-two Indian tribes in the United States and Canada,[2] and armed with this information ultimately hit upon the exceptional idea of launching a worldwide survey of kinship terminologies and systems. To do so, he sent out nearly a thousand questionnaires to missionaries, colonial administrators, and other officials, and amassed information on the kinship terminologies, marriage rules, and descent reckoning followed in hundreds of societies. With this unique set of data, he set about comparing the terminologies, and discovered that they were all variants of a few basic categories that he named "punaluan" or "turanian" and so on (which, following George Peter Murdoch, are known today as "Hawaiian," "Dravidian," "Iroquois," "Eskimo," and so forth).

Having compared these hundreds of terminologies collected in the field, in totally different languages, Morgan went on to determine that they could be grouped into a mere six different types.[3] In so doing, he systematically discovered that a multitude of social realities stated in different languages, from societies that had no history of contact with each other, made sense when they were viewed from the vantage point of underlying rules that defined and classified kinship relations between consanguines and affines. In essence, Morgan observed that the terminology used by the Seneca was identical to that used by other groups on other continents so far as its formal structure was concerned, regardless of the different words that were used. He also discovered that the ancient Latin kinship terminology, which employed terms such as *pater* and *mater*, was comparable in structure to that of groups living in Sudan, and had been supplanted in Europe by the system in use today, which is also employed by the Inuit. All of these facts were obviously unknown to the populations and individuals concerned. Morgan's contribution was thus the outcome of a theoretical undertaking that rested on information collected in the field, which was later analyzed to discover the underlying rules of construction—in short, the social and mental logic. Herein lies the key to anthropologic research.

Anthropological data thereby consists of material collected by taking part in the life of the populations observed. It is the result of what has been called "participant observation," but, it must be stressed, this approach does not lead anthropologists to identify totally—that is socially, emotionally, and intellectually—with the culture in which they immerse themselves for long periods of time. This is the first current that we find in Morgan's work, as he temporarily suspended his Western notions of kinship, descent, and family, and in so doing was willing and able to observe and listen to individuals living in other forms of society. But there were also missionaries and government officials living in these societies whose observations are often irreplaceable, providing they are reinterpreted according to their context. Such ethnography was not yet ethnology, however, because it was not possible to tease out the rules for constructing social relations that lie elsewhere, but in other forms, on the basis of a single example, and in the absence of rigorous hypotheses and methods of analysis. It is with this passage that the break occurred, and always occurs, between the spontaneous observations of onlookers and the ethnology developed by anthropologists.

Having summarized the results of his work in the enormous *Systems of Consanguinity and Affinity of the Human Family* (1871), Morgan sought to fit these results into a general theory of the social progress of humankind. The result was *Ancient Society* (1877), in which he placed the different groups he had studied, either personally or through the observations of others, at points along a scale measuring humanity's advancement from an initial "savage" state through a shorter "barbarian" state to the ultimate "civilized" state. In Morgan's view, this final state had been emerging in Western Europe since antiquity, and ultimately blossomed forth in Anglo-Saxon North America, free of the aftereffects of feudalism that hampered most Old World societies in Morgan's time.

This explains why Morgan chose the Latin term *gens* to designate the Iroquois descent group, as he believed that they had reached the stage in their history comparable to that which Romans had attained in antiquity (and then surpassed, since they had gone on to create a state and an empire). The Iroquois thus became an example of the first stage of the *gens*-based (that is, clan-based) society, which followed a matrilineal descent rule; in the next stage of social evolution, characterized by patrilineal descent, children were assigned exclusively to their father's clan. By contrast, Hawaiians seemed to illustrate the "savage" state, because they used a single term for brothers and cousins; according to Morgan, the fact that all were thus classified as brothers and sisters meant that the Hawaiians had just emerged from the primitive state of animal-like promiscuity, and that groups of brothers had only recently stopped marrying groups of sisters. In short, the far-flung populations with whom they shared the world in the nineteenth century appeared to Morgan and many of his contemporaries as arrested examples of the process of development that culminated in European and Euro-American societies. The history of Europe and the United States thus became the mirror in which all of the stages in the progress of humanity could be contemplated, and which served as the measure of this evolution:

Commencing, then, with the Australians and Polynesians, following with the American Indian tribes, and concluding with
the Roman and Grecian, who afford the highest exemplifications
respectively of the six great stages of human progress, the sum of
their united experiences may be supposed fairly to represent that
of the human family from the Middle Status of savagery to the
end of ancient civilization. Consequently, the Aryan nations will
find the type of the condition of their remote ancestors, when in
savagery, in that of the Australians and Polynesians; when in the
Lower Status of barbarism in that of the partially Village Indians
of America; and when in the Middle Status in that of the Village
Indians, with which their own experience in the Upper Status
directly connects. So essentially identical are the arts institutions and mode of life in the same status upon all the continents,
that the archaic form of the principal domestic institutions of
the Greeks and Romans must even now be sought in the cor-
responding institutions of the American aborigines, as will be
shown in the course of this volume. This fact forms a part of the
accumulating evidence tending to show that the principal institutions of mankind have been developed from a few primary germs
of thought; and that the course and manner of their development
was predetermined, as well as restricted within narrow limits of
divergence, by the natural logic of the human mind and the necessary limitations of its powers. Progress has been found to be
substantially the same in kind in tribes and nations inhabiting
different and even disconnected continents, while in the same
status, with deviations from uniformity in particular instances
produced by special causes. The argument when extended tends
to establish the unity of origin of mankind.

In studying the conditions of tribes and nations in these several
ethnical periods we are dealing, substantially, with the ancient
history and condition of our own remote ancestors.[4]

Yet Morgan does not include either China or Japan in this view
of social evolution, and reduces the Muslim world to the Arab
tribes. And he does not take a critical view when speaking of

the West and the "progress" of civilization, scarcely mentioning the existence of slavery in antiquity or serfdom in the Middle Ages. Here we find the second current in Morgan's work, as he ceased producing pieces of scientific knowledge and was instead engaged in constructing an ideological vision of the social progress of humankind. Anthropological discourse became a mere illusion, a hallucinatory vision of others produced by the West, from whom it had diverged and was no longer a part. This is the paradox of Borges's mirror.[5]

Morgan's successors, who were determined to get anthropology back on track, set about dismantling his evolutionary vision of history (a task that was ultimately accomplished by Franz Boas). Morgan's life and work thereby highlight the situation that anthropology (and the other social sciences) had to confront in order to establish itself as a scientific discipline.

⋊ ⋊ ⋊

The lesson is clear: Anthropology cannot a priori establish any culture, form of society, or epoch as the measure of human social progress. Anthropologists must go into the field and gather material through carefully controlled, systematic observations that are conducted in the course of extended immersion in another society. They must employ appropriate methods to disentangle the rules for constructing the social organization and the modes of thought of the society that they are observing. And they must analyze the impact that these ways of living and thinking have on the historical development when these societies are faced with internal change or intrusions from outside, and their consequences for the individual destinies of their members.

In short, if anthropology is to continue to exist and develop, anthropologists must construct a new mode of awareness, which is no longer centered on their society and culture of origin, be they Chinese, Hindu, German, American, or from any number of other backgrounds. And they must be cognizant that this kind of awareness cannot be taken for granted, for every day the assumptions and preconceived ideas of the anthropologist's society can crop up in a new context at the heart of his or her practice and writing.

Like the other social scientists—most particularly historians and sociologists—the anthropologist must therefore endeavor to "break the mirror of the Self." But what do we mean by the "Self"? Put simply, the Self is the sum total of the various egos that make up an individual. The Intimate Ego, comprised of all traces of desire, suffering, and joy that have accompanied an individual's reactions to his or her unique history, is largely unconscious, and remains in the background as we act and react with regard to others. But there is another ego, a Social Ego, which comes into existence at birth and is always inseparably bound to the Intimate Ego, shaped by life events and our relations with others. The Social Ego, through no design of its own, happens to find itself in a particular society, at a specific time, and thus occupies a certain position from whence its life will unfold and through which it will experience its various transformations. The Social Ego is never a single entity; it too is made up of several or more egos. An individual may be a man or a woman; may believe in one or several gods or in none at all; may live in the country where he or she was born or be an immigrant in another country; and may be for or against the separation of church and state. There are as many selves as there are identities that a person shares with other individuals and groups, many of which are changeable, and some of which can be radically altered. One may be born a Catholic, and choose to reject religion altogether or convert to Islam, by way of example.

But a person who wants to become an anthropologist (or a historian or sociologist) must also construct a Cognitive Ego, one that will enable him or her to acquire the knowledge and understanding essential to this chosen profession, which in many cases is equally a passion. This ego is usually constituted by learning the concepts, theories, and methods that define the discipline the individual wants to practice. To be sure, these theories and methods can be at odds and can determine opposing approaches. But it is often with this set of abstract tools that the anthropologist sets off into the field and begins to carry out observations and analyses. Though it is not essential for an anthropologist to have read or learned "everything," he or she must be ready to abandon or modify predetermined concepts and theories if the facts observed do not fit the pigeonholes, and come up with principles and approaches that correspond more closely to the new ways of thinking and acting found in the field.

× × ×

I will try to briefly show how my experience as an anthropologist has affected these egos. I have spent a total of seven years in the field, over a span of twenty years, during which, among other things, I carried out eight major systematic studies. I made two house-by-house censuses of each village, and recorded the genealogies of all members of the Baruya tribe—some 2,000 people, spanning up to four generations at least—which I updated on each visit. I measured over 600 gardens and studied the distribution of the land between the clans and families (which took over six months). I studied work times, and even conducted an experiment to measure the comparative efficiency of stone and steel tools, since many Baruya still knew how to use stone tools in 1967. I took part in two major male initiations, in several female initiations, and in a rare initiation of new shamans (adult men and women thirty and older), which occurs once every twenty years. I also spent several weeks recording the dreams of a number of Baruya friends when they woke up in the morning. During the course of my fieldwork, which was conducted almost always in the same valley and with the same people, I found that life presents you, day in, day out, with recurring or exceptional situations that you eventually come to understand. Every day people are born and people die and couples get married, and you take part in these events, where gestures, words, and practices are repeated. But alongside life as it is lived on a daily basis, events occur that bear on the society as a whole and mobilize all clans, villages, and generations, such as the male initiations that are held every three or so years. And then there are all the unexpected events, which in reality are only to be expected—a hunting accident, a clash between two lineages over a piece of land, the murder of a woman by her husband. So if you stay long enough, if you understand the language well enough, and if the community allows you attend numerous events and actions, you are eventually drawn into the way they live and think. The anthropologist cannot always be the victim of his or her hallucinating Western Ego.

When you subject yourself to this kind of regimen, analyzing the results as they come with the people with whom you're living, I can affirm that bit by bit you learn something about others, about their reasons and motives for acting, about the nature of their interrelations, about the ideas they have about themselves and others—in short, something that cannot be reduced to the ethnocentric projection of Western ideas onto what others "are," something that really belongs to them and that does not spring from the West's hallucinations or misapprehensions. The paradox of all this is that, when you reach this point, you discover that these others are somehow like you because they ask themselves some of the same questions about life—about power, about relations with the hereafter, about birth—that we ask ourselves. They simply come up with different answers.

What the Baruya showed me of themselves changed me as a person, but it also changed the theoretical preconceptions I had been carrying around about points that had seemed obvious, at least in the West. Changing such ideas clearly means modifying, for myself and perhaps for those around me, the status of anthropological and other theories we have in our heads when we go into the field. But since these ideas encompass a range of concerns—the relationship between the imaginary and the symbolic, the role and status of the economy, gender relations and male domination, the impact of violence and consent in establishing relations of power and hierarchy between social groups and the genders—altering our preconceptions no longer concerns anthropology alone, but the other social sciences as well. Anthropology does not have a monopoly on the analysis of social and historical realities, and to account for these, it relies on or must ally itself with other disciplines. More than any other field of study, anthropology simply cannot go it alone.

I will touch only briefly on some of the changes, those that affected me simultaneously as a person and as an anthropologist, among the many that I experienced in the field. In chapter 4,[6] I briefly described Baruya gender relations and the role that male homosexuality plays in legitimizing the men's domination of the women. For years I had observed these practices and listened to the discourses that supported them, and had drawn several theoretical and personal conclusions. Principally, I found full-fledged domination of one sex over the other in a society without class or caste divisions or the state. This led me to question the naive theoretical views I had taken with me when I left for New Guinea in the 1960s. At the time, I believed that egalitarian gender relations would be possible once other relations of domination and exploitation—for example, those of class or caste—had been abolished. In the field, I was obliged to admit that, even without these other social hierarchies, Baruya women were still subordinated to the men, and were even made responsible for their own subordination because their menstrual blood is considered unclean, sapping men's strength and threatening the social and cosmic orders. And when I was back in Paris, where I decided to help out the feminist movement and was appointed head of science policy for the Department of Humanities and Social Sciences of the Centre National de la Recherche Scientifique, the first thing I did was to launch a research program entitled "Researches on Women" and "Feminist Research." These two lines of research—the place of women as it now stands and women's demands for a different place in society—positive and normative, are equally legitimate, and the program made a few waves at the time.

But the Baruya also showed me, in their ideas about the body and through initiation rites designed to engender boys anew outside a woman's womb and without their mothers, the extent to which an imaginary core lies at the heart of such hierarchical practices. This alerted me to the importance of the imaginary and the symbolic in the creation of relations of power and domination. The imaginary is not the symbolic—even though the two cannot be separated—since it consists of shared ideas and beliefs whose meaning is expressed in signs and symbols and therefore does not exist solely in the mind. It is symbolically inscribed in bodies, in the things people make, in monuments, in the organization of space and time. But the explicit aim of these imaginary constructions and symbolic practices is neither purely imaginary nor purely symbolic. The Baruya clearly told me that the aim of male initiation was to grow men and to glorify them to the detriment of women, and so legitimize the right of one sex to represent humanity as a whole and the right of men to govern society. Thus the imaginary and the symbolic entailed in these relations of power have very real social consequences.

It is by virtue of their unclean state, which saps men's strength, that Baruya women are barred from owning and using weapons (which are tools in the service of power), are not permitted to transmit ancestral land to their children (because land circulates only among men), do not produce the salt money used in exchanges (even though they can use it in such transactions), and do not have direct access to the Sun, the Baruya's protector god and "father." Women therefore occupy a subordinate position when it comes to controlling the means of production, or the means of destruction, or the means of exchange between humans (in the form of currency) or between humans and gods (through ritual),[7] and this domination is thus not solely mental or symbolic.

For Baruya men, the denigration and segregation of women— all the symbolic, psychological, and quite often physical forms of violence directed toward them—are simply the way things are and the condition of the common good. On a number of occasions, I also observed that, insofar as the women shared these cultural and social representations, they thought of themselves not only as victims but also as guilty parties responsible for their fate, since their bodies harbor a source of disorder for society and the cosmos. On a more general theoretical level, these analyses led me to criticize the Lévi-Straussian thesis of the primacy of the symbolic over the imaginary, and to conclude that if we had consider one of these very real dimensions as preeminent, it should clearly be the imaginary. Symbols die once they have lost their meanings—not merely that from which they sprang, but all those that have accrued to them in the course of their existence.

⋊ ⋊ ⋊

This brings us to a substantive issue: the role of violence and consent in the formation of social relations of domination, or exploitation, in human societies. Here again the Baruya pointed me to one of the possible ways that such relationships might be formed, through a monopoly exercised by one fraction of society, not over land or material used to produce subsistence and wealth, such as labor, but over sacred objects and secret knowledge, through which human beings appeal to the powers that control the reproduction of the universe and bring men success in hunting or horticulture. We might well ask archeologists and historians whether this sort of cosmological monopoly historically preceded the control of land, labor, or products in antiquity. Whereas the Baruya masters of the initiations work their own gardens like everyone else and claim no privileges other than the right not to fight in the front line of a battle (for fear that they might be killed and their secret formulas lost), groups devoted exclusively to such social functions as war and religious sacrifices emerged in other societies, as in the Indian caste system.

I do not mean to say that religion gave rise to castes, classes, and forms of the state—that would be absurd—but rather where new social divisions such as castes appear, which bear little resemblance to the clan divisions prevailing among the Baruya, religious beliefs may have provided the models that defined the figures who embodied the new forms of power: the humans who were thought to be closer to the gods than the rest of humanity, or the gods in human form living among mortals. From a certain standpoint, it can be said that the myths and religious beliefs populated by imaginary characters, gods, spirits, and ancestors—which the rites translate to the world of the senses— served as a "medium" where a new set of political and economic relations crystallized, in forms unknown in such relatively egalitarian tribal societies as the Baruya. It was along these avenues of history that the new forms of power sprang up that were embodied in the figures of the pharaoh or the Inca, Inca-Inti, the Inca son of the Sun.

My work among the Baruya similarly enabled me to address other theoretical problems and to criticize certain bits of received wisdom. For instance, the Baruya had a category of objects— the sacred *kwaimatnie*, a term that comes from *kwala-nimatnie*, meaning "to grow men"—that could not be sold or given, but which had to be kept in order to be passed on to subsequent generations. The Sun gave these objects to the ancestors of the conquering Baruya clans, who used them in their male initiations and thus placed their magical powers at the service of all the other clans to produce new generations of men and warriors. In addition to objects excluded from circulation, the Baruya also produced a form of money, bars of salt that they exchanged for goods such as weapons, stone tools, and feathers, which were produced by neighboring tribes. The salt bars thus served as a commodity-currency that detached itself from its owners when exchanged, whereas the *kwaimatnie* remained attached to the clans that owned them. Salt bars were never used as money between Baruya, however. They were produced by specific clans and then redistributed in the form of gifts to their allies. Thus the same object circulated as a gift between Baruya, but as a commodity between the Baruya and their neighbors. So too, Baruya marriage alliances were contracted through the direct exchange of a woman for a woman between lineages. There was no bridewealth among the Baruya, nor was there competitive, agonistic gift-giving, like the Kwakiutl potlatch made famous by Franz Boas and Marcel Mauss.

Years after I had returned from the field, these facts led me back to the analysis of gift-giving and noncommercial exchanges.[8] I realized that neither Mauss (who had focused exclusively on the potlatch, the competition between clans to outgive each other and thus capture a title and a rank), nor Lévi-Strauss (who saw kinship as the product of an exchange of women) had taken into account the existence of a third category of objects, those that must neither be sold nor given, but must be kept to transmit. The whole picture of the relationship between commodity and gift was altered by the existence of this third category of objects. The first category consists of objects that are sold and detach themselves completely from the persons and the groups that sell them, and are thus alienable and alienated and circulate as commodities. The second category is made up of objects that are given and are thus alienated, but remain unalienated insofar as something of the giver remains inside the thing given, thereby making the recipient indebted to the donor and obliging him, for example, to give in turn. This is the point that Annette Weiner summed up in her book, *Inalienable Possessions*, by the phrase "keeping-while-giving." The last category comprises the inalienable and unalienated objects, which function as fixed points for a collective identity and even a social system.

This is the case of sacred objects, like the *kwaimatnie*, which are transmitted within a clan, but it is also true of the constitutions of democratic regimes. You can buy votes in an election, but you cannot buy a constitution at the supermarket, and hence it is not a commodity. And so even in our globalized liberal economy, you cannot argue that "everything is for sale" (as per the title of a recent book by Robert Kuttner, the *Business Week* commentator). But we must take care to remember that we are not discussing ownership of objects; when we say that an object is alienable or inalienable, we are referring to a property with which they are endowed by the nature of the social relations in which they circulate. It is possible to purchase an object in order to make a gift, and thus the same object can circulate in different social spheres and each time take on different attributes.

In a number of Oceanic societies, certain valuables are

hoarded away as clan treasure, such as particular pieces of shell money that are kept out of circulation but enable other shells of the same kind to circulate as money. This is reminiscent of the role of gold, which sat in the bank so that commodities could be bought or sold on the market and served as the standard and guarantee of their value in the nineteenth century. The formula in this instance would be "keeping-in-order-to-sell," while that of the sacred objects whose use benefits society as a whole would be "keeping-in-order-to-give." We can also find some interesting tidbits in the etymology of such words as *buy* and *sell*. *Sell* comes from the Gothic word *saljan*, which can be translated as "to offer something in sacrifice to a god," and *buy* from *bugjan*, which means "to buy someone out of slavery."[9] In the origin of these terms, we find evidence that money was once the equivalent of a human life or a relationship with the gods, as it still is today in Melanesia.

Another important point that we must bear in mind is that the human origin of sacred objects is concealed. It is unlikely that it was really the Sun who gave the ancestor of the Kwarrandariar Baruya clan the objects and sacred formulas used in the initiations, a point that touches on a basic aspect of the way societies function. Humans conceal the fact that they create various types of social orders, which therefore rest not on the transparency but the opacity of the relations that people have with each other, on a misapprehension of their human origin that must not be recognized as such. Thus we face the whole problem of ideologies—the systems of representations and practices that legitimize and are part of an existing social order and were born with and not after it—when we consider the customs of the Baruya, and of other societies.

⨯ ⨯ ⨯

Having set out for New Guinea with the idea that the economy was probably the primary force that shaped societies and made them prosper or disappear—a notion borrowed from Marx but shared by many non-Marxists as well, particularly in this age of economic globalization which was believed would bring about uniformization of the ways people live and think the world over—I came to conclude while in the field that there was no visible, direct, causal link between the Baruya manner of production (their economy) and, for instance, their social manner of self-reproduction (their kinship system). By no means could anyone claim that this system, with such features as its patrilineal descent rule and Iroquois terminology, was a superstructure that corresponded to their mode of production. The Baruya's neighbors, the Kenaze, who had the same production techniques, had an entirely different kinship system. In short, an idea espoused by Marx and other theorists that had met with great success in the West—the role of the economic determinant in the way societies evolve—did not seem to apply here. But if there was no visible correspondence between the economic system and the kinship system, neither do we see any connection between Christianity, which emerged in late antiquity in the Middle East, and the economic systems that have succeeded each other in the Western world from the end of the Roman Empire through feudalism to the present-day capitalist system. This is not to say that economic and political activities and structures do not exert extremely strong pressures on the way societies function and develop. But there are no visible relations of cause and effect or any direct correspondences linking all the institutions that make up a society, as functionalists, Marxists, and structuralists claimed. In short, the attempts at scientific explanations put forward by contemporary anthropologists and other social scientists must differ from those espoused in the last century, or by Morgan the century before.

✕ ✕ ✕

Anthropology is not in crisis, then, even if many anthropologists may be, and it is no longer indissolubly tied to the West where it was born. Since the Second World War, the discipline has demonstrated its ability to turn around and apply methods invented for understanding other cultures to Western society. We are starting to see an anthropology of firms, churches, political parties, education, health, and even the state, and all these endeavors have a bright future. Furthermore, not just anthropology but all the social sciences seem to be better equipped than they were a half-century ago to address the complexities of history. If researchers are willing, these varied disciplines are capable of taking into account the symbolic as well as the imaginary, the mental as well as the material aspects of the social realities they analyze. They know how to sort out the complex puzzle of interlocking interests and power relations present in all human societies, and have learned to measure the distance as well as the contradictions between what actors say and what they do. Our era will be an era of enlightened pragmatism. But pragmatism is not eclecticism, since pragmatism means using everything in the various theories useful to analyzing aspects of complex realities without claiming to explain everything.

In short, although the great paradigms and metatheories of yesterday—functionalism, structuralism, Marxism—have faded away, they have left us many ideas that are "good to think" and many hypotheses that are good to think with. There has been a lot of talk in the last twenty years about deconstructing the social sciences; postmodernism even made a specialty of it, and garnered a great deal of power in universities, particularly in the United States and a few other countries. In France, we are well acquainted with this body of theory, since we were the ones who disseminated it in the works of such theorists as Jacques Derrida, Michel Foucault, Gilles Deleuze, and Jean-François Lyotard. But although we are major exporters, we are relatively minor consumers, or rather we consume only those parts of their work that seem to be of use in analyzing the complexity of the facts. But we do not, or we no longer, look on these authors as social science gurus.

American and European "hard" scientists do not doubt their conceptual, methodological, or technological capacities to advance their understanding of the complexities of matter, such as the structure of the human genome. In the social sciences, by contrast, a number of voices have denied that we can truly understand other cultures. According to Mary Douglas, in her response to a book of postmodernist inspiration by Marilyn

Strathern, it seems that to most intellectuals any social science theory looks like a form of Western domination, and that one can analyze facts without ever having had to distinguish or classify them, and therefore without ranking and especially without comparing them.[10] In certain circles, the definitions, questions, and theories have even become highly suspect.

✕ ✕ ✕

I have tried to show that the task of constantly deconstructing the concepts and theories we initially take with us into the field is a vital part of scientific work, because the facts collected in the course of research often challenge our views and cultural prejudices. We must therefore have a very broad, solid, empirical basis if we hope to construct and deconstruct a scientific discipline and carry it forward. But that is not enough. We must also develop new paradigms with which to interpret these facts. There are two ways that we can go about deconstructing the sciences; one ultimately leads to their destruction, and the other to their reconstruction at a more complex level of rigor and inquiry. The lesson is clear: scientific endeavor requires a constant state of critical vigilance and regular reexamination of our cultural prejudices, our concepts, our hypotheses, our methods, and our conclusions.[11]

8

Excursus: Combining the Pleasures
of Art and Knowledge for the
Museumgoing Publics

Social anthropology—or ethnology, as it was still known in
the last century—owes its birth and its destiny to Western
expansion, and the need that arose in certain European countries for a better knowledge of two very different historical and
social realities. First, there were the ways of living and thinking of the peoples of Africa, Asia, and pre-Colombian America,
who Europe discovered and gradually subjected to its trade, its
religion, or simply its armed force as it conquered their territories. In order to govern, trade, or evangelize in these countries, soldiers, missionaries, and civil servants were obliged to
set about learning what were as a rule unwritten languages, as
well as customs, mores, and strange beliefs, if only to eradicate
them. They did so because they saw themselves as entrusted
with a mission to bring civilization to the non-European world,
to ensure the progress that accompanies trade and industry, and
to spread the "true" religion, Christianity. Second, there were
the customs of such groups as the Basques, Slovenes, and Valacs
within Europe itself, which the emerging nation-states from the
sixteenth century on dispatched individuals to inventory because
they conflicted with the newly prevailing national and trade laws
and needed to be reformed or abolished. And so a spontaneous ethnography emerged to serve these historical objectives,
and remained centered on the West until the second half of the
nineteenth century, when ethnology was reborn as a new social
science discipline through the work of such founding fathers as
Lewis Henry Morgan and Edward Tylor (see chapter 7).

During the four hundred years in which this colonial and global expansion occurred, hundreds of thousands of objects were collected from the four corners of the earth, and made their way first into the *cabinets de curiosité* of kings, nobles, and merchants, and then into museums, which were initially public rather than private institutions.

The British Museum was founded in 1753 with pieces collected by such great explorers as Captain James Cook and Joseph Banks. In France, the Musée de la Marine et d'Ethnographie was created by royal decree in 1827 and housed in the galleries of the Louvre. Later a national education minister, Jules Ferry, who was famous for his "free and compulsory" state school system, decided that these collections should be transferred from the Louvre to the museum on the Place du Trocadero, in order, he asserted, to separate "Art" from the objects illustrating savage mores and customs. It was not until the year 2000 that one hundred and twenty of these masterpieces returned to the Louvre, to take their place alongside examples of Greek and medieval art and the paintings of Rembrandt and Velasquez, where perhaps at last they have found a permanent home.

✕ ✕ ✕

It happens that I was personally involved in the creation of the new French museum on the left bank of the Seine, next to the Eiffel Tower, to replace two other museums: the old Musée de l'Homme, formerly part of the venerable Musée d'Histoire Naturelle, created in the eighteenth century by Georges Buffon; and the Musée des Arts d'Afrique et d'Océanie, the old Musée des Colonies, which was renamed by André Malraux in 1960 when he was de Gaulle's minister of culture and acutely aware of the need to avoid the word "colonies" as decolonization followed the Second World War.

When I was appointed head of science policy for the new museum, a position I held from 1997 to 2000, I immediately concluded it should offer its publics the pleasures of both art and knowledge. I had become convinced that the Musée de l'Homme, which had been dying a slow death for decades, could not be saved, because there were no funds to complete, restore, and digitize collections for broader dissemination over the Web, and as a consequence of changes in anthropological theory. Since the end of World War II, French anthropologists (with the exception of Claude Lévi-Strauss[1]) had increasingly abandoned the study of so-called "art" objects and devoted themselves mainly to the study of such concerns as kinship systems, power structures, and gender relations. In short, the museum had been both materially and intellectually marginalized.

The guidelines I laid out for the new museum were as follows:

1. The museum was to be resolutely post-colonial, stepping back and taking a critical view of Western history. Not only France should be considered, but the other European countries that had also extended their influence over the world since the sixteenth century. One idea, for instance, was to provide maps showing the area of Spanish, Portuguese, Dutch, French, English, but also Russian expansion in 1630, 1730, 1830, and so on.

2. The museum was also to draw heavily on history, and especially the history of the societies whose objects were held in our museums. This history should be at once that of a distant past, for cultures are not born in a day and social and mental structures often subsist for centuries, changing all the while. But it was also to be the history of a more recent past, that of the colonial period, and to merge into the history of the present, since most of the societies from which we have objects still exist alongside our own. The museum was thus to look at once into the past and on to the present.

3. The museum was to strive to combine two pleasures: that of art and that of knowledge. The reason for this was simple. Objects of whatever kind are silent about themselves. Beyond perhaps moving us, they tell us nothing about the people who made them or about the societies that used them. The idea therefore was to provide this museum with the databases necessary for interpreting the objects and societies in

a way that lent itself to multiple approaches. The museum was thus also to be a center of research and higher learning that would train young people to be both curators and researchers, a combination that is still rare, thus enabling them to give the best of themselves to the public. A portion of the students were to come from Africa, Asia, Oceania, and the Americas, and were to be trained using the collections of objects from their own countries.

4. The museum was also to be the place and the opportunity for scientific and cultural collaboration with the countries from which the objects came. It was to provide a means to set up partnerships that had been impossible in earlier times, when relations between the countries concerned had been based more on domination than on cooperation, and to create the conditions for an exchange on the way we view others and others view us.

5. Last of all, in an increasingly multicultural Western country like France, where immigration-related racism and xenophobia not only still exist but are on the rise, the new museum was to fulfill a function that was both political and symbolic. I concluded that this museum should be called the MAC, the "Musée des Arts et Civilisations."

To bolster this political and symbolic character, the project would create both a new museum and a space within the Louvre where one hundred and twenty masterpieces from Africa, Asia, Oceania, and the Americas would stand alongside the Venus de Milo and the *Mona Lisa*, thereby fulfilling the dream of poets like Stéphane Mallarmé and artists such as Pablo Picasso and Max Ernst, who had been calling for the admission of the "Arts Nègres" since the early twentieth century. I was in complete agreement, and immediately upon taking up my post, proposed the creation of a space apart from but directly connected to the space where the objects were to be exhibited, which I called "espace d'interprétation." Here, having enjoyed the tangible, aesthetic pleasures of the objects in the exhibition hall, visitors would be able to experience them once again, aided by new technologies that allowed for the virtual representation of each object and a personal analysis. This "intellectual reappropriation" required the creation of a database of the one hundred and twenty masterpieces that were selected by Jacques Kerchache, and the production of a CD-ROM that was to be made available to visitors.

I suggested that each object should be analyzed from four standpoints:

First, by examining the reasons that the object is regarded as a masterpiece. This analysis took into account the nature of the materials used and the size, shape, and structure of the objects exhibited, and sought to understand their aesthetic value and impact.

Second, by reconstructing the history of the object, and the circumstances that led to its inclusion in the collections of a French museum. Was it plundered from a colony, donated by a generous collector, purchased in a market? This brought us back to the complex history of France's relations with the countries of origin, and with the singular stories and biographies of those persons who had contributed to get each object out of its own country and into ours. One example of colonial plunder is the Bidjogo statue now in the Louvre, which comes from the island of Karavela in the Bissagos Islands (Guinea Bissau) and represents a goddess. From what we know, it was kept in the house of a headman and was stolen by a French naval lieutenant at the start of the nineteenth century. On the order of the French government, the lieutenant had led a punitive expedition against the headman's group on the pretext that they had attacked a French ship, though in reality this attack had been a response to France's failure to pay for the meat and fresh water its ships regularly took on there. Several villages were laid waste, and the officer took some strange objects from one of the huts. A century later his descendants donated them to the Musée de l'Homme.

Third, by documenting the way the object had been used in the society from which it originated, and explaining by whom and for what purpose had it been made. Though the maker is usually very difficult to determine, and a date can sometimes prove equally elusive, cross-museum comparisons may point to an artist or to a workshop that produced similar objects in a given country at a given time. All objects can be classified by their social uses according to the five thematic axes outlined later in this chapter (see p. 184), which cut across all societies. For example, the sculpture of the embracing couple from Makira Island in the south Solomons is a representation of a man copulating with an evil spirit named Matorua, who had changed into a woman, and thus exemplifies one of the relations that humans entertain with the invisible, the ancestors, the spirits, and the gods.

Fourth, by providing a clear description of the society that produced the object for its own use, including a reconstruction of the broad outlines and salient events of its precontact history, where possible, and its subsequent development up to the present. Not surprisingly, this fourth approach includes material collected by anthropologists and historians about hierarchy and power found in these societies, as well as the nature of their social groups (such as castes and clans), economic activities, and kinship systems, and of course essential information about the world of their representations, the cultural symbols embedded in the relations between people, with the natural environment, and with the gods. It also considers the other forms of artistic creation—music, dance, poetry, theater—that may have existed in each particular society at the time the exhibited objects were made. And though it is obviously impossible to put a whole society on display by using only a few, highly selective reference objects, the ethnographic picture can be supplemented with databases and hyperlinks between various sources of information—such as films, interviews, maps, and other series of objects—posted on the Web.

The general idea behind these four points was not to make visitors believe they were seeing the objects through the same eyes as those who had made and used them, but rather to make them aware that discovering what the objects meant for these individuals takes a complex investigation, one that cautiously feels its way toward their point of origin and supports its con-clusions with evidence. But an object's story does not end with its first steps or its first uses; it takes on new meanings when it leaves the society that produced it, meanings that are pro-jected onto it at different periods by the various museumgoing publics who appropriate it. We are thus confronted with the "mystery" of objects—of an original meaning that is necessarily attached to a form, and a form that can shed its initial mean-ing and don another. An object can thus paradoxically continue to have meaning for viewers who have no cultural or historical connection with the people who produced it and the society that originally had need of it. It stands before us like a sort of quasi-subject, a material form imbued with a human meaning to which it continues to testify, even if this testimony needs to be deciphered. The museum object is thus not a "natural" object. It cannot be detached from humankind. It is lodged within humankind from its inception and from there draws its life. It sends out a message, even if we do not know its language or the code of its discourse.[2]

To provide the public with the most accurate information about these objects without hiding and misrepresenting our doubts and the gaps in our knowledge, we must employ a variety of means of storing and making such facts accessible: interac-tive terminals, rooms for screening films, a library, a mediathec, lecture series, cultural programs. In essence, we must pare down the information surrounding a displayed object to a minimum and create separate, comfortable spaces for interpretation, where visitors can reappropriate the objects they have just seen at their own pace and learn more, by other means, about the individuals who made them and the societies where they were produced. A museum is not a book whose pages are pasted up on the wall to be read. Nor is it a university where courses are taught. It is a place that offers pleasure and knowledge, open to all publics, where each person should be able to choose the most amenable approach and what he or she wants to take away. The spectrum of available knowledge ranges from minimal, almost meaningless tags, such as "Initiation mask from the Sepik region," to complex information available in a database, to the sort of poetic details that encourage dreaming and set the imagination free—the driving force that enables the individual to appropriate objects and awakens an interest in those who made them.

But it is not enough to put the objects into context, to discover the place, the time, the reasons, and the representations that accompanied their birth in their own cultures, and parts of the world. Human cultures are different responses to fundamental questions of life that confront every society at all times. That is why it is indispensable for a museum dedicated to the cultures and societies of the five continents to have a department in which these cultural, geographic, and ethnic divisions are transcended, or relegated to the background. We can compare and create a dialogue between cultures and societies by considering five axes that correspond to existential questions, which every society answers in a different way in accordance with its principles of organization and its imaginary. These ways of living and thinking always translate into symbols, some of which take the material form of an object.

The five chains of existential questions (which we considered at length in chapter 3), comprise the following concerns:[3]

1. Human relations with the invisible, including gods, spirits, and ancestors
2. The forms and figures of power in human societies
3. Being born, living, and dying
4. Wealth, exchange, and currencies
5. Thinking nature, acting on nature

These themes are interconnected. For instance, Tonga's paramount chief, the *Tu'i Tonga*, is presented as a descendant of the gods, a human god living among humans who has power of life and death over them (and thus brings together themes 1 and 2). In addition to this, the paramount chief in Tonga is also believed to impregnate all the women in the kingdom by means of his spermatic breath, and is thus in a way the universal father of all Tongans, who are born and owe their life to him (the essence of theme 3). This also explains why all the chief's subjects, including the nobles, must make an annual offering of the first fruits of all harvests to the Tu'i Tonga and to his sister, the Tu'i Tonga Fefine, since he controls the fertility of all the women *and* all of the land (the crux of theme 4). Thus we see that, for Tongans, the natural environment was not made up of things, but receives its life from the gods, from the spirits, from the ancestors (which brings us to theme 5).

A museum department focusing on these themes would thus permit real comparisons between cultures, societies, and historical periods, and would set the West alongside the rest of the world, placing the paramount chief of Tonga beside both a Melanesian Big Man and Sitting Bull—a shaman turned war chief—or General de Gaulle and Mao Zedong.

But comparison in a museum must be museological. How can each of these five axes be adapted to a museum setting? Yves Lefur (a curator friend of mine) and I, working together, imagined a museography suited to such a thematically organized department. By way of example, in order to illustrate the second axis, we thought of creating a different area to highlight the various forms of power, using objects to illustrate the social *functions* fulfilled by each, as well as the associated *institutions* and the *practices* that gave it life (such as the competitive exchanges of gifts and countergifts of pigs and valuables among the Melpa of New Guinea, where local groups vied with each other through their Big Men in the exchange cycle known as *moka*). Focusing on the signs and symbols that distinguish such functions, institutions, practices, and figures from those of other social relations, each area would thus be organized by making use of various media—objects, images, texts, sounds, and materials. Here too, several levels of information and access should be available, ranging from minimal tagging to descriptions that are more poetic or more scientific (and more complex in terms of detail and interpretation), accessible through interactive terminals, videos, films, and other sorts of documentation.

Generally speaking, it is therefore necessary to equip arts

and civilizations museums with large databases of scientific analyses, to be sure, but also with a series of reference objects and a range of significant historical documents. For the Quai Branly museum, I proposed creating a database covering 2,000 societies chosen from Africa, Asia, the Americas, and Oceania. This figure is greater than the number of societies (estimated at 600) represented by their objects in the two museums slated for fusion. We expanded this number because knowledge of the continents, and the histories of the individual societies and their interactions with other societies, nearby or far away, must not be represented by the haphazard collection of objects that has led to certain groups figuring more prominently than others. Choosing this sample of 2,000 societies and constructing an analytical grid that would permit their comparison are considerable tasks, which could be undertaken in the framework of a European Union project.

⨯ ⨯ ⨯

One day in 2002, through a combination of circumstances, I was given the opportunity to explain to representatives of the European Community that a large part of Europe's cultural heritage is composed of non-European objects. I suggested that it would be useful to carry out a systematic inventory of these objects, to which research programs requiring the cooperation of European researchers and curators, together with their colleagues from the countries whose objects formed the museum collections, could be added. The idea was accepted by the European Commission's Research Directorate General, and we set up the first project with the University College London, the British Museum, the Leiden Rijks Museum and the network of museums in the Netherlands, the Budapest Ethnographic Museum, and the Hungarian Academy of Sciences. This project was part of a large-scale European program coordinated by Berlin's Max-Planck Institute entitled European Cultural Heritage Online, or ECHO.

The project's aim was to create a confederation of European museums to accomplish such a systematic inventory, and later to elarge the consortium to include all of the major European museums: Berlin's Dahlem Museum, the Pitt Rivers Museum in Oxford, the Copenhagen museum, the museums in Rome and Madrid, and of course the Hermitage in St. Petersburg. The project also sparked a great deal of interest in the countries that are represented in the holdings of these museums, such as Brazil and Mexico. Funding has been earmarked for North-South partnerships, so that as European museums inventory all of the Bambara objects from Mali in their collections, they will also help Mali carry out its own inventory of the Bambara objects there. Little by little the extent and the rich detail of the cultural heritage of the societies, ethnic groups, and ancient or modern cultures would have been revealed, and with it their history and memory. Of course, putting these objects and what we know about them on the Web is a virtual way of restoring them to their countries of origin, and would create the opportunities for other, more tangible restitutions in the future. This is an open-ended process that is in keeping with our time, its new values—which are often in conflict with the old—and thus its contradictions.[4]

✕ ✕ ✕

I would like to close with a few observations on the so-called "art" object, which can be defined as a man-made object fashioned in order to materialize meaning (whether real or imaginary) in symbolic form. This meaning flows from the object's functions—communicating with the ancestors, making evident the presence of a god, embodying the tutelary spirit that helps the Inuit shaman lure a whale into the shallows where it will beach and offer itself up to the hunters' harpoons. But this definition can just as well fit technical objects or everyday objects made to fulfill certain functions. When the Musée de l'Homme opened, Marcel Mauss declared that a spoon tells us just as much about a society as a mask does. He may well have been right, save for one difference—they do not tell us the same things. What is this difference between objects that gives certain pieces an artistic dimension?

Perhaps art objects are defined by their non-utilitarian character, the fact that most of them are not used for everyday eating, drinking, sleeping, fishing, or hunting, but act as intermediaries, as bearers of signs and therefore of meaning in producing the relations between humans and with the invisible powers around them. These relations always have imaginary components that need to be represented in a perceptible way, and art is one of the means invented to get from the intelligible to the perceptible, to turn something imaginary into something real and material by endowing matter with a symbolic form. Every society has some kind of artistic activity, and up to a certain point everyone practices it. It begins when someone puts on make-up, or chooses a piece of jewelry or the color of an item of clothing, or is adorned with body and ceremonial painting, or tattoos like those that covered the entire body of the chiefs in the Marquesas Islands, forming a second skin. The artist, who does this better than others, finds a new way to capture an idea or a belief in sizes, shapes, colors, or sounds, and hence to represent imaginary and intelligible components of society. That is why, for the ancient Greeks, craftsmen and artists were on the same plane, and there was only one word—*technè*—for their craft or their art. The crucial difference between them was that the craftsman, whose model was furnished, made what he was told to make, whereas the artist created the model that others would copy.

It is therefore indispensable, in setting a strategy for choosing and presenting objects in an ethnographically oriented museum, to draw a clear distinction between the imaginary and the symbolic. Though they are always linked, these two realities must not be confused. Let us consider an example from ancient Egypt, one the first recorded state-based societies in human history, which was governed by a "god" living among men: the pharaoh. Who was the pharaoh? Egyptian myth tells us that he was born of the union of two gods, Isis and Osiris, who were brother and a sister, a divine coupling that would be regarded as incestuous in most other societies (save for ancient Persia).

But this narrative of the pharaoh's divine origin, which refers to a totally imaginary reality, became embodied in numerous forms and symbolic productions. On the cartouches of the temples and the pyramids, the pharaoh is represented as being enormous, and the human figures around him—the Egyptians or their enemies, set alongside a god—barely reach his knee. The pharaoh's double crown, which symbolizes the two capitals of the Upper and Lower Nile, likewise proclaims that he embodies the unity of a country once divided into two kingdoms. The pharaoh also represents the sacred Nile, and every year, when its water level fell, he would proceed up the river on his Sunboat (because he descended from the Sun) until the vessel could go no farther. There he would perform a ritual to make the waters return the following year, and sure enough, some time later the Nile would flood, bringing with it the silt that made the crops grow. It was as though, through this rite, the pharaoh each year restored the waters, life, and wealth to his kingdom.

This example can help us understand the relationship between imaginary and symbolic practices, and their relations to the actual power exercised over and within a society. The imaginary in this case consists of the beliefs shared by the pharaoh and his subjects (such as the pharaoh's divine nature, and all of the associated ideas). This imaginary is embodied in objects, institutions, and symbolic practices—rites, gestures, temples, palaces, ornaments, political-religious orders, and priestly and administrative castes—that convey it to human senses, inscribing the pharaoh's power in stone, in bodies, and in the calendar.

Likewise, when we look at statues of the ancient Greek gods, we may find them beautiful, but they have lost part of their power because the imaginary component—the world of myths and rites, the political and social stakes associated with them—has dissipated over time. We admire them without really understanding their original meaning, but this does not signal that they are devoid of significance; the paradox of objects is that, even removed from their original context, they continue to mean something, and thus that they can take on yet other meanings. What draws other meanings is the symbolic form that exists within the object, even when the intentions and needs that called it into being have vanished, which attracts other imaginary elements that will again infuse it with new significance. It is particularly telling that the famous feather headdress attributed to Moctezuma, which is kept in the Vienna museum, never actually belonged to the ruler. And yet the museum exhibits it with the tag "from Moctezuma's treasure," while at the same time it sells a very serious volume by Ferdinand Anders[5] which outlines why this attribution is clearly a fiction. Nonetheless, the public apparently needs to believe that this headdress once belonged to the Aztec emperor who was defeated and killed by Cortez. For today's Mexicans, Moctezuma has become the noble figure of the Indian who resisted the white man, and he is thus a hero in the pantheon of the Mexican Republic. His name also emblazons one of the most popular brands of Mexican beer. But this skein of significations that would have been improbable in Moctezuma's time is nonetheless an object of history and tells us something about ourselves, about what people and societies do with their thoughts and their desires.

⨯ ⨯ ⨯

Let me conclude by noting that there is a gaping hole in this discussion. The vision of a such a museum may give the impression that the hundreds of thousands of objects which are not used to communicate with the gods or to signify power—the humble tools used for cooking, or house-building, or sewing—have been discarded or discounted. To be sure, I have focused principally on political-religious objects, and those that share the same signs and meanings. But I have neither forgotten nor forsaken the others. I simply believe that museums dedicated solely to ethnography, which arose in the age of the Enlightenment and thrived through the turn of the millennium, will not survive far into the twenty-first century. It seems to me that we can no longer interest museumgoers as we once did by filling showcases or drawers with row upon row of objects classified by their use, which are of interest primarily because they form a series. We are going to have to spotlight objects that convey the salient features of their societies, and arouse the attention and the emotion of publics from many backgrounds in a way that will kindle their interest in cultures different from their own, and lead them to recognize the existence of other forms of creativity. It is not my intention to belittle what we used to call "material culture," but to show that other peoples, whose techniques are often less complex than our own, have created social relations and representations of the world and its forces that are nonetheless highly complex, and are embodied in symbolic worlds and objects.

I dream of a museology that would create flexible, attractive, and demonstrative links between these two dimensions that are intertwined in human society—the incessant production of both new objects and new social relations, and the symbolization and materialization of our relationships by means of these objects, regardless of whether they are everyday and ordinary, or are exceptional because they condense a critical moment in the life of the individual (such as his or her initiation) or a key aspect of the society (such as power structures, or the presence of gods).[6]

Notes

Introduction

1. Clifford and Marcus, eds., *Writing Culture*; Marcus and Fischer, *Anthropology as Cultural Critique*. James Clifford, who has written extensively on anthropology, reduces the discipline to the texts written by ethnologists to communicate the findings of their fieldwork, but he leaves entirely to once side the crucial moment in the ethnographer's work, which is precisely the fieldwork, the source of the original material that will subsequently be analyzed and published. Clifford's "omission" or silence may stem from the fact that he himself has never done any fieldwork, but rather has specialized in criticizing the books published by those who have, such as Malinowski and Leenhardt. Critical analysis of these texts is surely useful and necessary, but it does not get to the heart of the matter—the nature of the ethnologist's observations and of what he or she has understood and restored.

2. Rabinow, *Reflections on Fieldwork in Morocco*.

3. See the remarkable book by François Cusset, *French Theory. Foucault, Derrida, Deleuze & Cie et les mutations de la vie intellectuelle aux États-Unis*; Lyotard, *La Condition post-moderne* (English translation: *The Post-Modern Condition*); Baudrillard, *Simulacres et simulation* (English translation: *Simulations*); Deleuze, *Logique du sens* (English translation: *The Logic of Sense*); Ricoeur, *Le Conflit des interprétations. Essai d'herméneutique I* (English translation: *The Conflict of Interpretations*) and *Essai d'herméneutique II*.

4. Sahlins, "Goodbye to Tristes Tropes," *How Natives Think*, and "Two or Three Things That I Know about Culture."

5. Nicholas Thomas, "Becoming Undisciplined: Anthropology and Cultural Studies"; Johnson, "What Is Cultural Studies Anyway?"; Howell, "Cultural Studies and Social Anthropology."

6. Wilson, *The Noble Savage*; Meek, *Social Science and the Ignoble Savage*.

7. Tylor, *Researches into the Early History of Mankind and the Development of Civilization*.

8. Morgan, *Systems of Consanguinity and Affinity of the Human Family.* On the genesis of Morgan's work, see (among the many useful titles) Trautmann, *Lewis Henry Morgan and the Invention of Kinship*, and Godelier, *Métamorphoses de la parenté.*

9. Morgan, *Ancient Society.*

10. A spectacular example is that of the Kwaio, a small Solomon Islands society that for decades refused to submit to British colonial power or convert to Christianity. Its resistance was marked by bloodshed, including the death of a patrol officer and two missionaries, and has continued into the twenty-first century. See Keesing, *Custom and Confrontation.* The history of the forms of resistance offered up by the colonized peoples of Africa, America, Asia, and Oceania remains largely to be written, though a giant step was taken with the publication of the Oxford series Subaltern Studies.

11. Amselle and M'Bokolo, eds., *Au cœur de l'Ethnie*, pp. 38–39. See Luc de Heusch's critique of this work in "L'Ethnie, les vicissitudes d'un concept."

12. Asad, ed., *Anthropology and the Colonial Encounter*; Nicholas Thomas, *Colonialism's Culture.* In France: Leclerc, *Anthropologie et colonialisme*; Lewis, "Anthropology and Colonialism"; Ferro, ed., *Le Livre noir du colonialisme.*

13. Schmidt, *What Is Enlightenment.* It should not be forgotten that the publication of the French *Encyclopédie*, begun in 1751, was temporarily forbidden (1759–1765) by decree by King Louis XV on grounds of "irreparable damage to morality and religion," and that Pope Clement XIII threatened to excommunicate anyone who read or possessed it.

14. This raises the whole question of the forms taken by the transition from socialism to capitalism. Among the many titles, see K. Verdery, *What was Socialism and What Comes Next?*; Bafoil, *Europe centrale et orientale*; Godelier, ed., *Transitions et subordinations au capitalisme*, especially the chapter "Les Contextes illusoires de la transition au socialisme," pp. 401–21.

15. Fukuyama, *The End of History and the Last Man.*

16. Roy, *L'Islam mondialisé* (English translation: *Globalised Islam*); Khosrokhavar, *Les Nouveaux Martyrs d'Allah* (English translation: *Suicide Bombers*); Khosrokhavar, *Quand Al-Qaida parle.*

17. Saïd, *Orientalism* and "Representing the Colonized"; Rodinson, *Islam et capitalisme* (English translation: *Islam and Capitalism*); Breckenridge and van der Veer, eds., *Orientalism and the Postcolonial Predicament.* It should be noted that Edward Saïd never confused the accounts of travels in the East written by poets like Lamartine or novelists like Gustave Flaubert, or Western diplomats' reports to their governments, with the work of major Orientalists like Louis Massignon, Jacques Berque, or Maxime Rodinson, whom he cites abundantly, or of attentive observers of Islam in Indonesia and Morocco, such as Clifford Geertz.

18. See Gellner's rigorous critique, *Postmodernism, Reason and Religion.*

19. See Hall, "The Local and the Global," and Friedman, *Cultural Identity and Global Process.*

20. See Warren, ed., *The Violence Within;* Wolf, "Perilous Ideas."

21. Lincoln, *Holy Terrors;* Juergensmeyer, *Terror in the Mind of God;* Wallerstein, "America and the World"; Alagha, "Hizbullah, Terrorism and September 11."

22. Bhargava, ed., *Secularism and Its Critics;* Galanter, "Secularism, East and West"; Nandy, "An Anti-Secularist Manifesto."

23. Savarkar, *Hindutva, Who is a Hindu?*

24. See Jean-Luc Racine's remarkable overview, "La Nation au risque du piège identitaire."

25. The controversy over the Babri-Masjid mosque was (prior to its destruction in 1992) the object of a series of important publications brought together in Sarvelli, ed., *Anatomy of a Confrontation.*

26. See Meyer, "Des usages de l'histoire et de la linguistique dans le débat sur les identités à Sri Lanka." The same debate can be found in the nationalist strife in Sri Lanka between essentialists, constructivists, and postmodernists; Tambiah, *Leveling Crowds.*

27. See Shober, "The Theravada Buddhist Engagement with Modernity in Southeast Asia" and "Buddhist Just Rule and Burmese National Culture."

28. Boas, "The Method of Anthropology"; Firth, "Contemporary British Social Anthropology"; Barth, "The Analysis of Culture in Complex Societies"; Sahlins, "Two or Three Things That I Know about Culture" and "What Is Anthropological Enlightenment?"

29. Dumont, *Essais sur l'individualisme.*

30. Ong, *Flexible Citizenship.* See also *Reconstructing Nations and States,* special issue of *Daedalus,* vol. 122, no. 3.

31. Clifford, "Diasporas." Certain countries respond to the intensification of migratory flows and the imposed contact of human groups of different ethnic origin and cultures with particularly violent policies of ethnic "cleansing." Diasporas represent a mere 2 percent of the world's population and therefore are not a force signaling the impending end of nation-states, as Appadurai would have us believe. See Appadurai, *Modernity at Large;* Kearney, "The Local and the Global."

32. See Ferguson, *The Anti-Politics Machine.* This book unravels the role played by a number of NGOs in the development of Lesotho, one of Africa's poorest countries. Their interventions, together with those of the World Bank, had an unexpected result: state and police control of a hitherto unsubdued mountainous region.

33. Firth, *The Work of the Gods in Tikopia; We, the Tikopia;* and *Tikopia Ritual and Belief.*

34. Evans-Pritchard, *The Nuer*; E. R. Leach, *Political Systems of Highland Burma*.

35. See Srinivas, "The Insider versus the Outsider in the Study of Culture" and "Practicing Social Anthropology in India"; Assayag, "Mysore Narasimhachar Srinivas (1916–1999)."

36. Chatterjee, *Nationalist Thought and the Colonial World*.

37. Guha, *Dominance without Hegemony*; Subaltern Studies, vols. 1–12.

38. Pouchepadass, "Les Subaltern Studies ou la critique postcoloniale de la modernité" and "Que reste-t-il des Subaltern Studies?" pp. 67–79: "L'apport essentiel est d'ordre critique. Les Subaltern Studies ont fourni sans conteste une des expressions les plus percutantes du procès de l'ethnocentrisme dans les sciences sociales, de l'élitisme des approches 'par le haut', et de la 'version standard' de l'histoire, dont le cadre de référence est l'histoire nationale." [The essential contribution was a critical view. Subaltern Studies provided one of the most hard-hitting expressions of the process of ethnocentrism in the social sciences, of the elitism of "top-down" approaches, and of the "standard version" of history with national history as its frame of reference.] Ludden, ed., *Reading Subaltern Studies*.

39. For an extreme example of the denunciation of "cultural imperialism" purported to be typical of all anthropological research methods, see Linda Tuhiwai Smith, *Decolonizing Methodologies*.

40. Hall, "Old and New Identities, Old and New Ethnicities."

41. See Knauft, "Pushing Anthropology Past the Posts": "The replacement of detailed exposition and social analysis by pastiche and irony is thus cause for concern. The echoes of fragment writing from Nietzsche, deconstruction and Baudrillard encourage post-modernism and contemporary cultural studies to evade declarative argument and sometimes to shrink from authorial responsibility" (141).

42. As early as 1990—a few years after the first studies published by Marcus, Fischer, Clifford, and others—David Harvey made the following observation in *The Condition of Postmodernity:* "In challenging all consensual standards of truth and justice, of ethics and meaning, and in pursuing the dissolution of all narratives and meta-theories into a diffuse universe of language games, deconstruction ended up, in spite of the best intentions of its more radical practitioners, by reducing knowledge and meaning to a rubble of signifiers. It therefore produced a condition of nihilism that prepared the ground for the re-emergence of a charismatic politics and even more simplistic propositions than those which were deconstructed" (350).

43. Marcus, *Ethnography Through Thick and Thin*, p. 110.

44. Tyler, "From Documents of the Occult to Occult Document," pp. 131, 138–39.

45. De Man, *The Resistance to Theory*, pp. 12, 19–20. De Man's theory of the absolute autonomy of language, as a place where tropes and figures circulate uncontrolled and cut off from the world of human intentions and representations, was acclaimed as a fundamental revolution in thinking as early as 1971 by Wlad Godzich, who makes the following observation in his introduction to the second edition of de Man's first book of collected essays, *Blindness and Insight*: "Once upon a time, we all thought we knew how to read, and then came de Man" (xvi). Hence Derrida's admiration for de Man and the 1979 publication of Bloom's *Deconstruction and Criticism*, which brought together de Man, Derrida, Harold Bloom, Geoffrey Hartman, and J. H. Miller.

46. Clifford and Marcus, eds., *Writing Culture*, p. 136. See Pool, "Postmodern Ethnography?"; Roth, "Ethnography without Tears."

47. Firth, "Outline of Tikopia Culture" (1930), reprinted in *Tikopia Ritual and Belief*, pp. 15–30.

48. Firth, *The Work of the Gods in Tikopia*.

49. Geertz, *The Interpretation of Cultures*; Lévi-Strauss, *La Pensée sauvage* (English translation: *The Savage Mind*) and *Mythologiques* (English translation: *Mythologiques*); Turner, *The Forest of Symbols*; Wagner, *Symbols That Stand for Themselves*; Izard and Smith, *La Fonction symbolique*; and the special issue of the *Revue du MAUSS*, *Plus reel que le reel, le symbolique*.

50. *Translator's note:* In Martin Thom's excellent translation of Professor Godelier's book *L'Idéel et le materiel* (*The Mental and the Material*), a publisher's note that succinctly states the problem of trying to find an adequate translation for the French term *idéel* precedes the preface: "We have translated—for lack of a better alternative—the word 'idéel' as 'mental' but we are aware that this partly distorts what Maurice Godelier intended by using the word 'idéel', which is rarely used in French except in philosophical discourse. Godelier's intention was to take into account thought in all its forms and processes, conscious and unconscious, cognitive and noncognitive. 'Mental' tends to underplay the unconscious aspects of thought and to reduce its conscious aspects to abstract and intellectual representations alone" (vi).

51. Godelier, *L'Idéel et le matériel* (English translation: *The Mental and the Material*).

52. Frankfort, *Kingship and the Gods*; Bonhême and Forgeau, *Pharaon*, chap. 3, pp. 101–20.

53. See Geertz, "An Interview with Clifford Geertz": "The way we mostly thought of it [symbolic anthropology] was in terms of the culture/social-structure opposition. We wanted to get culture, however defined, back in the picture" (605).

54. Godelier, *The Mental and the Material*, pp. 152–53. In chapter 3 of this work, I discussed four main functions of thought: (1) to make realities that

are external and internal to humankind, including thought itself, *present in thought* (to re-present them); (2) to thus *interpret* what is presented, giving it one or several meanings; (3) to *organize the relations* human beings entertain with each other and with their natural environment; and (4) to *legitimize these relations.* I have called everything involved in the construction of the various forms of social realities down through history, which depend directly or indirectly on the exercise of these four functions of thought, the "mental" or "conceptual" part (*la part idéelle*) of social reality.

55. See Lévi-Strauss, "Introduction à l'oeuvre de Mauss" (English translation: "Introduction to the Work of Marcel Mauss"): "The symbols are more real than what they symbolize, the signifier precedes and determines the signified" (37). This affirmation is the consequence of Lévi-Strauss's groundless postulate, namely that "man has from the start had at his disposition a signifier-totality . . . a surplus of signification which he shares out among things in accordance with the laws of . . . symbolic thinking" (62). This postulate would necessarily entail the disappearance of the subject, as the author clearly states in *Le Cru et le cuit* (English translation: *The Raw and the Cooked*): "I therefore claim to show, not how men think in myths, but how myths think themselves in men's minds without their being aware of the fact" (12). See my critique in *L'Enigme du don*, pp. 39–44 (English translation: *The Enigma of the Gift*, pp. 25–29).

56. Roger Keesing had formulated a similar idea in "Anthropology as Interpretive Quest" and in "Theories of Culture Revisited." Jean-François Billeter, the translator of Chuang-Tseu—perhaps the greatest but certainly the most difficult Chinese thinker to interpret and therefore to translate—demonstrates the same refusal to consider the specific characteristics of a non-Western society as manifesting absolute otherness with regard to the West. He has shown that, depending on the context, the famous notion of "Tao" should be translated in five different ways in order to make it perfectly intelligible to the Western mind, whereas most Sinologists simply throw in the towel and leave the word Tao in quotation marks. See Billeter, *Contre François Jullien*, especially pp. 82–84.

I would also note here that the objective of the social sciences is not to seek to know the Intimate Ego of the billions of individuals that make up today's human population, which is of course impossible, utopian, and perhaps pointless. That being said, other disciplines (such as psychoanalysis) and other modes of knowledge, combined with artistic creation and implemented by poets, novelists, playwrights, and the like, enable us to represent, up to a point, the complex inner workings of an individual.

57. See the references cited in note 64 to the findings of research done sixty years after Malinowski in the islands to the east of New Guinea, where the kula was and continues to be practiced.

58. Godelier, "L'Occident—miroir brisé" and "Mirror, Mirror on the Wall."

59. Clifford and Marcus, eds., *Writing Culture.*

60. Sanjek, ed., *Fieldnotes.*

61. Marcus, *Ethnography Through Thick and Thin*, p. 110.

62. A typical example of this way of thinking is found in the work of George Peter Murdoch, who in 1949 (the year Lévi-Strauss published his *Elementary Structures of Kinship*) brought out a book entitled *Social Structure* that was almost entirely devoted to analyzing the different forms of family and kinship systems. The starting point was the "nuclear family" as the fundamental unit of any kinship group, and kinship structures were seen as the basic social structures.

63. Geertz, *Works and Lives.*

64. Malinowski, *Argonauts of the Western Pacific;* Leach and Leach, eds., *The Kula;* Munn, *The Fame of Gawa;* Weiner, *Women of Value, Men of Renown* and *Inalienable Possessions.*

65. Damon, "Representation and Experience in Kula and Western Exchange Spheres."

66. Firth, "The Creative Contribution of Indigenous People to their Ethnography," p. 245.

67. Firth, "The Sceptical Anthropologist?"

68. This is what appears from reading the assessments of anthropology proposed, among others, in 1984 by Sherry B. Ortner ("Theory in Anthropology since the Sixties"), in 1994–97 by Bruce Knauft ("Pushing Anthropology Past the Posts," *Genealogies for the Present in Cultural Anthropology*, and "Theoretical Currents in Late Modern Cultural Anthropology"), and in 1999 by Henrietta L. Moore (*Anthropological Theory Today*).

69. Verdery, *What Is Socialism and What Comes Next?*

70. See note 15 above on Francis Fukuyama

71. See the work by the great neo-Confucian philosopher Mou Zongsan (1909–1995), *Spécificités de la philosophie chinoise*, with a long introduction by Joël Thoraval on Chinese neo-Confucianism today (pp. 1–65). See also the special issue of *Revue Extrême Orient—Extrême Occident* on the theme "Is There Still a Chinese Philosophy Today?" particularly Thoraval's article, "Sur la transformation de la pensée néo-confucéenne en discours philosophique moderne," pp. 91–118.

72. Godelier, "L'Anthropologie sociale est-elle indissolublement liée à l'Occident, sa terre natale?"

1 Some Things One Keeps, Some Things One Gives, Some Things One Sells, and Some Things Must neither Be Sold nor Given but Kept to Pass On

The present chapter is an expanded version of the keynote address to the American Association of Economic Anthropology meeting in Toronto in April 2002. In it, I outlined the main ideas of my book *L'Enigme du don* (English translation: *The Enigma of the Gift*). The association invited me because I had started out my academic career by teaching economic anthropology, a field that was practically unknown in France at the time (with the exception of Claude Meillassoux's *Anthropologie économique des Gouro*). In 1974, I published a selection of texts under the title *Un domaine contesté: l'anthropologie économique*, and in 1991, I edited a volume entitled *Transitions et subordinations au capitalisme*.

1. Panoff, "Objets précieux et moyens de paiement chez les Maenge de Nouvelle-Bretagne." The Maenge hoarded or circulated shell rings (*page*), carved from the shell of the *Tridacna gigas*, and lengths of shell-beads intertwined with other shells (*tali*).

2. Mauss, "Essai sur le don" (English translation: *The Gift*).

3. Kuttner, *Everything for Sale*.

4. For the biography of Mauss, see Marcel Fournier's henceforth indispensable *Marcel Mauss*, and the articles by the same author: "Marcel Mauss, l'ethnologue et la politique" and "Bolchevisme et socialisme selon Marcel Mauss."

5. Best, *Forest Lore of the Maori*, p. 439.

6. Lévi-Strauss, "Introduction à l'oeuvre de Mauss," p. xxxviii.

7. Ibid., p. xxxii.

8. "What power resides *in* the object given that causes its recipient to pay it back?" Mauss, "Essai sur le don," p. 148 (*The Gift*, p. 2; my emphasis).

9. Mauss, "Essai sur le don," pp. 160 and 162n2 (*The Gift*, pp. 12 and 92n38).

10. Ibid., p. 275 (pp. 79–80).

11. Ibid., p. 153 (p. 6).

12. Godelier, *L'Enigme du don*, pp. 59–62 (*The Enigma of the Gift*, pp. 41–43).

13. See Godelier and Strathern, eds., *Big Men and Great Men*.

14. Andrew Strathern, *The Rope of Moka*.

15. Feil, *Ways of Exchange*.

16. Boas, *The Social Organization and the Secret Societies of the Kwakiutl Indians;* Boas and Hunt, *Ethnology of the Kwakiutl*.

17. Mauss, "Essai sur le don," pp. 209–10 (*The Gift*, pp. 39–40).

18. Ibid., p. 212n2 ("L'idéal serait de donner un potlatch et qu'il ne fût pas rendu") (p. 114n143).

19. Ibid., p. 224n1 (p. 134n245).

20. Ibid.

21. Weiner, *Inalienable Possessions* and "Inalienable Wealth."

22. Malinowski, "The Primitive Economy of the Trobriand Islanders" and *Argonauts of the Western Pacific*.

23. Mauss, "Essai sur le don," p. 184 (*The Gift*, p. 26).

24. Damon, "Representation and Experience in Kula and Western Exchange Spheres" and "The Problem of the Kula on Woodlark Island"; Munn, *The Fame of Gawa;* Leach and Leach, eds., *The Kula;* Liep, "The Workshop of the Kula"; Persson, *Sagali and the Kula.*

25. Mauss, "Essai sur le don," p. 179 (*The Gift,* p. 102n32).

26. Godelier, "Quelle est la place des sociétés à Potlatch dans l'histoire?," *L'Enigme du don,* pp. 212–21 (*The Enigma of the Gift,* pp. 153–61).

27. Godelier, *La Production des Grands Hommes,* pp. 155–56; (English translation: *The Making of Great Men,* pp. 95–96).

28. Ibid., pp. 117–18 (p. 70).

29. On the distinction between the beautiful and the sublime, see Burke, *On Taste;* Hegel, *Aesthetics;* Longin, *Du sublime.*

2 No Society Has Ever Been Based on the Family or on Kinship

Page-Barbour Lecture 1. This theme is developed at greater length in Godelier, *Métamorphoses de la parenté,* chap. 9, pp. 325–44.

1. For material on the Yanomami see Lizot, *Le Cercle des feux,* and Chagnon, *Yanomamö, the Fierce People.*

2. Sinclair, *Behind the Ranges.*

3. For additional history and background, see Godelier, *La Production des Grands Hommes* (English translation: *The Making of Great Men*).

4. Godelier, *Rationalité et irrationalité en économie* and *Horizon, trajets marxistes en anthropologie.*

5. After reconstructing the story with the Baruya and calculating the number of generations since the events, I conclude that the events probably transpired in the eighteenth century CE.

6. Lloyd, "The Angan Language Family."

7. Cf. Lemonnier, "Mipela wan bilas."

8. Cf. Godelier, *L'Idéel et le materiel,* chap. 2, pp. 99–167: "Territoire et propriété dans quelques sociétés pré-capitalistes" (English translation: *The Mental and the Material,* chap. 2, pp. 71–121: "Territory and Property in Some Pre-capitalist Societies").

9. Barth, *Ethnic Groups and Boundaries.*

10. For example, Amselle and M'Bokolo, eds., *Au Coeur de l'ethnie.* See the vigorous critique of this book by Luc de Heusch, "L'Ethnie, les vicissitudes d'un concept."

11. Godelier, *La Production des Grands Hommes*, pp. 155–56 (*The Making of Great Men*, pp. 95–96).

12. Ibid., pp. 144–46 (pp. 87–89).

13. Cf. Godelier, "La Monnaie de sel chez les Baruya de Nouvelle-Guinée" (English translation: "Salt Currency and the Circulation of Commodities among the Baruya of New Guinea").

14. Cf. Turnbull, *The Forest People*.

15. Cf. Meggitt, "Understanding Australian Aboriginal Society."

16. See the work by Laurent Dousset, "Diffusion of Sections in the Australian Western Desert" and *Assimilating Identities*.

17. Yan Thomas, "A Rome, Pères citoyens et cité des pères," "Le 'Ventre', corps maternel, droit paternel," and "Remarques sur la juridiction domestique à Rome."

18. Cf. the Jajmani system in India: Mayer, *Caste and Kinship in Central India*; Wiser, *The Hindu Jajmani System*.

19. See the large body of work on the transition from feudalism to capitalism: Godelier, ed., *Transitions et subordinations au capitalisme*; Anderson, *Passages from Antiquity to Feudalism*; Hilton, ed., *The Transition from Feudalism to Capitalism*.

20. Kuttner, *Everything for Sale*.

3 It Always Takes More Than a Man and a Woman to Make a Child

Page-Barbour Lecture 2. This theme is developed at greater length in Godelier, *Métamorphoses de la parenté*.

1. Saladin d'Anglure, "'Petit-ventre', l'enfant géant du cosmos Inuit, Ethnographie de l'enfant dans l'Arctique central Inuit."

2. Saladin d'Anglure, "Nom et parenté chez les Esquimaux Terramint du Nouveau-Québec (Canada)."

3. Saladin d'Anglure, "L'Élection parentale chez les Inuit."

4. It is important to note that the Baruya's representations of the part played by the man, the woman, and the Sun in making babies is not found in all of the societies that belong to the same linguistic family and make up the ethnic group now known as the Anga. For instance, the Ankave (a small society studied for the past twenty years by Pierre Lemonnier and Pascale Bonnemère, which occupies the southern tip of the Anga territory, an area located in the mountains overlooking the mangrove swamps and the coast of the Gulf of Papua that is home to populations having a number of cultures and speaking different languages) believe that the fetus is made at once by the man's semen and the woman's blood. Thus, the importance of semen is diminished while that of the mother's blood increases, and homosexuality is not part of the initiation rites (which similarly do not tear the boys and young men away from the women's world or segregate them for a long period). For the Ankave, the role of the Sun tends to disappear

as well. These differences suggested transformations and social practices associated with changes in the nature of the kinship relations and with the existence of much more individualistic forms of authority and power than among the Baruya. See Bonnemère, "Maternal Nurturing Substance and Paternal Spirit" and *Le Pandanus rouge*.

5. Malinowski, *The Father in Primitive Psychology; Sex and Repression in Savage Society*, chap 10, pp. 253–80; and *The Sexual Live of the Savages*, pp. 15–44.

6. See chapter 1, note 25. Weiner, "The Reproductive Model in Trobriand Society," "Trobriand Kinship from Another View," and *The Trobrianders of Papua New Guinea*; Campbell, "Kula in Vakuta."

7. Hua, *Une société sans père ni mari*.

8. For example, among the Khumbo of Nepal, see Diemberger, "Blood, Sperm, Soul and the Mountain"; Levine, "The Theory of Rü Kinship, Descent and Status in a Tibetan Society."

9. Panoff, "Patrifiliation as Ideology and Practice in a Matrilineal Society."

10. Panoff, "The Notion of Double Self among the Maenge."

11. Jorgensen, "Mirroring Nature?"

12. Douaire-Marsaudon, "Le Meurtre cannibale ou la production d'un homme-dieu," "Je te mange, moi non plus," and "Le Bain mystérieux de la Tu'i Tonga Fefine."

13. Rogers, "The Father's Sister [Futa-helu] Is Black."

14. Schmitt, "Le Corps en chrétienté."

15. E. R. Leach, "Virgin Birth."

16. Godelier, "Inceste, parenté, pouvoir."

17. See pp. 129–35 of this volume for a more detailed discussion of this point.

18. Godelier, *Métamorphoses de la parenté*, chap. 10 ("De l'inceste et de quelques autres mauvais usages du sexe," pp. 345–418) and chaps. 11 and 12 ("Sur les origines et les fondements de l'inceste," pp. 419–510).

4 Human Sexuality Is Fundamentally A-social

A longer version of this chapter was published in the *Revue internationale de psychopathologie*, 1995, special issue, "Qu'est-ce qu'un acte sexuel?"

1. In Tonga, "both men and women seem to have little knowledge of what we call delicacy in Amours; they rather seem to think it unnatural to suppress an appetite originally implanted in them perhaps for the same purpose as hunger or thirst, and consequently make it often a topic of public conversation, or what is more indecent in our judgement, have been seen to cool the ardour of their mutual inclinations before the eyes of many spectators" (Cook, *Journal on Board of His Majesty's Bark Resolution*, p. 45).

Labillardière tells that one day, in Tonga, having chanced to enter a native dwelling, he surprised a member of his crew allowing himself *the greatest liberties with one of the prettiest persons on the island*, and that under the gaze of the head of the house, calmly sitting in the midst of his household (*Relation du voyage à la recherche de la Pérouse*, p. 130).

2. Concerning the notions of "society" and "culture," see Godelier, "Introspection, rétrospection, projections."

3. See above, chapter 3.

4. Male homosexuality, as practiced in the context of initiations, was very widespread in New Guinea. Gilbert Herdt (who conducted fieldwork among the Sambia, a society belonging to the same ethnic and linguistic groups as the Baruya) and Jadran Mimica (who studied the Iqwaye, another Anga group) have each described and analyzed these relations, which involve both eroticism and violence, between older givers and younger receivers of semen. See Herdt, *Guardians of the Flutes*; Mimica, *Intimations of Infinity* and "The Incest Passions." Herdt has also written or edited a number of works on ritualized homosexuality in Melanesia which are standard references in the field: Herdt, ed., *Rituals of Manhood* and *Ritualized Homosexuality in Melanesia*; Herdt and Stoller, *Intimate Communications*. See also Knauft, "Homosexuality in Melanesia." Female homosexuality connected with initiation rites also exists, but we know very little about it. Some information can be found in Florence Brunois' thesis on the Kasua of New Guinea, "Le Jardin du casoar."

5. Baruya representations do not oppose nature and culture (a juxtaposition that is important to Lévi-Strauss and other Western thinkers), and women are thought to have originally and spontaneously created items that in the West would be considered part of the realm of culture, such as weapons, clothing, and musical instruments.

6. See the remarkable book by Erik Porge, *Jacques Lacan, un psychanalyste*. From 1971, Lacan maintained that "there is no such thing as a sexual relation" in *D'un discours qui ne serait pas un semblant*, book 18. He returns to the theme in *Les Non-dupes errent*, book 21.

5 How an Individual Becomes a Social Subject

The present chapter includes elements of discussions with my psychoanalyst friends André Green and the late Jacques Hassoun. André Green invited me to give a lecture on 21 November 1993 to the Paris Société de Psychanalyse (SPP), which subsequently appeared [under what title?] in *Le Journal des anthropologues*, no. 64–65 (1996): 49–63. For two years, Jacques Hassoun and I led a seminar in which some thirty psychoanalysts and anthropologists participated and which resulted in the publication of a volume of essays, *Meurtre du père*, that we edited together.

1. The question of whether such signs ever existed in the common ancestor that gave rise to humans, chimpanzees, and bonobos is still open.

2. Vincent, *Biologie des passions*.
3. Freud, *Totem und tabu*, p. 174.
4. Bourdieu, *Esquisse d'une théorie de la pratique*.
5. Tort, *La Fin du dogme paternel*.

6 What Is a Society?

1. Of course I checked these details with the Andje and the other tribes neighboring the Baruya, some of which are friends and others enemies. All confirmed the account of the Baruya's flight and their arrival in the Marawaka Valley, as well as the ambush they had laid for their hosts and the subsequent massacre.

2. I would like to dispel some confusion that may arise concerning the question I pose in this chapter. It has nothing to do with the question philosophers and other theorists are fond of asking: namely, what are the foundations of human society in general, and of the social bond? In my opinion, this question is nearly meaningless, for all human activities, and all of the interrelations people produce or will produce are at the same time the content and the basis of their social existence, of their life in society. Humans are "naturally"—that is to say, by virtue of natural evolution—a social species, who did not have to make any contract, or do anything else (kill a father, for instance) to start living in society. Nonetheless, as I have already observed, we do not merely live in society, but produce new forms of social existence, and therefore society itself, in order to go on living.

3. I have left to one side the analysis of the role of the female initiations, which bring together hundreds of women and form a complement to their male counterpart to produce the order that holds sway in the society, which is in turn governed by men.

4. It may interest the reader to know that I "discovered," after the fact in my fieldnotes, that a Baruya had supplied the answer to my question: "And then we built out own *tsimia* and we initiated our boys ourselves." But I understood the importance and the pertinence of these few words only after I had become convinced—having eliminated, successively, the Baruya's kinship and economic relations—that the "political-religious" relations alone tied everyone to everyone else and constituted the basis of their overarching, tribal identity.

5. This system is not homogeneous, however. Economists distinguish various kinds of capitalism—Anglo-American, Scandinavian, Japanese—and maintain that the presumed convergence of the world's economic systems toward Anglo-American neoliberal capitalism is by no means inevitable. See Amable, *Les Cinq capitalismes*, pp. 101–51.

6. See Godelier, *L'Idéel et le materiel*, chap. 2: "Territoire et propriété dans quelques sociétés précapitalistes," pp. 99–163 (*The Mental and the*

Material, chap. 2: "Territory and Property in Some Pre-Capitalist Societies," pp. 71–121).

7. Sinclair, *Behind the Ranges*.

8. This state was created after the First World War through the fusion, under the authority of Australia, of two former European colonies: British Papua in the south and the German Neue Guinea in the north. See Ryan, ed., *Encyclopaedia of Papua and New Guinea*.

9. For example, for Sieyès, on the eve of the French Revolution, "the Nation is the source of Everything . . . it is the Law itself. It is the community of citizens conscious of their belonging and equal in rights" (*Qu'est-ce que le Tiers-Etat?*).

10. Firth, *The Work of the Gods in Tikopia*. I will return later in this chapter to his formula, which does not seem to me to exactly fit the beliefs and ritual practices Firth described in minute detail.

11. Firth, "Outline of Tikopia Culture" (1930), reprinted in *Tikopia Ritual and Belief*, pp. 15–30.

12. All men were and had to be at the same time warriors, hunters, and gardeners, even if very few were regarded as great warriors, great hunters, or great gardeners.

13. Firth, *Rank and Religion in Tikopia*.

14. Ibid. In many religions, the gods are conceived primarily as humans who have been deified after death for any number of reasons, such as for the wonders and good works they performed when they were alive. In China, the emperor granted or refused divine status to those individuals who local populations wished to worship after they died. Following an investigation, if the emperor acceded to such a request, he would sign a decree authorizing the construction of an altar and a temple in honor of the deceased, and would assign him a rank somewhere in the hierarchy of the countless gods of the Chinese pantheon. For generations, and even centuries to come, subsequent emperors would either promote or demote the god, depending on the positive or negative effects people continued to attribute to his intervention. Such modes of thought and practices are diametrically opposed to those of religions that affirm the existence of a single, omnipotent, and omniscient god who created everything from nothing and thus is infinitely removed from humankind. The relations that men—be they princes or kings—entertain with such a god must be ones of submission, of prayer that their desires may be realized and thanksgiving when this is so; there is no room for "cooperation," for any sharing of action with god. On the opposition between the Chinese and the Judeo-Christian visions of god, see Jullien, *Procès ou création*.

15. Valeri, *Kingship and Sacrifice*; Kirch and Sahlins, *Anahulu*; Kirch and Green, *Hawaiki, Ancestral Polynesia*.

16. Gifford, *Tongan Myths and Tales* and *Tongan Society;* Douaire-Marsaudon, *Les Premiers Fruits.*

17. See note 2 of this chapter.

18. Quesnay, *Tableau économique de la France;* Adam Smith, *An Inquiry into the Nature and Causes of the Wealth of Nations;* Godelier, "Ordres, castes et classes," *L'Idéel et le materiel,* pp. 296–317 ("Estates, Castes and Classes," *The Mental and the Material,* pp. 227–44).

19. I will merely suggest that the appearance of different forms of state stemmed, in certain cases, from those contexts where the government and administration of a large chiefdom could no longer be managed directly by the paramount chief and his kin in cooperation with the local chiefs (who were their subordinates and often related by marriage). Such situations may fostered the desire to dispose of those social groups, comprised of individuals unrelated by kinship to the paramount chief and the noble families of the tribe, who more or less entirely replaced the local chiefs, administering them on behalf of the paramount chief and his inner circle. This kind of administration would have produced resistance from the local chiefs who were thus stripped of part of their authority and their power over their dependents, and prompted the central power to call upon armed forces to impose such change and quell any unrest. Such a process was probably at work in Hawaii before the Europeans landed, culminating in the 1790s when one of the paramount chiefs, Kamehameha, garnered a monopoly on the purchase of European weapons and was thus able to vanquish, one by one, the remaining unsubdued local chiefs and groups and bring them under his power. As Marshall Sahlins concludes: "In Hawaii, the continuous redistribution of lands among the ruling chiefs preempts any local lineage formation, reducing genealogical memories among the common people largely to personnal recollections" ("Other Times, Other Customs," p. 524).

See also Sahlins on the Chinese emperor and the paramount chiefs of Hawaii: "And if the great Hawaiian chiefs competed to distinguish themselves by taking on European identities, it was because unlike the Celestial Emperor, the Unique Man, they confronted each other as perpetual rivals who in their own divinity were virtual doubles" ("Cosmologies of Capitalism," p. 29).

20. Dumont, *La Civilisation indienne et nous* and *Homo hierarchicus;* Khilnani, *L'Idée de l'Inde;* Mishra, *Temptations of the West.*

21. Maspero, *La Chine antique,* esp. pp. 75–81; Vandermeersch, *Wangdao ou la Voie royale;* Granet, *La Religion des Chinois;* Chang, *Art, Myth, and Ritual.*

7 Social Anthropology Is Not Indissolubly Tied to the West, Its Birthplace

Page-Barbour Lecture 3. In preparing this lecture, I realized the importance of elaborating the notion of a Cognitive Ego, as distinct from a Social Ego and an Intimate Ego. I consider this concept at length in the introduction.

1. Much has been published on the history of ethnology in the past two decades, particularly by George Stocking and Adam Kuper. See Stocking, *Race, Culture, and Evolution, Functionalism Historicized,* and *Victorian Anthropology*; Kuper, *Anthropologists and Anthropology* and *The Invention of Primitive Society*. Robert Lowie's book *The History of Ethnological Theory* is still worth reading for its discussion of the German precursors of the late eighteenth and the early nineteenth centuries, Meiners-Klemm and Waitz, both of whom have been forgotten today. Paradoxically, Lowie does not consider Herder, who is recognized as the precursor to Boas and cultural anthropology; he refers to a few quotations in passing, but glosses over Herder's pronouncements on Jews, Africans, Asians, and the like, as well as his constant reference to the will of God to explain History. Herder, *Une autre philosophie de l'Histoire*. See also Sternhell, *Les anti-Lumières*.

2. Trautmann, *Lewis Henry Morgan and the Invention of Kinship* and "The Whole History of Kinship Terminology in Three Chapters."

3. In fact Morgan, for reasons discovered by Trautmann, had not seen the differences between the Iroquois and the Dravidian terminologies: both distinguish between parallel and cross cousins in generation G-0, but only the Dravidian terminology maintains this distinction in generations G-1 and G-2. Cf. Trautmann, *Lewis Henry Morgan and the Invention of Kinship*.

4. Morgan, *Ancient Society*, chap. 1, pp. 17–18.

5. Borges, *Les Miroirs Voilés*.

6. See pp. 101–24 of this volume.

7. The same is true of the place of women in the Roman Catholic and Greek Orthodox churches, and in Islam.

8. See pp. 45–61 of this volume, for a more detailed development of this analysis.

9. Benvéniste, *Vocabulaire des institutions indo-européennes*, t. 1, pp. 132–33.

10. Marilyn Strathern, *The Gender of the Gift*; Douglas, "Une déconstruction si douce," p. 113.

11. A final word or two about today's Baruya, whose life has changed a great deal since I first turned up in 1967. In 1960 they were forcibly subsumed in a colonial state, and in 1975 became citizens of an independent, emerging nation. They have been partially Christianized, but still hold initiation ceremonies. They produce coffee they do not drink for an inter-

national market they do not control. Salt money has been replaced by the Papuan national currency, the kina, which is tied to the Australian dollar. Many social relations that once called for noncommercial exchanges today depend on exchanges of money, which has replaced all of the traditional forms of wealth, including shells and feathers. The last time I visited the Baruya, many told me they wanted to become "modern," to "Behainim Jisas" and "Mekim bisnis" (to follow Jesus and to go into business). In short, they have truly become a fragment of a globalized world dominated by the West.

8 Excursus

Page-Barbour Lecture 4. This chapter charts another direction in which I was drawn for several years in my work, as head of program planning for a new museum devoted to the arts and civilizations of Africa, Asia, Oceania, and the Americas to be created in Paris. When this became official, I continued to serve in the same capacity until the end of 2000, when, in the wake of various conflicts and pressures, I was finally obliged to bow out.

The task of imagining a new museum devoted to several hundred non-Western societies and cultures, each represented by a objects unearthed from the collections of the two public museums that were to be merged into the new institution, was for me a new and exciting experience. I immediately grasped the cultural and political scope and the scientific importance of a museum that would be open to people from all walks of life, in an era marked by the disappearance of colonial empires and the multiplication of new, independent nations that, rightly laying claim to their own destinies, refused to let others, particularly people from the West, define their culture and their history.

A few words by way of background. The project, which would replace both the Musée de l'Homme and the Musée des Arts d'Afrique et d'Océanie (the former Musée des Colonies, renamed by André Malraux while he was culture minister under Charles de Gaulle), was announced by Jacques Chirac as one of his campaign promises during the 1985 presidential elections. The idea had been suggested to him by his friend, Jacques Kerchache, an important collector and dealer in "primitive" art. Like the Louvre Pyramid and the new François Mitterand National Library, such ambitious projects are vestiges of the monarchy that continues to permeate the French Republic.

When the plans were made public, they met with opposition from the majority of French anthropologists, who were worried about the prospect of the Musée de l'Homme disappearing. A few, including Claude Lévi-Strauss and myself, took the opposite position, arguing that if such a project were to be launched, it should receive our support. Why did I react in this way when I was not in the same political camp as Jacques

Chirac? Principally because I had carried out an assessment of the state of the Musée de l'Homme as the request of Lionel Jospin (then the national education minister) before the new museum was conceived, and had concluded that this once venerated institution had been dying for some time and, barring radical transformations, could not be resuscitated. A few years later, Jacques Chirac was president of the Republic, the Left had returned to power, and Lionel Jospin was prime minister. Claude Allègre, then the national education and research minister, asked me what I thought about the new museum project, for which the president of the Republic was seeking the government's financial and administrative commitment. I told him to "go for it," but to take care to ensure a true balance and complementarity between esthetic and anthropological-historical approaches, and was appointed program director for the planning stage (a position that was renewed when the museum was officially created as a new public establishment).

A few years later, when it became apparent that the philosophy guiding the many choices involved in the project's construction and programming increasingly inclined toward a museum of fine arts, to the detriment of the means and the spaces required by a museum of civilizations, I was obliged to give up my post.

Thereafter, as part of the European Cultural Heritage Online (ECHO) project, I worked with Professor Roberte Hamayon (an expert on Siberian societies) and her team to produce the prototype of a database on the Tungus of Siberia. This database was realized through collaboration with several French museums (Bordeaux, Lyons, Musée de l'Homme in Paris), together with those in other European countries (Leiden, Budapest), and the École des Hautes Études en Sciences Sociales, the Centre National de la Recherche Scientifique and the Hungarian Academy of Sciences. The prototype (which can be consulted, free of charge, at www.necep.net) is what we had envisioned for the proposed Quai Branly Museum.

The new museum was at last inaugurated on 19 June 2006 by President Jacques Chirac in the presence of numerous foreign and French personalities, including Claude Lévi-Strauss, for whom the large amphitheater which serves as a lecture hall/theater is named. The library is housed in the Jacques Kerchache room, which honors President Chirac's friend and advisor, who originally suggested the creation of this new museum. I was invited as well, and though the museum is a great accomplishment, it confirms some of my fears. Beyond the superb objects on display, it remains to be seen whether visitors will gain a better understanding of the men and women who made them, and the societies that needed them in order to exist and to reproduce. It is now up to the public to judge.

1. See Lévi-Strauss, *La Voie des masques* (English translation: *The Way of the Masks*).

2. Godelier, "Préface" to *Arts primitifs, regards civilisés* (the second edition of the French translation of Sally Price's book *Primitive Art in Civilized Places*).

3. These axes are discussed in detail in chapter 3, pp. 80–100 of this volume.

4. By the end of 2004, our team had produced a prototype of a database focusing on the Siberian Tungus, "Objects and Societies," that was intended to serve as a model for museums to document their objects and the societies that produced them (see this chapter's introductory note). Unfortunately, the second phase of the project lacked funding and has not been realized.

5. Anders, *The Treasures of Montezuma*.

6. Our point of view concurs in part with that developed by Alfred Gell in *Art and Agency*, in particular the idea that the art object acts on us as a subject.

Bibliography

Alagha, Joseph. "Hizbullah, Terrorism and September 11." *Orient* 44, no. 3 (Sept. 2003): 385–412.

Amable, Bruno. *Les Cinq capitalismes*. Paris: Éditions du Seuil, 2005.

Amselle, Jean-Loup, and Elikia M'Bokolo. *Au cœur de l'ethnie: Ethnie, tribalisme et État en Afrique*. Paris: La Découverte, 1985.

Anders, Ferdinand. *The Treasures of Montezuma: Fantasy and Reality*. Vienna: Museum für Völkerkunde, 2001.

Anderson, Perry. *Passages from Antiquity to Feudalism*. London: New Left Books, 1974.

Appadurai, A. *Modernity at Large: Cultural Dimensions of Globalization*. Minneapolis: University of Minnesota Press, 1996.

Asad, Talal, ed. *Anthropology and the Colonial Encounter*. London: Ithaca Press, 1970.

Assayag, J. "Mysore Narasimhachar Srinivas (1916–1999)." *L'Homme* 156 (2000): 1–14.

Bafoil, François. *Europe centrale et orientale: mondialisation, européanisation et changement social*. Paris: Les Presses de la Fondation Nationale des Sciences Politiques, 2006.

Barth, Fredrik. "The Analysis of Culture in Complex Societies." *Ethnos* 54, no. 3–4 (1989): 120–42.

———. *Ethnic Groups and Boundaries*. Boston: Little, Brown and Company, 1969.

Baudrillard, Jean. *Simulacres et simulation*. Paris: Éditions Galilée, 1981. Translated by Paull Foss, Paul Patton, and Philip Beitchman as *Simulations* (New York: Semiotext[e], 1983).

Benveniste, Émile. *Vocabulaire des institutions indo-européennes*. 2 vols. Paris: Éditions de Minuit, 1969.

Best, Elsdon. *Forest Lore of the Maori*. Wellington E.C.: Keating Government Printer, 1977 [1909].

Bhargava, Rajeev. *Secularism and Its Critics.* Delhi/New York: Oxford University Press, 1998.

Billeter, Jean-François. *Contre François Jullien.* Paris: Éditions Allia, 2006.

———. *Études sur Tchouang-Tseu.* Paris: Éditions Allia, 2004.

Bloom, Harold. *Deconstruction and Criticism.* New York: Seabury Press, 1979.

Boas, Franz. "The Method of Anthropology." *American Anthropologist* 22 (1920): 311–21.

———. *The Social Organization and the Secret Societies of the Kwakiutl Indians.* Washington, DC: Government Printing Office, 1897.

Boas, Franz, and George Hunt. *Ethnology of the Kwakiutl.* 2 vols. Washington, DC: Government Printing Office, 1921.

Bonhême, M. A., and A. Forgeau. *Pharaon: les secrets du pouvoir.* Paris: Armand Colin, 1988.

Bonnemère, Pascale. "Maternal Nurturing Substance and Paternal Spirit: The Making of a Southern Anga Society." *Oceania* 64 (1993): 159–86.

———. *Le Pandanus rouge: Corps, différences des sexes et parenté chez les Ankavé-Anga.* Paris: Éditions du Centre national de la recherché scientifique/Éditions de la Maison des sciences de l'Homme, 1996.

Borges, Jorge Luis. "Les Miroirs Voilés." In *Œuvres Complètes de J. L. Borges,* volume 2, translated by Roger Caillois, Nestor Ibarra and Jean-Pierre Bernès, [pp?]. Paris: Gallimard (Bibliothèque de la Pleiade), 1999.

Bourdieu, Pierre. *Esquisse d'une théorie de la pratique.* Geneva: Droz, 1972.

Breckenridge, Carol A., and Peter van der Veer, eds. *Orientalism and Postcolonial Predicament.* Philadelphia: University of Pennsylvania Press, 1993.

Brunois, Florence. "Le Jardin du casoar." Doctoral dissertation, École des hautes etudes en sciences socials, Paris, 2001.

Burke, Edmund. *On Taste; On the Sublime and Beautiful; Reflections on the French Revolution; A Letter to a Noble Lord; with introduction, notes and illustrations.* New York: P. F. Collier, [c1909].

Campbell, Shirley F. "Kula in Vakuta: The Mechanics of Keda." In *The Kula: New Perspectives on Massim Exchange,* edited by Edmund Leach and Jerry Leach, 201–27. London: Cambridge University Press, 1983.

Chagnon, Napoleon. *Yanomamö, the Fierce People.* New York: Holt, Rinehart and Winston, 1968.

Chang, K. C. *Art, Myth, and Ritual: The Path to Political Authority in Ancient China.* Boston: Harvard University Press, 1983.

Chatterjee, P. *Nationalist Thought and the Colonial World: A Derivative Discourse?* London: Zed Books, 1986.

Clifford, James. "Diasporas." *Cultural Anthropology* 9, no. 3 (1994): 302–38.

Clifford, James, and George E. Marcus, eds. *Writing Culture: The Poetics and Politics of Ethnography*. Berkeley: University of California Press, 1986.

Cook, James. *Journal on Board of His Majesty's Bark Resolution*. In *The Journals of Captain James Cook on His Voyages of Discovery*, annotated and edited by J. C. Beaglehole, [pp?]. 4 vols. Cambridge: Cambridge University Press, 1955–74.

Cusset, François. *French Theory: Foucault, Derrida, Deleuze & Cie et les mutations de la vie intellectuelle aux États-Unis*. Paris: Éditions La Découverte, 2003.

Damon, Frederick. "The Kula and Generalized Exchange: Considering Some Unconsidered Aspects of the Elementary Structures of Kinship." *Man* 15 (1980): [pp?].

———. "The Problem of the Kula on Woodlark Island: Expansion, Accumulation, and Over-production." *Ethnos* 3–4 (1995): 176–201.

———. "Representation and Experience in Kula and Western Exchange Spheres (Or, Billy)." *Research in Economic Anthropology* 14 (1993): 235–54.

Deleuze, Gilles. *Logique du sens*. Paris: Éditions de Minuit, 1969. Translated by Mark Lester with Charles Stivale as *The Logic of Sense*, edited by Constantin V. Boundas (New York: Columbia University Press, 1990).

de Man, Paul. *Blindness and Insight: Essays in the Rhetoric of Contemporary Criticism*. 2nd ed., revised. Introduction by Wlad Godzich. Minneapolis: University of Minnesota Press (Theory and History of Literature Series 7), 1983.

———. *The Resistance to Theory*. Foreword by Wlad Godzich. Minneapolis: University of Minnesota Press, 1986.

Diemberger, H. "Blood, Sperm, Soul and the Mountain." In *Gendered Anthropology*, edited by T. del Valle, 88–127. London: Routledge, 1993.

Douaire-Marsaudon, Françoise. "Le Bain mystérieux de la Tu'i Tonga Fefine. Germanité, inceste et mariage sacré en Polynésie." Part I, *Anthropos* 97, no. 1 (2002): 147–69; Part II, *Anthropos* 97, no. 2 (2002): 519–28.

———. "Je te mange, moi non plus." In *Meurtre du père, sacrifice de la sexualité: Approches anthropologiques et psychanalytiques*, edited by Maurice Godelier and Jacques Hassoun, 21–52. Paris: Arcanes, 1995.

———. "Le Meurtre cannibale ou la production d'un homme-dieu." In *Le Corps humain, supplicié, possédé, cannibalisé*, edited by Maurice Godelier and Michel Panoff, 137–67. Amsterdam: Éditions des Archives Contemporaines, 1998.

———. *Les Premiers Fruits: parenté, identité sexuelle et pouvoirs en Polynésie*

Occidentale: Tonga, Wallis et Futuna. Paris: Éditions de la Maison des sciences de l'Homme/Centre National de la Recherché Scientifique, 1998.

Douglas, Mary. "Une déconstruction si douce." *Revue du MAUSS* 11 (1991): 113.

Dousset, Laurent. *Assimilating Identities: Social Networks and the Diffusion of Sections.* Sydney: Oceania Monograph 57, 2005.

———. "Diffusion of Sections in the Australian Western Desert: Reconstructing Social Networks." In *Filling the Desert: The Spread of Langages in Australia's West,* edited by M. Laughren and P. McConvell, [pp?]. Brisbane: University of Queensland Press, 2003.

Dumont, Louis. *La Civilisation indienne et nous: Esquisse de sociologie comparée.* Paris: A. Colin, 1964.

———. *Essais sur l'individualisme: une perspective anthropologique sur l'idéologie moderne.* Paris: Éditions du Seuil, 1983.

———. *Homo hierarchicus: Essai sur le système des castes.* Paris, Gallimard, 1966. Translated by Mark Sansbury, Louis Dumont, and Basia Gulati as *Homo Hierarchichus: The Caste System and Its Implications* (complete revised English edition, Chicago: University of Chicago Press, 1970).

Evans-Pritchard, E. E. *The Nuer: A Description of the Modes of Livelihood and Political Institutions of a Nilotic People.* Oxford: Oxford University Press, 1969.

Feil, Daryl Keith. "The Bride in Bridewealth: A Case from the New Guinea Highlands." *Ethnology* 20 (1981): 63–75.

———. *Ways of Exchange: The Enga Tee of Papua New Guinea.* Brisbane: University of Queensland Press, 1984.

Ferguson, J. *The Anti-Politics Machine: Development, Depolitization, and Bureaucratic Power in Lesotho.* Cambridge: Cambridge University Press, 1990.

Ferro, Marc, ed. *Le Livre noir du colonialisme: XVI–XXIe siècle: de l'extermination à la repentance.* Paris: Laffont, 2003.

Firth, Raymond. "Contemporary British Social Anthropology." *American Anthropologist* 53 (1951): 474–89.

———. "The Creative Contribution of Indigenous People to Their Ethnography." *The Journal of the Polynesian Society* 110, no. 3 (2001): 241–45.

———. *Rank and Religion in Tikopia.* London: George Allen and Unwin, 1970.

———. *Religion: A Humanist Interpretation.* London/New York: Routledge, 1996.

———. "The Sceptical Anthropologist? Social Anthropology and Marxist Views on Society." Inaugural Radcliffe-Brown Lecture in Social Anthropology. *Proceedings of the British Academy* 58 (1974): 177–214.

———. *Tikopia Ritual and Belief.* Boston: Beacon Press, 1967.

———. *We, the Tikopia.* New York: American Book Company, 1937.

———. *The Work of the Gods in Tikopia.* London: The Athlone Press, 1967.

Firth, Raymond, and Mervyn McLean. *Tikopia Songs: Poetic and Musical Art of a Polynesian People of the Solomon Islands.* London: Cambridge University Press, 1990.

Fournier, Marcel. "Bolchevisme et socialisme selon Marcel Mauss." *Liber* (1992): 9–15.

———. *Marcel Mauss.* Paris: Fayard, 1994.

———. "Marcel Mauss, l'ethnologue et la politique: le don." *Anthropologie et sociétés* 19, no. 1–2 (1995): 57–69.

Frankfort, Henri. *Kingship and the Gods: A Study of Ancient Near East Religion as the Integration of Society and Nature.* Chicago: University of Chicago Press, 1948.

Freud, Sigmund. *Totem und tabu.* Vol. 9, *Gesammelte Werke.* London: Imago Publishing Company, 1940.

Friedman, Jonathan. *Cultural Identity and Global Process.* London: Sage, 1994.

Fukuyama, Francis. *The End of History and the Last Man.* New York: Free Press, 1992.

Galanter, Marc. "Secularism, East and West." In *Secularism and Its Critics,* edited by Rajeev Bhargava, 234–67. Delhi/New York: Oxford University Press, 1998.

Geertz, Clifford, *The Interpretation of Cultures,* New York, Basic Books, 1973.

———. "An Interview with Clifford Geertz" by Richard Handler. *Current Anthropology* 32, no. 5 (1991): 603–12.

———. *Works and Lives: The Anthropologist as Author.* Stanford: Stanford University Press, 1988.

Gell, Alfred. *Art and Agency: An Anthropological Theory.* Oxford/New York: Clarendon Press, 1998.

Gellner, Ernest. *Postmodernism, Reason and Religion.* London: Routledge, 1992.

Gifford, Edward. *Tongan Myths and Tales.* Honolulu, HI: The Museum, 1924.

———. *Tongan Society.* Honolulu, HI: The Museum, 1929.

Godelier, Maurice. "L'Anthropologie sociale est-elle indissolublement liée à l'Occident, sa terre natale?" *Revue internationale des sciences sociales*, no. 143 (1995): 166–83.

———. "Les Contextes illusoires de la transition au socialisme." In *Transitions et subordinations au capitalisme*, edited by Maurice Godelier, 401–21. Paris: Éditions de la Maison des sciences de l'Homme, 1991.

———. "Corps, parenté, pouvoir(s) chez les Baruya de Nouvelle-Guinée." *Journal de la Société des Océanistes*, no. 94, (1992–1): 3–24.

———. "Correspondance avec Maurice Godelier." In *Jacques Hassoun*. Paris/Montréal: Editions de L'Harmattan (*Che vuoi?* new series no. 12), 1999.

———. *Un domaine contesté, l'anthropologie économique*. Paris: Mouton, 1974.

———. *L'Enigme du don*. Paris: Fayard, 1996. Translated by Nora Scott as *The Enigma of the Gift* (Chicago/Cambridge: University of Chicago Press/Polity Press, 1998).

———. *Horizons, Trajets marxistes en anthropologie*. Paris: Maspero, 1973. Translated by Robert Brain as *Perspectives in Marxist Anthropology* (Cambridge: Cambridge University Press, 1977).

———. *L'Idéel et le materiel*. Paris: Fayard, 1984. Translated by Martin Thom as *The Mental and the Material: Thought Economy and Society* (New York: Verso, 1986).

———. "Inceste, parenté, pouvoir." *Psychanalystes* 36 (1990): 33–51.

———. "Introspection, rétrospection, projections: un entretien avec Hosham Dawod." *Gradhiva*, no. 26 (1999): 1–25.

———. *Métamorphoses de la parenté*. Paris: Fayard, 2004.

———. "Meurtre du père ou sacrifice de la sexualité?" In *Meurtre du père, Sacrifice de la sexualité: Approches anthropologiques et psychanalytiques*, edited by Maurice Godelier and Jacques Hassoun, 21–52. Paris: Arcanes (Les Cahiers d'Arcanes), 1996.

———. "Mirror, Mirror on the Wall: The Once and Future Role of Anthropology, a Tentative Assessment." In *Assessing Cultural Anthropology*, edited by Robert Borofsky, 97–112. New York: McGraw Hill, 1993.

———. "La Monnaie de sel des Baruya de Nouvelle-Guinée." *L'Homme* 10, no. 2 (1970): 5–37. Translated as "Salt Currency and the Circulation of Commodities among the Baruya of New Guinea" (*Studies in Economic Anthropology*, AS7 [1971]: 52–73).

———. "L'Occident—miroir brisé: une évaluation partielle de l'anthropologie sociale assortie de quelques perspectives." *Annales E.S.C.*, no. 5 (1993): 1183–1207.

————. "Préface" in Sally Price, *Arts Primitifs, Regards Civilisés,* 2nd ed., 9–16. Paris: Éditions de l'École Nationale Supérieure des Beaux-Arts, 2006. Originally published as *Primitive Art in Civilized Places* (Chicago: University of Chicago Press, 1989).

————. *La Production des Grands Hommes: Pouvoir et domination masculine chez les Baruya de Nouvelle-Guinée.* Paris: Fayard, 1982. Translated by Rupert Swyer as *The Making of Great Men: Male Domination and Power among the New Guinea Baruya* (Cambridge: Cambridge University Press, 1986).

————. "Qu'est-ce qu'un acte sexuel?" *Revue internationale de psychopathologie,* no. 19 (1995): 351–82.

————. *Rationalité et irrationalité en économie.* Paris: Maspero, 1966.

————. "Le Sexe comme fondement ultime de l'ordre social et cosmique chez les Baruya de Nouvelle-Guinée: mythe et réalité." In *Sexualité et pouvoir,* edited by A. Verdiglione, 268–306. Paris: Payot, 1976.

————. "Sexualité et société." *Journal des anthropologues, anthropologie et psychanalyse,* no. 64–65 (1998): 49–63.

————. "Sexualité, parenté et pouvoir." *La Recherche,* special issue on sexuality, vol. 20, no. 213 (1989): 1141–55.

————, ed. *Transitions et subordinations au capitalisme.* Paris: Éditions de la Maison des sciences de l'Homme, 1991.

Godelier, Maurice, and Michel Panoff, eds. *Le Corps humain, supplicié, possédé, cannibalisé.* Paris: Archives Contemporaines, 1998.

————. *La Production du corps.* Paris: Archives Contemporaines, 1998.

Godelier, Maurice, and Marilyn Strathern, eds. *Big Men and Great Men: Personifications of Power in Melanesia.* Cambridge: Cambridge University Press, 1991.

Gopal, Sarvepalli, ed. *Anatomy of a Confrontation: The Babri-Masjid-Ramjanmabhumi Issue.* New Delhi/New York: Viking, 1991.

Granet, Marcel. *La Religion des Chinois.* Paris: Albin Michel, 1989.

Guha, Ranajid. *Dominance without Hegemony: History and Power in Colonial India.* Cambridge, MA: Harvard University Press, 1997.

Hall, Stuart. "The Local and the Global: Globalization and Ethnicity." In *Culture, Globalization and the World-System: Contemporary Conditions for the Representation of Identity,* edited by Anthony D. King, 1–39. Minneapolis: University of Minnesota Press, 1997.

————. "Old and New Identities, Old and New Ethnicities." In *Culture, Globalization and the World-System: Contemporary Conditions for the Representation of Identity,* edited by Anthony D. King, 41–68. Minneapolis: University of Minnesota Press, 1997.

Harvey, David. *The Condition of Postmodernity*. Oxford: Blackwell, 1990.

Hegel, Georg W. F. *Aesthetics: Lectures on Fine Art*. Translated by T. M. Knox. Oxford: Clarendon Press, 1975.

Herder, Johann Gottfried von. *Une autre philosophie de l'Histoire*. Paris: Aubier, 1964 [1774].

———. *Idées sur la philosophie de l'histoire de l'humanité*. Paris: Aubier, 1962.

Herdt, Gilbert. *Guardians of the Flutes: Idioms of Masculinity*. New York: McGraw Hill Book Company, 1981.

———, ed. *Ritualized Homosexuality in Melanesia*. Berkeley: University of California Press, 1984.

———, ed. *Rituals of Manhood: Male Initiation in Papua New Guinea*. Berkeley: University of California Press, 1982.

Herdt, Gilbert, and R. J. Stoller. *Intimate Communications: Erotics and the Study of Culture*. New York: Columbia University Press, 1990.

Heusch, Luc de. "L'Ethnie, les vicissitudes d'un concept." *Archives européennes de sociologie* 38, no. 2 (1997): 185–206.

Hilton, Rodney, ed. *The Transition from Feudalism to Capitalism*. London: New Left Books, 1976.

Howell, Sigue. "Cultural Studies and Social Anthropology: Contesting or Complementary Discourses?" In *Anthropology and Cultural Studies*, edited by Stephen Nugent and Cris Shore, 103–25. London: Pluto Press, 1997.

Hua, Cai. *Une société sans père ni mari: Les Na de Chine*. Paris: Presses Universitaires de France, 1997. Translated by Asti Hustvedt as *A Society without Fathers or Husbands: The Na of China* (New York: Zone Books, 2001).

Hübinger, P. E. *Bedeutung und Rolle des Islam beim Übergang vom Altertum zum Mittelalter*. Darmstadt: Wissenschaftliche Buchgesellschaft (Wege der Forschung 202), 1968.

Izard, Michel, and Pierre Smith. *La Fonction symbolique*. Paris: Gallimard, 1979.

Johnson, Richard. "What Is Cultural Studies Anyway?" *Social Text*, no. 16 (1987): 38–90.

Jorgensen, Dan. "Mirroring Nature? Men's and Women's Models of Conception in Telefolmin." *Mankind* 14, no. 1 (1988): 57–65.

Juergensmeyer, Mark. *Terror in the Mind of God: The Global Rise of Religious Violence*. Berkeley: University of California Press, 2004.

Jullien, François. *Procès ou création: Essai de problématique interculturelle*. Paris: Éditions du Seuil, 1989.

Kearney, M. "The Local and the Global: The Anthropology of Globalization and Transnationalism." *Annual Review of Anthropology* 24 (1995): 547–65.

Keesing, Roger. "Anthropology as Interpretive Quest." *Current Anthropology* 28, no. 2 (1987): 161–76.

———. *Custom and Confrontation: The Kwaio Struggle for Cultural Autonomy.* Chicago: University of Chicago Press, 1992.

———. "Theories of Culture Revisited." In *Assessing Cultural Anthropology*, edited by Robert Borofsky, 301–10. New York: McGraw Hill, 1993.

Khilnani, Sunil. *L'Idée de l'Inde.* Paris: Fayard, 2005.

Khosrokhavar, Farhad. *Les Nouveaux Martyrs d'Allah.* Paris: Flammarion, 2002. Translated by David Macey as *Suicide Bombers: Allah's New Martyrs* (London: Pluto Press, 2005).

———. *Quand Al-Qaida parle.* Paris: Grasset, 2006.

Kirch, Patrick, and Roger Green. *Hawaiki, Ancestral Polynesia: An Essay in Historical Anthropology.* Cambridge: Cambridge University Press, 2001.

Kirch, Patrick, and Marshall Sahlins. *Anahulu: The Anthropology of History in the Kingdom of Hawaii.* 2 vols. Chicago: University of Chicago Press, 1992.

Knauft, Bruce. *Genealogies for the Present in Cultural Anthropology.* New York: Routledge, 1996.

———. "Homosexuality in Melanesia." *The Journal of Psychoanalytic Anthropology* 10, no. 2 (1987): 155–91.

———. "Pushing Anthropology Past the Posts." *Critique of Anthropology* 14, no. 2 (1994): 117–52.

———. "Theoretical Currents in Late Modern Cultural Anthropology." *Cultural Dynamics* 9, no. 3 (1997): 277–300.

Kuper, Adam. *Anthropologists and Anthropology: The British School, 1922–1972.* London: Allan Lane, 1973.

———. *The Invention of Primitive Society: Transformations of an Illusion.* London: Routledge, 1988.

Kuttner, Robert. *Everything for Sale: The Virtues and Limits of Markets.* New York: A. Knopf, 1997.

Labillardière, J. J. H. de. *Relation du voyage à la recherche de la Pérouse fait sur l'ordre de l'Assemble constituante, pendant les années 1791, 1792 et pendant la 1ere et 2nde année de la République française.* 2 vols. Paris: Jansen, [1800].

Lacan, Jacques. *D'un discours qui ne serait pas du semblant.* Paris: Éditions du Seuil (Le Séminaire Livre XVIII), 1970–1971.

———. *Des Noms-du-Père.* Paris: Éditions du Seuil, 2005.

———. *Les Non-dupes errent.* Paris: Éditions du Seuil (Le Séminaire Livre XXI), 1974.

Leach, E. R. *Political Systems of Highland Burma.* London: Berg, 1973.

————. "Virgin Birth." *Proceedings of the Royal Anthropological Institute*, 1966: [pp?]. Reprinted in E. R. Leach, *Genesis as Myth and Other Essays* (London: Cape, 1968).

Leach, Jerry, and Edmund Leach, eds. *The Kula: New Perspectives on Massim Exchange*. London: Cambridge University Press, 1983.

Leclerc, G. *Anthropologie et colonialisme*. Paris: Fayard, 1972.

Lemonnier, Pierre. "Mipela wan bilas. Identité et variabilité socio-culturelle chez les Anga de Nouvelle-Guinée." In *Le Pacifique-Sud aujourd'hui: identités et transformations culturelles*, edited by S. Tcherkézoff and F. Marsaudon, [pp?]. Paris: Éditions du Centre National de la Recherche Scientifique, 1989.

Lévi, Jean. *Des fonctionnaires divins: politique, despotisme et mystique en Chine ancienne*. Paris: Éditions du Seuil, 1989.

Levine, N. E. "The Theory of Rü, Kinship, Descent and Status in a Tibetan Society." In *Asian Highland Societies in Anthropological Perspective*, edited by E. Fürer-Haimendorf, 52–78. New Delhi: Stirling, 1981.

Lévi-Strauss, Claude. *Le Cru et le cuit*. Paris: Plon, 1964. Translated by John and Doreen Weightman as *The Raw and the Cooked: Introduction to a Science of Mythology* (Chicago: University of Chicago Press, 1986).

————. "Introduction à l'oeuvre de Mauss." In Marcel Mauss, *Sociologie et anthropologie*, pp. I–LII. Paris, Presses Universitaires de France, 1950. Translated by Felicity Baker as *Introduction to the Work of Marcel Mauss* (London: Routledge and Kegan Paul, 1987).

————. *Mythologiques*. 4 vols. Paris: Plon, 1964–1971. Translated as *Mythologiques: Introduction to a Science of Mythology* (Chicago: University of Chicago Press, 1969–1981).

————. *La Pensée sauvage*. Paris: Plon, 1962. Translated as *The Savage Mind* (Chicago: University of Chicago Press, 1969).

————. *La Voie des masques*. Paris: Plon, 1979. Translated by Sylvia Modelski as *The Way of the Masks* (Seattle: University of Washington Press, 1982).

Lewis, Diane. "Anthropology and Colonialism." *Current Anthropology* 14, no. 5 (1973): 581–602.

Lienhardt, R. G. *Divinity and Experience: The Religion of the Dinka*. Oxford: Oxford University Press, 1961.

Liep, John. "The Workshop of the Kula: Production and Trade of Shell Necklaces in the Louisiade Archipelago, Papua New Guinea." *Folk*, no. 23 (1981): 297–309.

Lincoln, Bruce. *Holy Terrors: Thinking about Religion after September 11*. Chicago: University of Chicago Press, 2003.

Lizot, Jacques. *Le Cercle des feux: faits et dits des Indiens Yanomami.* Paris: Éditions du Seuil, 1976.

Lloyd, R. G. "The Angan Language Family." In *The Linguistic Situation in the Gulf District and Adjacent Areas, Papua New Guinea,* edited by K. Franklin, 1–110. Canberra: Australian National University Press, 1973.

Lombard, Maurice. *L'Islam dans sa première grandeur.* Paris: Flammarion, 1971.

Longin. *Du sublime.* Paris: Rivages, 1991 [1939].

Lowie, Robert. *The History of Ethnological Theory.* New York: Holt, Rinehart and Winston, 1937.

Ludden, David, ed. *Reading Subaltern Studies: Critical History, Contested Meaning and the Globalisation of South Asia.* New Delhi: Permanent Black, 2001.

Lyotard, Jean-François. *La Condition post-moderne.* Paris: Éditions de Minuit, 1979. Translated by Geoff Bennington and Brian Massumi as *The Post-Modern Condition: A Report on Knowledge* (Minneapolis: University of Minnesota Press, 1980).

Malinowski, Bronislaw. *Argonauts of the Western Pacific.* London: Routledge, 1922.

———. *The Father in Primitive Psychology.* New York: Norton, 1927.

———. "The Primitive Economy of the Trobriand Islanders." *Economic Journal* 31, no. 121 (1921): 1–16.

———. *Sex and Repression in Savage Society.* London: Routledge and Kegan, 1927.

———. *The Sexual Life of Savages.* London: Routledge and Kegan, 1929.

———. *The Sexual Life of Savages in Northwestern Melanesia.* London: Routledge and Kegan, 1931.

Marcus, George. *Ethnography Through Thick and Thin.* Princeton: Princeton University Press, 1996.

Marcus, George, and Michael Fischer. *Anthropology as Cultural Critique: An Experimental Moment in the Human Sciences.* Chicago: University of Chicago Press, 1986.

Maspero, Henri. *La Chine Antique.* Revised edition. Paris: Presses Universitaires de France, 1965.

Mauss, Marcel. "Essai sur le don. Forme et raison de l'échange dans les sociétés archaïques." *L'Année sociologique,* nouvelle série, 1, 1925. Reprinted in Marcel Mauss, *Sociologie et anthropologie,* Paris: Presses Universitaires de France, 1950. Translated by W. D. Halls as *The Gift: The Form and Reason for Exchange in Archaic Societies.* Foreword by Mary Douglas. New York/London: W. W. Norton, 1990.

————. *Manuel d'ethnographie*. Paris: Payot, 1947.

————. "Origine de la notion de monnaie." *Anthropologie* (Revue de l'Institut français d'anthropologie) 3, no. 1 (1914): 14–20.

————. *Sociologie et anthropologie*. Paris: Presses Universitaires de France, 1950.

Mauss, Marcel, and Henri Hubert. "Essai sur la nature et la fonction du sacrifice." *L'Année sociologique*, tome 2 (1899): 29–138.

Mayer, Adrian. *Caste and Kinship in Central India*. London: Routledge, 1960.

Mead, Margaret. *Sex and Temperament in Three Primitive Societies*. New York: Morrow Quill Paperbacks, 1931.

Meek, Ronald L. *Social Science and the Ignoble Savage*. London: Cambridge University Press, 1976.

Meggitt, Mervyn. "Understanding Australian Aboriginal Society: Kinship or Cultural Categories?" In *Kinship Studies in the Morgan Centennial Year*, edited by P. Reining, 64–87. Washington, DC: Anthropological Society, 1972.

Meigs, Anna S. *Food, Sex, and Pollution: A New Guinea Religion*. New Brunswick, NJ: Rutgers University Press, 1984.

Meillassoux, Claude. *Anthropologie économique des Gouro*. The Hague: Mouton, 1964.

Meyer, Éric. "Des usages de l'histoire et de la linguistique dans le débat sur les identités à Sri Lanka." *Purusartha* (2001): 91–126.

Mimica, Jadran. "The Incest Passions: An Outline of the Logic of Iqwaye Social Organization." *Oceania* 61 (1991): 34–58 and 81–113.

————. *Intimations of Infinity: The Mythopoeia of the Iqwaye Counting System and Number*. With an afterword by Roy Wagner. Oxford: Berg, 1988.

Mishra, Pankaj. *Temptations of the West: How to Be Modern in India, Pakistan, Tibet and Beyond*. New York: Farrar, Straus and Giroux, 2006.

Moore, Henrietta L., ed. *Anthropological Theory Today*. Cambridge: Polity Press, 1999.

Morgan, Lewis Henry. *Ancient Society, or Researches in the Lines of Human Progress from Savagery through Barbarism to Civilization*. Reprinted with a foreword by Elisabeth Tooker. Tucson: University of Arizona Press, 1985 [1877].

————. *Systems of Consanguinity and Affinity of the Human Family*. Washington, DC: Smithsonian Institution (Smithsonian Contributions to Knowledge no. 218), 1871.

Mou, Zongsan. *Spécificités de la philosophie Chinoise*. Paris: Éditions du Cerf, 2003.

Munn, Nancy. *The Fame of Gawa*. London: Cambridge University Press, 1986.

Murdock, George Peter. *Social Structure*. New York: MacMillan, 1949.

Nandy, A. "An Anti-Secularist Manifesto." *Seminar,* no. 314 (1985): 14–24.

Ong, Aihwa. *Flexible Citizenship: The Cultural Logics of Transnationality*. Durham, NC: Duke University Press, 1999.

Ortner, Sherry. "Theory in Anthropology since the Sixties." *Comparative Studies in Society and History* 26, no. 1 (1984): 126–86.

Panoff, Michel. "The Notion of Double Self among the Maenge." *Journal of the Polynesian Society* 77, no. 3 (1968): 275–95.

————. "Objets précieux et moyens de paiement chez les Maenge de Nouvelle-Bretagne." *L'Homme* 20, no. 2 (1980): 6–37.

————. "Patrifiliation as Ideology and Practice in a Matrilineal Society." *Ethnology* 15, no. 2 (1976): 175–88.

Persson, Johnny. *Sagali and the Kula: A Regional Systems Analysis of the Massim*. Lund, Sweden: Department of Sociology (*Lund Monographs in Social Anthropology* no. 7), 1999.

Plus réel que le réel, le symbolique. Special issue of *La Revue du MAUSS*, no. 12 (1998).

Pool, Robert. "Postmodern Ethnography?" *Critique of Anthropology* 11, no. 4 (1991): 309–31.

Porge, Erik. *Jacques Lacan, un psychanalyste*. Paris: Éditions Eres, 2000.

Pouchepadass, Jacques. "Que reste-t-il des Subaltern Studies?" *Critique Internationale*, no. 24 (2004): 67–79.

————. "Les Subaltern Studies ou la critique postcoloniale de la modernité." *L'Homme*, no. 156 (2000): 161–85.

Quesnay, François. *Tableau économique de la France*. Paris: Calman Lévi, 1969.

Rabinow, Paul. *Reflections on Fieldwork in Morocco*. Berkeley: University of California Press, 1977.

Racine, Jean-Luc. "La Nation au risque du piège identitaire: communalisme, post-modernisme et neo-sécularisme." In *La Question identitaire en Asie du Sud*, 11–46 and 373–407. Paris: Purusartha, 2001.

Reconstructing Nations and States. Special issue of *Daedalus*, vol. 122, no. 3 (1993).

Ricoeur, Paul. *Le Conflit des interprétations: Essai d'herméneutique I*. Paris: Éditions du Seuil, 1969. Translated as *The Conflict of Interpretations*, edited by Don Ihde (Evanston: Northwestern University Press, 1974).

————. *Essai d'herméneutique II*. Paris: Éditions du Seuil, 1986.

Rodinson, Maxime. *Islam et capitalisme*. Paris: Éditions du Seuil, 1966. Translated by Brian Pearce as *Islam and Capitalism* (New York: Pantheon Books, 1974).

Rogers, Garth. "The Father's Sister [Futa-Helu] is Black: A Consideration of Female Rank and Power in Tonga." *Journal of the Polynesian Society* 86 (1977): 157–82.

Roth, Paul A. "Ethnography without Tears." *Current Anthropology* 30, no. 5 (1989): 555–69.

Roy, Olivier. *L'Islam mondialisé*. Paris: Éditions du Seuil, 2002. Translated as *Globalised Islam: The Search for a New Ummah* (London: C. Hurst, 2002).

Ryan, Peter, ed. *Encyclopaedia of Papua and New Guinea*. 2 vols. Melbourne: Melbourne University Press, 1972.

Sahlins, Marshall. "Cosmologies of Capitalism: The Trans-Pacific Sector of the World-System." The Radcliffe-Brown Lecture in Social Anthropology. *Proceedings of the British Academy*, 1989: 1–51.

———. "Goodbye to Tristes Tropes: Ethnography in the Context of Modern World History." *Journal of Modern History* 65 (1993): 1–35.

———. *How Natives Think: About Captain Cook, For Example*. Chicago: University of Chicago Press, 1995.

———. "On the Sociology of Primitive Exchange." In *The Relevance of Models for Social Anthropology*, edited by Michael Banton, 139–236. London: Tavistock Publications, 1965.

———. "Other Times, Other Customs: The Anthropology of History." *American Anthropologist* 83 (1983): 517–44.

———. "Poor Man, Rich Man, Big Man, Chief." *Comparative Studies in Society and History* 5 (1963): 285–303.

———. "The Spirit of the Gift: une explication de texte." In *Echanges et communications; mélanges offerts à Claude Lévi-Strauss à l'occasion de son 60ème anniversaire*, [pp?]. Leiden: Mouton, 1970.

———. "Two or Three Things That I Know about Culture." *Journal of the Royal Anthropological Institute* V, no. 3 (1999): 399–421.

———. "What Is Anthropological Enlightenment? Some Lessons of the Twentieth Century." *Annual Review of Anthropology* 28 (1999): 1–23.

Saïd, Edward. *Orientalism*. New York: Viking, 1978.

———. "Representing the Colonized: Anthropology's Interlocutors." *Critical Inquiry* (1989): 205–25.

Saladin d'Anglure, Bernard. "L'Élection parentale chez les Inuit: fiction empirique ou réalité virtuelle." In *Adoptions, ethnologie des parentés croisées*, edited by Agnès Fine, 121–49. Paris: Éditions de la Maison des Sciences de l'Homme, 1998.

————. "Nom et parenté chez les Eskimos Tarramint du Nouveau-Québec (Canada)." In *Échanges et communications: Mélanges offerts à Claude Lévi-Strauss*, edited by J. Pouillon and P. Maranda, 1013–38. The Hague: Mouton, 1970.

————. "'Petit-ventre', l'enfant géant du cosmos Inuit, Ethnographie de l'enfant dans l'Arctique Central Inuit." *L'Homme* 20, no. 1 (1980): 7–46.

Sanjek, R., ed. *Fieldnotes: The Making of Anthropology*. Ithaca: Cornell University Press, 1996.

Sarvelli, Gopal, ed. *Anatomy of a Confrontation: The Babri-Masjid-Ramjanmabhumi Issue*. New Delhi: Penguin Books India, 1991.

Savarkar, V. D. *Hindutva; Who is a Hindu?* Delhi: Bjarti Sahitya Sadan, 1969 [1924].

Schmidt, James. *What Is Enlightenment: Eighteenth-Century Answers and Twentieth-Century Questions*. Berkeley: University of California Press, 1996.

Schmitt, Jean-Claude. "Le Corps en chrétienté." In *La Production du corps*, edited by Maurice Godelier and Michel Panoff, 224–356. Amsterdam: Éditions des Archives Contemporaines, 1998[339–56 in chap. 3, n. 13].

Schneider, David M. *A Critique of the Study of Kinship*. Ann Arbor: University of Michigan Press, 1984.

————. "The Theravada Buddhist Engagement with Modernity in Southeast Asia." *Journal of Southeast Asian Studies* 26, no. 2 (1995): 307–35.

Shober, Juliane. "Buddhist Just Rule and Burmese National Culture: State Patronage of the Chinese Tooth Relic in Myanmar." *History of Religions* 36, no. 3 (February 1997): 218–43.

————. "The Theravada Buddhist Engagement with Modernity in Southeast Asia." *Journal of Southeast Asian Studies* 26, no. 2 (1995): 307–35.

Sieyès, Emmanuel Joseph. *Qu'est-ce que le Tiers-Etat?* Paris, 1787.

Sinclair, James. *Behind the Ranges: Patrolling in New Guinea*. Melbourne: Melbourne University Press, 1966.

Smith, Adam. *An Inquiry into the Nature and Causes of the Wealth of Nations*. London: Printed for W. Strahan and T. Cadell, 1776 (New York, A. M. Kelley, 1966).

Smith, Linda Tuhiwai. *Decolonizing Methodologies: Research and Indigenous Peoples*. London/New York: Zed Books; Dunedin NZ: University of Otago Press, 1999.

Srinivas, M. N. "The Insider versus the Outsider in the Study of Culture." In *Collected Writings*, 553–60. Delhi: Oxford University Press, 2002.

————. "Practicing Social Anthropology in India." *Annual Review of Anthropology* 26 (1997): 1–24.

Sternhell, Zeev, *Les anti-Lumières: du XVIIIe siècle à la guerre froide*. Paris: Fayard, 2006.

Stocking, George. *Functionalism Historicized: Essays on British Social Anthropology*. Madison: University of Wisconsin Press, 1984.

———. *Race, Culture, and Evolution: Essays in the History of Anthropology*. New York: The Free Press, 1968.

———. *Victorian Anthropology*. New York: The Free Press, 1987.

Strathern, Andrew. "Alienating the Inalienable." *Man*, no. 17 (1982): 548–51.

———. "The Central and the Contingent: Bridewealth among the Melpa and the Wiru." In *The Meaning of Marriage Payments*, edited by J. L. Komaroff, 49–66. London: Academic Press, 1980.

———. "Finance and Production: Two Strategies in New Guinea Exchange Systems." *Oceania*, no. 40 (1969): 42–67.

———. "Finance and Production Revisited." In *Research in Economic Anthropology* 1 (1978): [pp.?].

———. "The Kula in Comparative Perspective." In *The Kula: New Perspectives on Massim Exchange*, edited by Jerry Leach and Edmund Leach, 73–88. London: Cambridge University Press, 1983.

———. *The Rope of Moka: Big Men and Ceremonial Exchange in Mount Hagen, New Guinea*. Cambridge: Cambridge University Press, 1971.

———. "Tambu and Kina: 'Profit', Exploitation and Reciprocity in Two New Guinea Exchange Systems." *Mankind*, no. 11 (1978): 253–64.

Strathern, Marilyn, ed. *Dealing with Inequality: Analysing Gender Relations in Melanesia and Beyond*. Cambridge: Cambridge University Press, 1987.

———. *The Gender of the Gift*. Berkeley: University of California Press, 1988.

Subaltern Studies: Writings on South Asian History and Society, 12 vols. (1982–2005). Delhi/New York: Oxford University Press (vols. 1–10); New York: Columbia University Press (vol. 11); New Delhi: Permanent Black/Ravi Dayal (vol. 12).

Tambiah, Stanley J. *Leveling Crowds: Ethnonationalist Conflicts and Collective Violence in South Asia*. Berkeley: University of California Press, 1996.

Thomas, Nicholas. "Becoming Undisciplined: Anthropology and Cultural Studies." In *Anthropological Theory Today*, edited by Henrietta L. Moore, 262–79. Cambridge: Polity Press, 1999.

———. *Colonialism's Culture*. Cambridge: Polity Press, 1994.

Thomas, Yan. "Remarques sur la juridiction domestique à Rome." In *Parenté et stratégies familiales dans l'Antiquité Romaine*, 449–74. Rome: École Française de Rome, 1990.

———. "A Rome, pères citoyens et cité des pères." In *Histoire de la famille*, tome 1, edited by A. Burgière, Ch.F. Klapisch, M. Segalen and F. Zonabend, 193–223. Paris: Armand Colin, 1986.

———. "Le 'Ventre', corps maternel, droit paternel." *Le Genre humain* 14 (1986): 211–36.

Thorval, Joël. "Le Néo-Confucianisme chinois aujourd'hui." Introduction to Mou Zongsan, *Spécificités de la philosophie chinoise*, pp. 1–65. Paris: Éditions du Cerf, 2003.

———. "Sur la transformation de la pensée néo-confucéenne en discours philosophique moderne." Special issue of *Revue Extrême Orient— Extrême Occident* ("Y a-t-il une philosophie chinoise?"), no. 27 (2005): 91–118.

Tort, Michel. *La Fin du dogme paternel.* Paris: Aubier, 2005.

Trautmann, Thomas R. "The Gift in India: Marcel Mauss as Indianist." Paper delivered at the 36th Meeting of the Society of Asian Studies, 1986.

———. *Lewis Henry Morgan and the Invention of Kinship.* Berkeley: University of California Press, 1987.

———. "The Whole History of Kinship Terminology in Three Chapters: Before Morgan, Morgan and after Morgan." *Anthropological Theory* 1 (2001): 268–87.

Turnbull, Colin. *The Forest People: A Study of the Pygmies of the Congo.* New York: Simon and Schuster, 1962.

Turner, Victor. *The Forest of Symbols.* New York/Ithaca: Cornell University Press, 1967.

Tyler, Stephen, "From Documents of the Occult to Occult Document." In *Writing Culture: The Poetics and Politics of Ethnography*, edited by James Clifford and George E. Marcus, [pp?]. Berkeley: University of California Press, 1986.

Tylor, Edward B. *Primitive Culture.* 2 vols. New York: Brentano's, 1924 [1871].

———. *Researches into the Early History of Mankind and the Development of Civilization.* Edited by Paul Bohannan. Chicago: University of Chicago Press, 1964 [1865].

Valeri, Valerio. *Kingship and Sacrifice: Ritual and Society in Ancient Hawaii.* Chicago: University of Chicago Press, 1985.

Vandermeersch, Leon. *Wangdao ou la Voie royale: Recherches sur l'esprit des institutions de la Chine archaïque.* 2 vols. Paris: Maisonneuve, 1977.

Verdery, K. *What Was Socialism and What Comes Next?* Princeton: Princeton University Press, 1996.

Vernant, Jean-Pierre, ed. *La Cité des images: religion et société en Grèce antique.* Paris: Fernand Nathan, 1984.

Vincent, Jean-Didier. *Biologie des passions*. Paris: Odile Jacob, 2002.

Wagner, Roy. *Symbols That Stand for Themselves*. Chicago: University of Chicago Press, 1986.

Wallerstein, Immanuel. "America and the World: The Twin Towers as Metaphor." In *Understanding September 11*, edited by Craig Calhoun, Paul Price, and Ashley Timmer, 345–60. New York: The New Press, 2002.

Warren, Kay, ed. *The Violence Within: Cultural and Political Opposition in Divided Nations*. San Francisco: Westview Press, 1993.

Weiner, Annette. *Inalienable Possessions: The Paradox of Keeping-while-Giving*. Berkeley: University of California Press, 1992.

———. "Inalienable Wealth." *American Ethnologist* 12, no. 2 (1985): 210–27.

———. "Plus précieux que l'or: Relations et échanges entre hommes et femmes dans les sociétés d'Océanie." *Annales E.S.C.*, no. 2 (1992): 222–45.

———. "The Reproductive Model in Trobriand Society." *Mankind* 11 (1978): 175–86.

———. *The Trobrianders of Papua New Guinea*. New York: Holt, Rinehart Winston, 1988.

———. "Trobriand Kinship from Another View: The Reproductive Power of Women and Men." *Man* 14 (1979): 328–48.

———. *Women of Value, Men of Renown: New Perspectives in Trobriand Exchange*. Austin: University of Texas Press, 1976.

Weiner, Annette, and Jane Schneider, eds. *Cloth and Human Experience*. Washington, DC: Smithsonian Institution Press, 1989.

Wilson, Bryan. *The Noble Savages: The Primitive Origins of Charisma and Its Contemporary Survival*. Berkeley: University of California Press, 1975.

Wiser, Willem Henricks. *The Hindu Jajmani System*. Lucknow: Lucknow Publishing House, 1936.

Wolf, Eric. "Perilous Ideas: Race, Culture, People." Sydney Mintz Lecture for 1992. *Current Anthropology* 35, no. 1 (1994): 1–12.

Index

Abaogdu, 88
Aborigines, 59, 75, 76, 97
Adam, 95
adultery, 103
adzes, 74
affection, 122
affinity, 88, 161
Afghanistan, 10, 41, 69
Africa, 13, 33, 35, 154, 177, 186;
 arts and civilizations of, 180,
 209n; Central, 28; representations of procreation, 81; resistance in, 194n10; students from,
 180
afterlife, 11, 94, 95, 96
age-grades, 68, 141
Alagha, Joseph, 195n21
Allègre, Claude, 210n
alliances, 74, 88, 123, 139, 171
al Qaeda, 8, 10, 194n16
Althusser, Louis, 7
Amazon, 62
America, 145, 164; pre-Columbian,
 144, 154, 177; resistance in,
 194n10
Americans, 18
Americas, 33, 35, 186; arts and civilizations of, 180, 209n; students
 from, 180

Amselle, Jean-Loup, 194n11,
 201n10
analysand, 103. *See also* psychoanalysis
analysis, structural, 8
analyst, 103. *See also*
 psychoanalysis
ancestors, 20, 26, 58, 88, 141, 142;
 Baruya, 111; divinized, 151;
 imaginary male, 118; male, 91;
 relations with, 80, 182
Andavakia, 67, 72, 141
Anders, Ferdinand, 190, 211n5
Andje, 65, 138, 141, 205n1
Anga, 202n4, 204n4
Ankave, 202n4
anthropological truths, death of,
 19–26
anthropologist(s), 15; and other
 social scientists, 26; and psychoanalysts, 101; responsibilities of,
 36–39
anthropology: assessments of,
 199n68; of churches, 174; crisis
 of, 3–4, 39, 174; economic, 61,
 200n; of education, 174; of
 firms, 174; of health, 174; major
 axioms of, 62; no longer measure and mirror of human prog-

Berque, Jacques, 194n17
Best, Elsdon, 47, 200n5
Bharatiya Janata Party (BJP), 10
Bhargava, Rajeev, 195n22
Bidjogo statue, 181
Big Man, 185; Big-Man societies,
52
"big name" (Baruya), 65
Billeter, Jean-François, 198n56
Bissagos Islands, 181
Black struggles, 17
blood: menstrual, 91, 116, 118,
120, 134, 168, 202n4; woman's,
81–99. *See also* procreation; sub-
stances, male and female
Bloom, Harold, 197n45
Boas, Franz, 12, 52, 171, 195n28,
200n16, 208n1
body, 134, 168; language of, 135;
shared representations of, 102
Bolshevism/Bolsheviks, 46. *See also*
revolutions: Bolshevik
bones, 109. *See also* procreation
Bonhême, M. A., 197n52
Bonnemère, Pascale, 203n4
bonobos, 204n1 (chap. 5)
Bordeaux, 210n
borders, 5, 6, 13, 21, 69, 73, 79,
142, 146
Borges, Jorge Luis, 208n5
Bosnia, 9
Bougainville, Louis-Antoine de,
101
Boulakia, 66
Bourdieu, Pierre, 136
bourgeoisie, 40
bows and arrows, 74
Brahman(s), 29, 77, 155
Bravegareubaramandeuc, 65, 70,
137
Brazil, 43, 187

breath: cosmic, 81; of life, 81;
spermatic, 184. See also *khâ*
bridewealth, 55, 171
British Empire, 145
British Museum, 178, 186
British Papua, 206n8
Brunois, Florence, 204n4
Budapest, 210n
Buddha, 11, 35
Buddhism, 11, 13; Mahayana, 26;
Theravada, 11, 28
Buffon, Georges, 178
bugjan, 173
Bulgaria, 7
bull-roarers, 57, 118, 119
Burke, Edmund, 201n29
Burma, 11

Campbell, Shirley, 85, 203n6
Canada, 7
cannibals, 94
canoes, 54
capital, 42, 60, 143
capitalism, 8, 41, 194n14, 205n5
(chap. 6); capitalist market economy, 8, 142–43; capitalist system, 9, 13, 39, 40, 42, 60–61,
143, 174; capitalist world economy, 7, 42, 47, 79, 157; Western
world, 6, 7
cash crop, 15
cassowary, 65, 72, 118; great
hunters, 118
caste(s), 17, 20, 29, 43, 59, 62, 77,
79, 124, 128, 133, 142, 156, 165,
168, 182, 189; definition of,
153–55; emergence of, 156; as
identity, 142; system, 142, 155,
171. *See also* class(es); orders
Castilians, 158
Catalans, 158

images, as part of mental world, 22
imaginary, 18, 19, 54, 55, 76, 97, 99, 118, 168; cores, 20, 22, 149, 169; primacy of, 21–26, 48; and the real, 48, 96, 107, 127, 188; relationship with symbolic, 19, 21–26, 59, 97, 108, 167, 169–70, 188, 189; representations (as components of society), 20, 22, 55, 59, 70, 76, 82, 97, 108, 117, 118, 120, 121, 144, 147, 150, 157, 168, 171, 175, 184, 188, 189. *See also* symbolic
Immaculate Conception, 97
imperialism, cultural, 196n39
impurity, 154, 155
Inamwe, 141
Inca-Inti, 148, 171
Inca(s), 59, 144, 171
incest, 73, 100, 109, 111–12, 114, 129, 130, 188; taboo, 100, 111, 129
independence, 5, 6, 15, 40, 145
India, 16, 43; caste system, 77, 142, 153. *See also* caste(s)
Indian tribes, 160
individual(s), 17, 102, 123, 191; not source of society, 126; promotion of, 6; as social subject, 125–37
Indonesia, 43; Islam in, 194n17
industry, as vector of European civilization, 177
inequalities, 154
inequality, gender, 133
informants, 18, 30, 31, 38, 54, 103, 125, 138
initiation(s), 68, 90, 92, 107, 109; Baruya, 46, 57, 64, 69–75, 83, 84, 103, 113, 116, 118, 137, 138, 140–42, 145, 150, 166, 168, 170,

171, 173, 202n4, 204n4, 208n11; masters of, 57, 65, 69, 71, 72, 115, 116, 128, 141, 150, 170; of shamans, 65, 68, 73; stages, 71
insects, 94
insemination. *See* homosexual relations; semen
insignia, of rank, 139
institutions, 22, 127
instruments, musical, 204n5. *See also* flutes
integration, of economies into capitalist system, 12
International Monetary Fund, 13
interpretation: representations as, 22; spaces for, in museum, 183
intervention, Western, 13
intimacy, impersonal, 134
Inuit, 74, 161, 187, 202n1, 202n3; representations of conception and gestation, 81–83
invisible, relations with the, 80, 184
Iqwaye, 204n4
Iran, 143
Iraq, 41
Irian Jaya, 62
Iroquois. *See under* kinship terminologies
Isis, 23, 155, 188
Islam, 10, 13, 194nn16–17; Islamic world, 41; pre-Islamic ideology, 35; radical, 42
Israel, 21, 69, 143
Izard, Michel, 197n49

Jajmani system, 202n18
Japan, 43, 143, 163
jargon, scientific, 28
jati, 155. *See also* caste(s)
Jaurès, Jean, 46

Kwaio, 194n10
Kwakiutl, 45, 47, 53, 171
Kwarrandariar, 70, 71, 149, 173

Labillardière, J. J. H. de, 203–4n1
labor: division of, 102, 150, 152;
forced, 156; process, 78; role of,
78
Lacan, Jacques, 123, 204n6
Lamartine, Alphonse de, 194n17
land, 23, 58, 88, 94, 145, 152, 153,
160; access or rights to, 26, 65,
66, 67, 72, 74, 75, 86, 97, 144,
150, 151, 166, 167, 169, 207n19;
denied to women, 117; ownership, 6, 11, 59, 89, 96, 117, 120,
133, 170
language, 139; autonomy of,
197n45; as basis of society, 66;
coded, 110
Latin America, 13
law, 53, 123, 131, 145, 159, 177,
198n55, 206n9
Law of the Father, 136
laws, Russian, 146
Leach, Edmund, 14, 97, 196n34,
199n64, 201n24, 203n15
Leach, Jerry, 37, 54, 199n64,
201n24
Lebanon, 69
Leclerc, G., 194n12
Leenhardt, Maurice, 193n1
Lefur, Yves, 185
legend, 70
Leiden, 210n
leisure, reserved for nobles, 152
Lemonnier, Pierre, 201n7
Lesotho, 195n32
Levine, N. E., 203n8
Lévi-Strauss, Claude, 7, 22, 25,
197n49, 198n55, 200n6, 204n5,

209n, 210n, 210n1; on exchange,
172; on gift-exchange, 47–49; on
symbolic and imaginary, 170
Lewis, Diane, 194n12
liberalism, 13, 46
libido, 131
Liep, John, 54, 201n24
life: breath of, 23, 81, 85, 94–95;
equivalents of, 48, 55, 173; powers of, 58, 68, 77, 90, 91, 93, 94,
108, 119, 152; source of, 23, 60,
73, 82–84, 93, 95, 104, 114, 121,
134, 185
Lincoln, Bruce, 195n21
lineage(s), 38, 51, 54, 65, 67, 71,
74, 75, 78, 84, 89, 90, 91, 110,
112, 114, 119, 121, 123, 134,
137–40, 153, 167, 171, 207n19
Lizot, Jacques, 201n1
Lloyd, R. G., 201n6
local cultures, 61
local groups, 40, 72
local societies, 9
Longin, 201n29
Louis XV (king), 194n13
Louvre Pyramid, 209n
love, 115
Lowie, Robert, 208n1
Ludden, David, 196n38
Lumumba, Patrice, 6
Lutheran Mission, 63
Lyons, 210n
Lyotard, Jean-François, 2, 7, 8,
175, 193n3

Macbeth, 37
Maenge, 45, 87, 89, 200n1
Makira Island, 182
Malaysia, 39
Mali, 187
Malinowski, Bronislaw, 27, 37, 38,

other(s) (*continued*)
164, 165–67; understanding,
26–28, 31–36, 43, 125, 175, 180
otherness, 8, 26–27, 33

Pacific: Central, 142; South, 142
pacification, 63
page, 200n1. *See also* seashells
Pakistan, 69
Palestinians, 143
Panoff, Michel, 45, 200n1,
203nn9–10
Papua New Guinea, 32
participant observation, 30–32,
161
Pashtun, 69
pater familias, 77
patrifiliation, 89
patrol post, 93
peasants, caste, 78
penis, 84, 97, 109, 111, 113, 121;
water, 87, 91
"people of the same bone," 88
Persia, 188
Persson, Johnny, 201n24
Peru, 43
pharaoh, 23–24, 59, 148, 155, 171,
188–89
philosophers, 205n2 (chap. 6)
philosophy, means of conferring
meaning, 35
physiocrats, 153
Picasso, Pablo, 180
Pitt Rivers Museum, Oxford, 187
Pizarro, Francisco, 144
plants, cultivated, 117
playwrights, 198n56
poetry, 182; poets, 198n56
Poland, 7
political-religious relations, 21, 24,
33, 56, 81, 83, 140, 141, 149,

152, 153, 157, 189, 190, 205n4
(chap. 6); as basis of society,
62–79. *See also under* relations
pollution, female, 114
Polynesia, 62, 92, 142, 148;
Polynesians, 101, 163
Pool, Robert, 197n46
populus romanus, 77
Porge, Erik, 204n6
Portugal, 5, 39; Portuguese
expansion, 179
possessions, inalienable, 53–60. *See
also* objects: sacred
postmodernism, 19, 29, 39, 175;
postmodern condition, 7; postmodernists, 8, 195n26
poststructuralism, 29
potlatch, 45, 49, 50, 52, 56, 171,
172, 200n18. *See also* Kwakiutl
Pouchepadass, Jacques, 196n38
poverty, 18
power, 6, 27, 35, 49, 52, 56, 80, 94,
97, 102, 126, 151, 152, 167, 182,
189, 190, 207n19; beliefs as
source of, 48; colonial, 5, 6, 16,
37, 40, 41, 69, 145, 194n10;
forms and figures of, 30, 34, 40,
59, 79, 80, 148, 170, 171, 184,
185; legitimization of, 59; military, 42; objects as source of, 57,
190; political, 21, 60, 144; relations, 20, 37, 50, 88, 90, 91, 113,
127, 133, 143, 151, 167, 169,
175; representations of, 59; spiritual, 73, 150; structure(s), 46,
149, 179, 191
powers: centralized, 62; female
(creative, life-giving), 5, 7, 57,
58, 90, 116, 118, 119; male (of
death), 57, 58, 91, 117, 119;
political-religious, 152; super-

natural, 43, 70, 83, 85, 86, 88,
92, 93, 96, 108, 112, 146, 148,
151, 170, 171, 188
practices, symbolic, 107, 150, 189
pragmatism, enlightened, 175
preconceptions, theoretical, in
ethnography, 167
pregnancy, 81–99, 106; intercourse
during, 134. *See also* procreation
prestige, 150
Price, Sally, 211n2
priests, 147, 156
primal time, 58. *See also*
Dreamtime
primitive, 15, 19
procreation, 108; indigenous theories of, 80–99; Inuit beliefs
about, 81–83; Na beliefs about,
87–89; representations of, 80–
99; —, in Africa, 81; —, in Asia,
81
production: of knowledge, 7;
means, conditions of, 6, 78, 117,
153, 169; of means of subsistence, 64, 74, 77, 140, 154;
mode of, 78, 139, 153, 174; of
social relations, 24, 59, 75, 154;
of wealth, commodities, goods
and services, capital, 40, 42, 59,
64, 79, 139, 153, 155
professional conduct, code of,
37
progress, 163; human, 4, 18, 50,
101, 159, 162–63, 164; social,
157–76
prohibitions, 74
property, private, 13. *See also* possessions, inalienable
prophet, 41
psychoanalysis, 124, 128, 129,
198n56

psychoanalysts, 101, 102, 125, 136;
and anthropologists, 204n
Pukapuka, 21, 149
purity, 154, 155
python, 142

Quesnay, François, 153, 207n18
questions, existential, addressed by
all societies, 80, 184

Rabinow, Paul, 1, 19, 193n2
Racine, Jean-Luc, 195n24
racism, immigration-related, 180
Radcliffe-Brown, A. R., 15
Raja, functions, 155
Rama, 11
Ranapiri, Tamati, 47
rank(s), 14, 52, 54–55, 92–94, 133,
139, 153, 172, 206n14
ranked society, 77, 85, 141, 149,
154, 155, 176
real, 18, 19, 22, 25, 48, 59, 96, 98,
107, 108, 118, 127, 150, 187,
188, 197–98n54. *See also* imaginary; symbolic
rebirth, male, 84. *See also*
initiation(s)
recipient, in gift-exchange, 47
redistribution, of resources, 51
refugees, Baruya, 65
regime, military, 143
reincarnation, 86
relations, 19, 129, 157; chains of,
5; economic, 78, 139, 157; —,
not basis of society, 19, 64; —,
role of, 77; family, 129; gender,
167, 168, 179; hierarchical, 141;
noncommercial, 46; opacity of,
173; political-religious, origin
of, 154–56 (*see also* political-
religious relations); power, 127;

Strathern, Marilyn, 175, 200n13,
 208n10
structuralism, 7, 8, 29, 39, 47, 175
structure, of society, 127
structures, unconscious, of the
 mind, 48, 49
Subaltern Studies, 16, 194n10,
 196n38
subcontinent, Indian, 16
subject: death of, 7; disappearance
 of, 198n55; resurgence of, 8;
 social, 125–36
"subjectification," 8
subjectivity, 132; inner, 100
sublime, 58
subordination, 11, 97, 120, 132,
 207n19; of sexuality, 98–99, 121,
 132; of women to men, 97, 120–
 21, 132, 168–69. *See also*
 domination
subsections, Aborigines, 75
subsistence, 139; means of, 151
substances, male and female,
 81–99, 114, 121. *See also*
 procreation
substitutes, symbolic, for life, 48
Sudan, 161
suicide, 119
Sukarno, 6
Sumer, 146
Summer Institute of Linguistics,
 63
Sun, 70; Baruya representations of,
 85, 95, 96, 98, 108, 134, 139,
 142, 169, 171, 173; bird of the,
 107; father of the Baruya, 84;
 role in making babies, 202n4;
 son of the (Inca), 146
Sun-boat, 189
Sunni, 12
superstructure, 174

surpluses, 74, 139
symbolic: practices, 20, 22, 26; primacy of, 21–26, 48; relationship
 with imaginary, 19, 21–26, 167,
 169, 170, 188 (*see also* imaginary)
symbolization, of relationships by
 means of objects, 191
symbols, 25, 48, 127, 198n55; cultural, 182; as translation of ways
 of living and thinking, 184
Syria, 69

taboo(s), 94, 100, 116, 150; incest,
 100, 111, 129; sexual, 98, 101
Tahiti, 92, 151
Taiwan, 43, 143
tali (shells), 200n1. *See also*
 seashells
Tambiah, Stanley J., 195n26
Tamil, 11
Tangaloa, 151
Tao, 198n56
Tapache, 137
taro, 117; "taro" people, 90
tattoos, 188
Te Ariki Kafika, 14, 149
tee, 52
Telefolmin, 90–92, 98
television, 18
territory, 65, 66, 67, 68, 72, 111,
 138, 141, 157, 202n4; authority
 over, 66–67, 92, 146; definition
 of, 145–46; hunting, 72, 74; and
 identity, 127; sovereignty as
 defining a society, 21, 66, 67, 69,
 71, 127, 143, 144, 145, 147, 148,
 155 (*see also* sovereignty)
theater, 182
things and persons, 53
Third Estate, 153
third world, 6

Thomas, Nicholas, 193n5, 194n12
Thomas, Yan, 202n17
Thoraval, Joël, 199n71
thought: deep structures of
(Baruya), 109; functions of,
197n50; reflexive, 34
Tibet, 88
Tikopia, 14, 39, 148–51, 155;
Tikopians, 21
titles, 52–53, 92, 93, 172
tjuringas, 59
Tlingit, 45
tolerance, religious, 10
Tonga, 21, 90, 148, 151; representations of procreation, 92–94;
sexual activity in, 203–4n1
total prestations, 49–50
trade: international, 78; as vector
of European civilization, 177
traditions: local, 9; rediscovered or
reinvented, 15
transmission, of goods, statuses,
powers, 97
Trautmann, Thomas R., 194n8,
208n2
travelers, 158
treasure, clan, 53, 173
tribe(s), 43, 45, 53, 63, 64, 65, 66,
67, 70, 71, 72, 74, 76, 78, 81,
105, 112, 113, 127, 128, 137,
138, 139, 140, 144, 166, 205n1,
207n19; American Indian, 163;
Arab, 163; Bedouin, 35; Celtic,
69; definition of, 68; North
American, 160, 163; Pashtun, 69
tribute, 78, 156
Trobriand Islanders, 49, 97, 134;
representations of procreation,
85–87
Trobriand Islands, 27, 95

truth, self-evident, 19, 33
truths, anthropological, 19–20
tsimia, 68, 70, 71, 119, 140, 205n4
(chap. 6)
tsimie, 139
Tu'i Tonga, 92, 93, 94, 95, 151, 184
Tu'i Tonga Fefine, 151, 185
Tuma, 85
Tungus, 211n4
Tupileta, 86
Turnbull, Colin, 202n14
Turner, Victor, 22, 197n49
Twin Towers, 8. *See also* September
11, 2001 (9/11)
Tyler, Stephen, 1, 18, 19, 196n44
Tylor, Edward, 4, 159, 177, 193n7

Ukraine, 9
unconscious, 122, 127, 132, 135
United Nations, 9, 13, 63
United States, 7, 9, 13, 16, 18, 142,
160, 175; as mirror of progress,
162
University College London, 186
urine, 87
USSR, 39; disintegration of, 13

vagina, 91, 104, 109, 113, 116,
118, 134
Vaishya, 15
Valacs, 177
Valeri, Valerio, 206n15
valuables, 48, 55–56, 172
value, imaginary, 55–56
values: bourgeois, 6; modern, 41
Vandermeersch, Leon, 207n21
varna, 155
vaygu'a, 54–55
Velasquez, Diego, 178
vengeance, 112

ventriloquist's dummy, body as, 20, 135
Venus, powers of, 57
Venus de Milo, 180
Verdery, K., 194n14, 199n69
victims, women as, 169
Vienna museum, 190
Vietnam, 7, 39, 143
Vincent, Jean-Didier, 130
violence, 9, 17, 34, 58, 66, 109, 116, 118, 156, 204n4; and origin of Baruya society, 137; and political relations, 41, 46, 66, 118, 133, 137, 146, 155–56; real, 117–18; in relations of domination, 24, 41, 116–19, 156–57, 167, 169–70, 204n4 (*see also* consent); symbolic, 118
Virgin Mary, 97
Vishnu, 11

Wagner, Roy, 22, 197n49
Wahhabism, 10
Waitz, 208n1
wai waya (spirit-child), 86
Wallerstein, Immanuel, 195n21
wandjinia, 107, 119
Wang ("Unique Man"), 148, 156, 207n19
Wantekia, 66
warfare, 68, 76, 89, 139, 146; reserved for nobles, 152
Warren, Kay, 195n20
warrior(s), 48, 51, 65, 70, 72, 76, 115, 137, 140, 141, 146, 150, 155, 171, 206n12
wars: First World War, 5, 46, 206n8; Second World War, 5, 6, 39, 63, 174, 179; Vietnamese War, 6

wealth, 80, 102, 151, 184
weapons, 45, 204n5; denied to women, 117
Weiner, Annette, 27, 37, 49, 53, 54, 85, 134, 172, 199n64, 201n21, 203n6
West, the, 28, 159, 174; as birthplace of anthropology, 39–43, 158–76; capitalist, 7; influence of, 14; as measure and mirror of human progress, 3, 18; and the rest, 39
Western Desert, Australia, 76
Western domination, 3, 8, 40, 176
Western empires, 158
Western lifestyle, rejection of, 8, 10
Western mind, 4, 41, 51, 110, 161, 167, 198n56
Western world, 6, 95, 174
"white man's peace," 145
wild woman, 118
Wilson, Bryan, 193n6
Wiser, Willem Henricks, 202n18
Wolf, Eric, 195n20
womb, 80, 83–88, 91, 95–97, 106–9, 116, 168. See also procreation
women, world of, among the Baruya, 57
Wonenara Valley, 65
Woodlark, 49
work: of the gods, 21, 149, 150; with the gods, 151, 156; times, as part of fieldwork, 166
World Bank, 13, 195n32
World Trade Center, 41
World Trade Organization, 13
"Writing Culture," 2
writing ethnography, 37